The Adaptability Quotient

The Adaptability Quotient

REWIRING YOUR MIND FOR SUCCESS IN THE NEXT HUMAN ERA

Alec Litowitz

DISRUPTION BOOKS

Washington, DC

Published by Disruption Books
Washington, DC
www.disruptionbooks.com

Distributed by Disruption Books

For information about special discounts for bulk purchases, please contact Disruption Books at info@disruptionbooks.com.

Cover image used under license from Adobe Stock: synthetick/1516296853

Cover and book design by Sheila Parr

Library of Congress Cataloging-in-Publication Data available

Printed in the United States of America

Print ISBN: 978-1-63331-155-8
eBook ISBN: 978-1-63331-156-5

First Edition

10 9 8 7 6 5 4 3 2 1

For Jennifer, and for Jack, Luke, Nick, and Jude—with love for the questions we ask and the paths we explore together.

Contents

Author's Note . . . ix

Introduction . . . 1

1: Out of Chaos, Order . . . 9

2: The Anatomy of Adaptation—Why Your Human System Needs an Update . . . 35

3: Steering Through the Storm . . . 55

4: Thinking About Thinking . . . 79

5: On Self-Awareness . . . 105

6: Max Entropy . . . 131

7: From Hunch to Hypothesis . . . 155

8: Designing the Experiment . . . 177

9: Launch, Learn, Repeat . . . 201

10: Back into the Loop . . . 219

11: Leading at Altitude . . . 243

12: Authors of the Future . . . 263

13: The Most Extraordinary Machine . . . 287

Acknowledgments . . . 307

Notes . . . 311

Glossary of Terms . . . 313

About the Author . . . 329

Author's Note

And you may ask yourself,
"Well, how did I get here?"

—Talking Heads

I did not set out to write this book.

For most of my life, I was too busy building things to pause long enough to name what I was doing. I worked inside fast-moving environments—markets, businesses, teams—where decisions had to be made before the data was complete and before the consequences were clear. Over time, some of those decisions worked out. Others didn't. What mattered most was not intelligence, or even experience, but something harder to define: the ability to adapt—to reframe a problem, update one's thinking, and act decisively under uncertainty.

Only later did I realize that this pattern repeated across very different domains. Building investment businesses. Supporting entrepreneurial spinoffs. Creating a nonprofit focused on financial literacy. Opening a neighborhood restaurant. Helping turn around and sell a software company. The contexts were different, but the underlying mode of thinking was strikingly similar.

I began to see that what separated progress from paralysis was not foresight, but adaptability.

In retrospect, some of this way of thinking began much earlier. I grew up as the son of not one but *two* psychoanalysts, with a mother who also held a PhD in linguistics. Questioning assumptions was not an activity in our household; it was the atmosphere. I learned early that the surface of one's thoughts—and even the language used to express them—were only the outermost layer of something deeper. Ideas could be unpeeled. Meanings reframed. Causes traced beyond appearances.

I was taught, implicitly, that understanding required movement: telescoping up and down between levels of abstraction, not just zooming in for detail, but zooming out to see structure and context. That habit—of shifting perspective, testing interpretations, and resisting the comfort of first explanations—shaped how I came to see the world. It made pattern recognition feel less like intuition and more like disciplined curiosity.

This disposition followed me into professional life, where uncertainty was not an exception but the norm. Over time, I noticed that the people who navigated such environments best were rarely those with the most impressive credentials or the most refined models. They were those who could hold uncertainty without freezing, learn without overfitting, and act without waiting for perfect information. What is often described as intuition or vision was, more precisely, an adaptability of mind.

I began calling this capacity the Adaptability Quotient, or AQ. What follows is a framework for cultivating and exercising that capacity under real-world uncertainty.

This realization came at a moment of transition. After decades spent helping build firms and organizations, I stepped back from day-to-day leadership and began thinking more deliberately about what comes next—not just for me, but for all of us. The world entering the next decade does not look like an extension of the last one. The convergence of data, compute, artificial intelligence, material science, and networked media represents a genuine discontinuity—a punctuated equilibrium rather than a smooth curve.

In such moments, the skills that brought success in the past often become liabilities. Linear thinking fails. Static playbooks break. Optimization gives way to exploration. And yet, most of us are still taught to think and decide as if the world were stable.

As I searched for guidance, I found no shortage of excellent books. I read widely—across psychology, philosophy, sociology, anthropology, cognitive science, neuroscience, systems thinking, information theory, and decision theory. Many works offered deep insight into specific traits: grit, curiosity, beginner's mind, expertise, judgment. Others were rigorous but narrowly academic. What I could not find was a single integrated guide that connected these domains into a practical framework for adapting to rapid change.

The knowledge existed—but it lived in silos.

This book is my attempt to bring those strands together through consilience: to connect ideas across disciplines and translate them into a usable way of thinking and deciding under uncertainty. It reflects both how I was taught to question the world and how I have learned to operate within it. It is not a formula, but a field guide—drawn from experience, failure, reflection, and exposure to others who excel at this mode of thinking.

I wrote this book because I believe that gap now matters. As artificial intelligence accelerates and automates many forms of analytical and technical work, human agency—our ability to frame problems, revise mental models, and exercise judgment in novel situations—becomes more important, not less. Unlike intelligence or emotional sensitivity, adaptability is not fixed. It can be learned. It can be practiced. And it can be taught.

This book is written for those who sense that the rules are changing faster than the instructions. It is meant as a practical guide to upgrading how we think and decide—so that we can navigate what comes next with greater agency and clarity.

To see a world in a grain of sand
And a heaven in a wild flower,
Hold infinity in the palm of your hand
And eternity in an hour.

—William Blake in "Auguries of Innocence,"
a poem written in 1803
(at the peak of the First Industrial Revolution)

Introduction

Be water, my friend.

—Bruce Lee

The factory was an empty shell. That was the headline when my colleague Charlie called from the outskirts of a provincial city in China. He was standing in what was supposed to be a humming, fully functioning plant. Instead, the place looked almost completely abandoned: weeds pushing up through the cracked pavement, boxes with a visible coat of dust, machines sitting idle like stage props that hadn't been touched in months.

A handful of workers were milling around, but even they seemed staged. Charlie swore he watched them get shuffled from one part of the plant to another, as if to create the illusion of productivity.

"This is *bad*, Alec," he told me on the phone. His voice was flat, grim. "Fraud. There's nobody here."

At the time, the market already agreed. On paper, the company certainly looked like a fraud. The CFO—brother of the CEO—was rumored to have committed some kind of financial crime; the stock had cratered from eighteen dollars to eight dollars, almost overnight. Analysts were pulling coverage. Shorts were piling on. To most people, this was case closed.

But we hadn't sold—at least not yet.

The truth was, nobody in the United States actually knew what was real and what wasn't. Investor relations were outsourced. Calls went unanswered. And most of what passed for "due diligence" was speculation echoing through conference calls and trading desks thousands of miles away.

The company was part of a broader wave of 300–400 Chinese "reverse mergers" that had flooded US markets between 2006 and 2010—small manufacturers, chemical firms, and dairy processors that had gone public overnight by merging into dormant American shell corporations. It was a cheap shortcut to Wall Street capital. China's domestic markets were still immature and tightly controlled by the state; listing in New York offered credibility and a pipeline to US investors desperate for exposure to Chinese growth.

But by 2011, the tide had turned. Scandals were breaking across the sector—phantom factories, ghost assets, nonexistent revenue streams. Short sellers like Muddy Waters had detonated one exposé after another, from theft on the part of a billion-dollar timber company called Sino-Forest to fertilizer plants that didn't fertilize. Stocks that once traded at twenty-five dollars were collapsing to four dollars, then zero.

The company Charlie was visiting was caught in that storm. Yet amid the chaos, its CEO announced something almost unthinkable: He planned to buy out the company himself, to take it private (via a form of merger offer) at a steep premium of roughly twenty-four dollars a share.

It was a defiant move, the kind of gesture that could signal either supreme confidence or a last-ditch attempt to keep the fraud alive. Ninety percent of all merger offers eventually close, according to a near-ironclad law of markets stretching back decades. But stocks trading at one-third of their offer price don't reflect normal merger risk. They reflect existential doubt; they are the market's way of saying *this might not exist at all.*

So I did what seemed obvious, even if I appeared to be just about the only person who thought this way.

I sent someone.

Charlie didn't speak Mandarin. He had no point of contact at the company. But when the data collapses and the story doesn't add up, you don't wait for clarity to descend like divine inspiration. You poke the system. You run another loop. You test a new hypothesis.

So Charlie boarded a plane to China.

His first call back nearly confirmed everyone's worst fears.

"There's no business here," he told me. "No throughput. No evidence of demand. If this is their state-of-the-art factory, we've got a problem."

Most people would've sold on the spot. I told him to keep digging. Given the CEO's talk of taking the company private, we needed to know whether he knew something we didn't. What information, if true, would make these facts logical?

What followed was part corporate investigation and part surreal spy thriller. At one plant, Charlie was given the facility tour any visiting investor would receive, but this one was given by the CEO himself—trailed by the man's elderly father, who worked on the factory floor. At another, the accounting staff were literally roused from midday naps and made to stand at attention by their desks while the potential investors walked past.

At one point, Charlie noticed giant metal parts that had been pressed into shape—but no sign of the massive industrial presses that should've been doing the work. He asked where the presses were. The company minder shut him down fast, saying, "We'll talk about that later." That was the moment Charlie suspected something was hidden: There must be another factory, located somewhere else in the city, that wasn't on any of the official listings.

And there was.

The real revelation came as one of our Chinese colleagues with deep local ties diligently pored over public property records, leaving no stone unturned. That "missing factory"? It existed, all right, but not in an industrial zone. It was in the heart of bustling Xi'an, sitting on premium commercial land. That single plot of real estate was worth more than the entire company's market cap.

The short sellers were right about one thing: The factories alone weren't worth much. But they had missed the bigger picture. This didn't seem to be a fraud at all—it was a real-estate play, plain and simple. The company wasn't taking itself private to save a dying motor business. It was a merger offer aimed at unlocking hidden value under its feet.

We bet on the merger closing. It did—everything was legit. The trade was a win.

But this story isn't about the trade. It's about the mindset that made it possible: the ability to step back, question the obvious, stay nimble when the ground shifts beneath your feet. To hold your assumptions lightly, resist the herd when everybody else has already decided, keep probing when the evidence looks damning but remains incomplete.

That kind of cognition—nimble, pattern-driven—is what separates luck from design. It's what allows you to recognize when the map in your hands no longer matches the terrain beneath your feet, or when yesterday's winning play becomes tomorrow's blind spot.

At its core, it's deceptively simple: It's *adaptive thinking.*

And that, more than anything, is what this book is about.

A Hidden Code

What does it take to operate, let alone succeed, in an environment where the pace is relentless, the stakes are massive, and every decision carries a risk of failure, at least on some scale? How do you orient yourself when you *know* you can't rely on the past to inform your sense of what might happen next? How can you hold deep-seated biases at bay, keep your emotions in check, and step outside of your own perspective—"telescope up," as I like to say—when it's time to pull the trigger and execute on your decision? And what if all of the above presupposes that you're not just comfortable, but confident, navigating turbulence and uncertainty as essentially a default state of being?

Succeeding under these and similar conditions demands not a certain type of person, but a certain *way of thinking*.

I've spent the past thirty-plus years building and leading investment organizations—first as a trading executive, later as a founder and investor—working in environments where decisions are made quickly, under uncertainty, and with real consequences for getting them wrong. Over the course of three decades spent in the daily practice of fast-cycle decision-making—as well as the close study of how others, in and far beyond my industry, make decisions—I started to notice something: The people who consistently outperformed weren't always the smartest, or the boldest, or even the most experienced. They were the most adaptive: the ones who knew how to mentally "simulate" a potential course of action before they acted, learned fast enough to course-correct mid-flight, and had the humility to pivot and adjust without ego. In fact, I've come to believe that the *most* successful people, especially serial entrepreneurs and those who rack up wins across industries, use a common set of tools and processes, either knowingly or unknowingly. People who employ these techniques may appear to be lucky, but—in reality—they're not placing random bets; they're *making their own luck*. They're stacking the odds in their favor like a casino. They're leveraging superior decision-making to increase their chance of success and minimize the risk of total (fatal) catastrophe.

This is high Adaptability Quotient, or AQ. There's nothing innate about it—just as serially successful people aren't lucky, by and large (barring the rare exception), they're not geniuses either. They come equipped with the same mental "hardware" as the rest of us; all they're doing is engaging that hardware differently and running it more actively, not unlike a learnable operating system for making better decisions under uncertainty. They have a kind of secret, shared playbook—and a hidden code, running quietly in the background of the most consistently successful among us.

This also means that the discipline of cultivating high AQ—the mental architecture behind consistent success, even in chaos—isn't reserved for the elite. It's a learnable discipline.

Intelligence, Upgraded

What follows is a field guide for developing your practice of this discipline—and building the mental architecture behind consistently better outcomes.

It's built from decades of observation and pattern recognition inside live markets, the high-growth startup environment, tight-loop experimental systems. It's grounded in a blend of many disciplines, where the secret lies at the intersections between them—from cognitive science to systems thinking to evolutionary psychology, and even including my own upbringing.

But this book is far from a memoir. And it's not a self-help book—at least, not exactly. It's more like a manual, a practical handbook for navigating complexity, and a manifesto for reclaiming the singular advantage that we, as human beings, still possess in a world increasingly optimized for autopilot. Because here's the truth: We're not just living through an age of disruption. We're living through the quiet but steady erosion of human agency.

More and more, as a species, we're deferring to algorithms. Outsourcing our judgment to artificial intelligence (AI). Submitting (and subsuming) our tastes and preferences and wants and desires to recommendation engines. What we call "progress" often amounts to little more than elegant, comfortable surrender.

The machine uprising won't come in the form of some real-world analog of Skynet hunting us down with Terminator-like killer robots. It's already here—in the form of complacency, delegation, default settings. The real threat isn't that the machines wake up; it's that *we* allow ourselves to drift tranquilly off to sleep.

Every week, it seems, the half-life of expertise gets shorter. Industries rise and fall in the span of product cycles. A generation once shaped by change now finds itself outpaced by it. The curve is steepening—not just rapidly but exponentially—and the difference between those who adapt and those who don't is no longer measured in years, but in updates. We've entered an era where the only sustainable advantage is the ability to learn faster than the world around us is changing.

What we need, and what this pivotal moment demands, is an adaptive uprising. Not to overthrow the machines—but to reclaim what makes us human in the first place.

This isn't about resisting change. Quite the opposite: It's about becoming fluent in it—mastering uncertainty and turning chaos into advantage.

Among other things, this means refusing to treat the future as something we passively inherit. At least for now, the future is still something we can build.

Let's get to work.

1

Out of Chaos, Order

Luck is the residue of design.

—Branch Rickey[i]

You do not rise to the level of your goals.
You fall to the level of your systems.

—James Clear

All our lives, we've been conditioned to chase the so-called right answer. From school exams to corporate boardrooms to geopolitical strategy sessions, one assumption quietly governs our decision-making: that success follows, or flows from, accuracy. *Hitting the right target. Making the correct call. Buying or selling at the optimal moment.* Get our facts straight, nail the right answer, and the future will reward us.

We build our careers, our companies, our institutions around this illusion. And in slow, stable environments, it sometimes even works. We *are* occasionally "right," or close enough that it makes little difference.

---

i Sometimes misattributed to John Milton.

But even a broken clock is right twice a day. In the world we now inhabit—to say nothing of the future that is swiftly dawning—this mode of thinking breaks down almost immediately. We were taught that success is linear, rational, even just. That the people who win are the ones who make fewer mistakes. That being smart and being right are, more or less, the same thing—and with enough intelligence, effort, and planning, we can make the world make sense.

We were misled.

Not out of malice—out of inheritance: Every human being is born with a mental tool kit designed for a different time than the one we're currently in. Human brains are wired for a world with slower cycles, longer feedback loops, fewer invisible hands tugging at our every perception.

That world is over. The one replacing it is faster, more chaotic, more interconnected—and, in many cases, more adversarial—than anything our species has faced before.[ii]

For most of history, our biggest leaps forward were about power and production. The first Industrial Revolution harnessed steam and mechanical force, multiplying human muscle. The second wired the world with electricity and assembly lines, scaling factories and supply chains. The third transformed information itself into infrastructure, using silicon and code to calculate, store, and transmit knowledge at scale. All three transformed how we worked and what we could build—but the substrate, the basic medium of human thought, stayed the same. By contrast, the first Cognitive Revolution had happened much earlier, when humans became capable of using language and began encoding ideas outside our brains, turning private perceptions and insights into shared symbols and collective memory.

The ongoing (and accelerating) Fourth Industrial Revolution didn't just raise the stakes; it rewrote them. For the first time since the birth of language, we've created a new cognitive medium: systems that don't just process information, but learn from it, predict with it, and feed it

---

ii At least cognitively. In terms of *physically adversarial* situations our species has faced, it's hard to rival a lion on the savanna.

back into our perception. Artificial intelligence, machine learning, and generative models don't simply extend our muscles or our memory; they coauthor, curate what we consider plausible, and decide which options even appear on the mental menu. This moment, therefore, also represents a Second Cognitive Revolution: a threshold beyond which cognition *itself* becomes a shared space between humans and machines. The result is not simply faster progress but a fundamental shift in the architecture of human understanding.

Data, or at least noise, surrounds, suffuses, overwhelms us. Complexity compounds complexity. Machine learning systems optimize what we see, what we buy, what we believe—often without our awareness. We're being asked to make decisions faster, with less clarity and greater consequence, than any generation before us.

It bears emphasizing that the problem *isn't* our underlying hardware. The human brain is miraculous—arguably the most powerful pattern-recognition engine in the known universe. But our default programming? That was written during the Stone Age, on the savanna. For reasons we'll begin to unpack in chapter 2, it's spectacularly good at reacting to things like immediate physical threats, but not so great at reasoning through probabilistic chains of cause and effect, let alone sorting signal from noise in an environment engineered to manipulate your instincts.

Worse still: It can be hacked. Our brain—our decision-making engine—is vulnerable to phishing, nudging, priming, framing. Our fears can be triggered, our attention hijacked.

So the enemy isn't just noise. It's false clarity—the illusion of certainty where the real task is adaptation.

The Adaptability Quotient

How do you steer, in a world like this?

This is a question that has, in a sense, haunted me—first as a trader, trying to avoid losing money on broken deals, then as an entrepreneur, trying to build business after business under uncertainty, and eventually, as someone watching brilliant people fail, not from lack of talent, but from trusting the wrong mode of thinking at the wrong time.

Over time, I began to notice a pattern.

Some people, regardless of their field, seemed to perform unusually well in volatile, ambiguous, high-stakes environments. Not once, but repeatedly. They didn't freeze when things got messy. They didn't try to control what couldn't be controlled. They had something else to fall back on—not a religion, but not far from it, either: a system, a methodology, a (secular) code.

It wasn't raw intelligence. It wasn't charisma. It wasn't even confidence, though it sometimes looks like all of the above. It represents a deeper kind of intelligence—one that doesn't just tolerate chaos, but seems to grow stronger inside it.

These were people who didn't chase the right answer. They built systems that kept improving their answers over time. They didn't avoid failure. They absorbed it, learned from it, and iterated faster than everyone else.

They weren't just smart. They were *adaptive.*

They weren't geniuses—not in the way that word is usually meant. What they exhibited was a way of thinking, a method of making decisions on the way to achieving a goal that prioritized *learning* over *being right.* Speed without recklessness. Structure without rigidity. A framework for navigating uncertainty with discipline and creativity.

This is what I call Adaptability Quotient.

Unlike other aspects of intelligence, like IQ and EQ (as we'll discuss), it's not fixed. AQ is a learnable way of using your mind like a high-performance machine: to model risk, absorb feedback, make faster corrections, and create repeatable advantages in conditions where most people stall out—or drown.

You see elements of it in elite founders who treat every product launch as a live experiment. In top investors who reunderwrite their portfolios in real time. In battlefield commanders who adjust strategy on the fly when the fog of war rolls in.

It's not luck. And it's not magic. It's the operating system that serially successful people are already using—whether they can articulate it or not.

And once you start to see it, you'll see it's everywhere: Elon Musk blowing up rockets—loudly, publicly, if necessary—to accelerate learning curves. Ken Griffin structuring hedge fund teams like special ops units to maximize adaptability and minimize exposure. The best startup CEOs, poker players, intelligence analysts, crisis managers—they're not following any single rigid rulebook. They're building a dynamic framework and adjusting it constantly as the environment changes. Not to make perfect decisions, but to make decisions that get better with every outcome.

We'll spend the rest of the book breaking down this high-AQ methodology into its constituent parts and steps—so you can see it, use it, internalize it. Because adaptive thinking isn't just a nice-to-have skill anymore. In a world shaped by intelligent systems, rapid feedback loops, and engineered uncertainty, this kind of decision-making is a survival trait. Without it, your agency—the very ability to choose for yourself—will be steadily eroded by speed, confusion, and the subtle pull of algorithms trained to "know" you better than you know yourself.

But this isn't a TED Talk in hardcover. It's not life-hacking for productivity junkies. It's your guidebook for upgrading to a better operating system—one built to thrive amid chaos. To make this systematic, we will break down the AQ process into three distinct phases, which form the structure of this book:

PHASE I: METACOGNITION

First and foremost: You have to get to know the machine you're operating, the horsepower under the hood, and the problem-solving "tools" at your disposal. This starts with the realization that our brains—the same ultrapowerful supercomputers that helped our ancestors evade predators and organize societies—are still wired for a world that no longer exists. The result is that we rely, for nearly all decisions, on fast, reflexive mental processes, which evolved to make snap judgments in a much simpler, more stable environment.

But in the Fourth Industrial Revolution, this powerful shortcut leaves us uniquely vulnerable to manipulation, outdated assumptions, and blind spots in our own perception. So the first step is getting in touch with *how you think*: Why do your thoughts, biases, instincts, and intuitions work the way they do? When should you trust them—and when are they steering you off a cliff?

PHASE II: SIMULATION

Once you've arrived at a working understanding of how your mind operates, you can begin to model the world more effectively with it. This phase is about learning to ingest and absorb messy, often conflicting data, and then building a structured way to understand it and to explore your potential options—by constructing a decision tree or a mental prototype of what could happen next.

This is where *choice* emerges, as you chart various courses of action and create a large set of possibilities. This is where you map out the new territory we are living in, rather than relying on old assumptions or outdated maps. Only then can you form a hypothesis and begin to evaluate, by mentally simulating, various competing paths forward—with the goal of eliminating fatal risk and setting up a preliminary game plan upon which you can execute in pursuit of your ultimate objective.

PHASE III: EXPERIMENTATION

At last, it's time to test your hypothesis. Not mentally or in theory, as you've been doing, but out in the real world. This doesn't mean betting the farm—it means learning how to experiment without blowing up the rocket with a crew on board. It means running small tests, absorbing feedback quickly, and revising your model based on what actually happens.

The goal isn't to be right—it's to iterate in the right direction, maximizing learning, figuring out where you might go fatally wrong before it matters, and (ultimately) shortening the path to victory.

At some level, this isn't just a "decision framework." It's your life.

Strip away the stories, the resumes, and the headlines, and what you're left with is simple: A human life is a compounding series of decisions, made under uncertainty. Where you live, who you partner with, what job you take, which career path you pursue, what you work on, when you walk away, when you double down—every one of these is a fork in the road. Some you choose consciously, others you drift into. But in aggregate, they are the path; they add up to your life.

Seen that way, the core challenge of adulthood isn't finding the one right answer. It's learning how to navigate the tree of possibilities, it's generating real options instead of sleepwalking into defaults, and then it's methodically eliminating the branches that are misaligned with your goals or that carry unacceptable risk. AQ is that discipline, just formalized. It gives you a way to create choice on purpose, and then narrow it on purpose, instead of letting circumstance, inertia, or someone else's algorithm do the pruning for you.

You can't control the randomness that hits you along the way. But you can control how you decide, how you update, and how you keep steering. The phases that follow are not academic; they're the mechanics of how you turn a chaotic sequence of moments into an intentional trajectory.

The rest of this chapter will illustrate why this process—not chasing the right answer, but making decisions right—is essential for success, starting with how I discovered this principle in my own career and began to observe it across other high-stakes fields.

Process over Perfection

When we see success, we tend to lionize the lone genius, the decisive leader who makes the perfect call or places the winning bet under pressure. But in the real world—especially when the stakes are high and the variables unknown—that kind of clean resolution is more fantasy than formula.

The people who consistently make good decisions don't rely on brilliance. They rely, knowingly or unknowingly, on process—because they understand it's better to *make decisions right* than to *make the right decision* in any given case. One is repeatable; the other could be random.

To see this principle in action, consider a rescue effort that gripped the world. On the surface, it looked like a long shot: too many unknowns, too little time. Yet the outcome defied the odds and the experts—not because somebody came up with the right answer on day one, but because the people in charge knew how to adapt, iterate, and keep moving forward.

Here's what it looks like when a high-stakes system is built not around certainty, but around adaptive decision-making itself: In August 2010, a cave-in at the San José Mine, a copper-gold mine in northern Chile, trapped thirty-three miners more than two thousand feet underground. Initial efforts to locate them failed. The rock above their refuge was incredibly dense, the mine's maps were outdated, and at first no one even knew for sure whether the men had survived. From the outside, the situation looked hopeless.

There was no existing contingency plan, no map for how to solve the problem. So above ground, a small team—engineers, geologists, Chilean officials, and eventually even NASA specialists—began the grueling work of strategizing a rescue. They faced an agonizingly complex set of constraints: time, geology, equipment limitations, public pressure, and above all, the risk of making things worse. The first drill probes failed. One missed the miners' chamber entirely. But rather than lurching from one idea to the next, the team adapted their approach in real time—relying on a diverse decision-making process that emphasized parallel problem-solving, cross-disciplinary collaboration, and constant revision of their working knowledge of the terrain below.

They ran multiple rescue strategies—dubbed Plans A, B, and C—simultaneously on the theory that one might eventually succeed, even if the others didn't. As conditions changed, they further updated their working assumptions; when Plan B began to show promise, they focused additional resources there. Within seventeen days, that drill reached the cavity where the miners had taken shelter. But even then, the hardest part remained: extracting thirty-three men, one by one, through a narrow shaft that was not designed for human passage. Again, rather than improvise or fixate on finding *the* perfect solution, the team adapted. Engineers redesigned the rescue capsule on the fly. NASA advised them on human endurance in confined spaces, applying hard-won learnings gleaned across decades of manned spaceflight to a decidedly terrestrial challenge. Psychologists developed novel protocols for emotional triage.

Sixty-nine days after the collapse, all thirty-three miners were pulled to the surface—alive.

From the outside, the extraordinary Chilean mine rescue might appear to be just that—a singular miracle of survival or a feat of technical brilliance. But, with all due credit and commendation to the heroic rescue team, that's not the whole story.

What saved those men wasn't a stroke of genius at precisely the right moment, nor an act of bravery or physical courage, nor a heroic guess made in a flash of intuition. It was a disciplined and adaptive decision-making process that scaled under pressure: a flexible but principled framework for assessing risk, adjusting strategies, leveraging innovation and expertise, and moving forward even in the face of incomplete information. The team brought together people with diverse backgrounds and skill sets, all of whom were open to debate and intent on facing a novel problem with no preexisting assumptions. They didn't know exactly what would work, but they knew how to decide what to try next.

Had they waited for perfect information, or bet everything on a single strategy, or clung to the illusion that someone, somewhere, might know the "right" answer—they might still be drilling. Or, more likely, mourning. Instead, they trusted the process, using every tool at their disposal—technical, psychological, organizational—to guide decisions toward the most probable successful outcome.

That's not luck. That's what adaptive decision-making looks like in action—and it illustrates a key distinction: between *making decisions right* and *making the right decision*.

Making Decisions Right

This is where we begin to sharpen the distinction that will guide the rest of the book: Success doesn't come from one-time brilliance, but from repeatable processes. This is what Phase I (metacognition) and Phase II (simulation) make possible—so that when you finally act in Phase III, you're not gambling on perfection but feeding a system designed to keep improving.

Making the right decision is, of course, what we invariably set out to achieve—because we like to win. We prefer never to be wrong. But because that's not the world we live in—everybody gets to be wrong at least some of the time—*how and why* we arrive at a decision is vastly more important than the ultimate outcome. In special operations, elite military teams spend far more time on process than on action. But mission planning isn't about finding *the* perfect plan—it's about stress-testing every assumption, mapping contingencies, rehearsing failure. A successful outcome—a hostage rescued, a high-value target captured—doesn't validate the decisions made unless the process that led there was sound. In fact, teams are trained to debrief every mission the same way, regardless of whether it succeeded or failed, because what matters isn't *just* what happened, even when lives are on the line. It's whether the approach is repeatable, adaptable, resilient under pressure.

A raid that succeeds despite a sloppy plan is not treated as a success—it's both a warning and a learning opportunity. Because in this domain, getting it "right" once by luck can be fatal the next time. That's the true measure of a good decision-making process: not that it guarantees victory, but that it gives you the highest odds, over time, of surviving uncertainty. A CEO who makes bold, high-stakes calls without a structured decision-making process might get lucky once in a while or even more than once—but eventually luck runs out. By contrast, a leader who first and foremost builds a sound framework and culture—for gathering the right information, testing assumptions, considering second-order effects, and more—will sometimes make the "wrong" call, but should consistently make better decisions overall.[iii]

This is where the distinction between *making decisions right* and *making the right decision* becomes more than just semantics: It's the difference between static success and continual improvement. If your focus is on *making decisions right*—following a sound, repeatable process—then even when you happen to get it wrong, you still gain something enormously valuable: learning.

Think about how the best organizations, investors, and innovators operate. They don't expect perfection; they expect *iteration*. A bad decision isn't a failure—it's feedback. Which is why, at least in my experience, the best investors don't obsess over a single losing trade; they refine their models, get up the next day, and try again. The best entrepreneurs don't cling to a failed product launch; they extract insights, adapt, and move on.

Jeff Bezos famously described decision-making itself as a process of experimentation, saying, "If you know it's going to work, it's not an experiment." That's the mindset of someone who builds systems that allow for small, survivable failures—the kind that reveal blind spots, generate better data, and ultimately make you better at making decisions over time.

As I often remind myself, my kids, and my coworkers, *how you do anything is how you do everything*. At the macro level, this means that when you shift your focus from *Was this the right decision?* to *Did I make this decision right?*—when you optimize for learning rather than perfection—you set yourself up for something far more valuable than never being wrong. You set yourself up to be better on the next attempt, and the one after that. In the long run, this is what separates those who succeed from those who stagnate.

But it's important to state something clearly: *Making decisions right* doesn't mean there's one correct way to iterate. There isn't a universal checklist or perfect template. What it means is that you're engaging a

---

iii Culture here isn't just about morale or belonging—it's about shared cognitive methodologies. Later, we'll explore how building a "cognitive culture" means establishing a common way of thinking, problem-solving, and updating beliefs across a team.

process—one that is itself adaptable, testable, and designed to improve over time. A method, not a product.

Because, of course, it's not just about the *next* attempt. Pulling back the camera, if you consider each success or failure in isolation—a singular, barely contextualized data point, either *I was right* or *I was wrong*, plotted against a limitless void—it's not useful. But picture dozens, hundreds, thousands of data points coming into focus in relation to one another: *Now* you might begin to see patterns, be able to draw conclusions, and even advance broader hypotheses about how to string these small "wins" together, and learn from your small "losses," to help achieve your ultimate goal.

This focus on building a resilient, repeatable methodology—a process optimized for learning rather than perfection—is not just visible in high-stakes rescue operations or elite military teams, it is the exact discipline I was forced to build from scratch when confronting the market's chaos. Long before I had the language for AQ, I was living it in the world of finance.

How I Discovered It—Before I Had a Name for It

Before I could articulate the pattern I now call AQ, I had to build my way toward it—deal by deal, trade by trade, business by business.

What follows isn't a grand theory. It's not some tidy origin story either. Because long before I started to recognize high AQ in others—before I could see the patterns and trace it across industries, disciplines, and domains—I had to "wake up."

After all, I didn't set out to create a decision-making framework. I didn't even have the language for it, at first, and it took me years even to scratch the surface when it came to understanding and explaining the underlying science. What I started with, improbably enough, was a puzzle to solve—from scratch, under pressure, with consequences imposed by the market, which like the world around us is ever unforgiving, fast-moving, coldly indifferent to how clever we think we are.

Thus our story begins where this journey started for me—during the frigid Chicago February of 1994.

Where It All Began

When I walked into Wellington Financial Group that winter—just a few months before it changed its name to Citadel Investment Group—it was still a small firm. I believe there were seven other employees there on my first day.

Citadel's founder, the inimitable Ken Griffin, liked that I had a JD/MBA. But I think what Ken found in me most of all—and, over time, what I found in Ken—was someone whose mind worked in similar, or at least congruent, ways: We were both relentlessly analytical thinkers who loved to probe, deconstruct, and question, at times to the consternation of those around us.

With my fresh JD/MBA and a scant six months of mergers and acquisitions experience at JPMorgan, I was first set by Ken to work on learning the business of risk arbitrage, also known as merger arbitrage or risk arb—which, at the time, was an esoteric, poorly understood, mostly clandestine, and ad-hoc subarea of finance.

I'd never been aware of, let alone studied, hedge fund strategies; if you'd asked me what risk arb was during grad school or even my short stint at JPMorgan, I wouldn't have had the faintest idea. But I've always been a quick study, and what I soon learned is that risk arbitrage, in basic terms, means following announced mergers and acquisitions—agreed deals, letters of intent, rumored deals, hostile deals, etc.—and betting on whether they'll fall apart or close successfully.

To use an analogy I've deployed with investors over the years: Risk arb is like having a friend introduce you to a recently engaged couple, and then inviting you to bet on whether they will, in fact, get married or not. Wager ten dollars and lose it all if the couple calls off the engagement, but win eleven dollars from your friend if they *do* wind up tying the knot.

Let's say you take your friend up on this bet. Short of peering into the souls of the couple in question or eavesdropping on their private conversations, what evidence might you want to gather, before deciding whether and how much to wager, to determine the likelihood that this couple will get married or not?

Depending on the type of wedding they're planning, first and foremost I know they'll need to set a date, reserve a venue, get sized for wedding bands, hire florists and caterers, send invitations, possibly take a blood test, file paperwork for a marriage license, and more. Much of this unfolds along a (more or less) predictable timeline—which I'll be tracking closely if I do decide to take the bet, to ensure they're signing contracts with vendors, hiring the band or DJ, getting those save-the-dates in the mail on schedule. If there are three weeks to go until the couple's ostensible wedding day and no invitations have gone out, or if some other big piece is missing or looks wobbly—that's information that needs to be accounted for and might shift my thinking.[iv]

This is analogous to risk arb, which involves breaking mergers down into their constituent steps or parts, figuring out how to assess (based on publicly available information) whether those steps are proceeding as expected, and then watching those and any other indicators like a hawk to anticipate or monitor each party's commitment (as evidenced by progress).[v]

The trouble was that, when Ken decided I should learn how to build a risk-arb business in 1994, there was virtually nothing—and virtually

iv Each of these data points reduces uncertainty about the future—an idea rooted in Claude Shannon's work on information theory. As we'll explore more fully in later chapters (and particularly during Phase II), decision-making under uncertainty is ultimately a process of gathering information to narrow the range of possible outcomes.

v In a sense, this is a preview of another important concept that arises in Phase II: breaking down complex situations to first principles, then reasoning forward through patterns and probabilities. It's a disciplined way of seeing *before* deciding.

no one—to learn *from*. There were no textbooks, no how-to guides. Just a twenty-page pamphlet by Guy Wyser-Pratte, one of the earliest practitioners, which mostly gestured at concepts rather than showing how to apply them.

So I started the only way I knew how: Break the problem down, then build it back up again. No one asked me to do so, but then again no one told me *not* to. And then, with no small degree of urgency—and without an expert risk arbitrageur sitting over or steering me—I dove in, exercising a certain amount of freedom to proceed in whichever direction satisfied my curiosity.

I wasn't sure which factors mattered, so I began with what I much later understood as *maximum entropy*—a starting point that assumes all outcomes are equally likely because you have no basis yet for favoring one over another.[vi] It's the cleanest possible mental reset: maximum uncertainty, zero assumptions, full openness to signal. This meant beginning with the basics: building the complex tools I'd need to track various aspects of each deal (which would also form the foundations of a database), along with spreadsheets to take in live quotes and calculate key metrics. I called friends at the investment services firm Bear Stearns, to try to glean something from their expertise, but quickly found that wasn't good enough. I didn't just want to know, based on the considered opinion of some expert advisor, whether a given deal was likely to be approved or rejected; in the spirit of "teach a man to fish," I wanted to *understand why*, and be able to perform that analysis for myself, so I could operationalize it and make it repeatable. Thus, even as I was constructing my tools and spreadsheets and corralling my own rogues' gallery of experts, I was simultaneously reading as widely and deeply as I could, analyzing merger agreements cover to cover, so I could soak up as much nuance as possible. I also brushed up on Delaware state law, since almost all of the companies in question were

---

vi In information theory, the principle of maximum entropy states that the most unbiased prediction you can make, given limited information, is the one that assumes the widest possible distribution of outcomes. In other words: Don't assume structure that isn't there. We'll return to this idea later, when we explore how adaptive minds use entropy as a guide to navigate uncertainty.

headquartered there—and even researched the inner workings of non-antitrust regulatory bodies, from the Fed to health care regulators to state insurance regulators. And so on.

This gave me the ability to go back and interrogate the data for myself, starting from a blank-slate mental posture known as *beginner's mind.*[vii] Sometimes, I'd think I spotted a pattern—some repeatable signal hiding in the noise—and, sure enough, the data would confirm it. Other times, I'd have an intuition that turned out to be wrong, so I'd dig into the numbers and discover there was no real arbitrage opportunity after all. Not everything panned out. But the process sharpened my judgment and deepened my understanding.

In early 1995, we put together $1 million to form Titan Partners—the first fund I ever managed. I'll never forget my first trade, which I made the day after we started the fund. A company was doing a spin-off, so I called two brokers. One said the market was a four-dollar bid with a five-dollar ask per share. In other words, buyers were willing to pay four dollars per share while sellers would expect five dollars. Another broker said it was a six-dollar bid with seven dollars offered. Both were ten thousand shares up.

I put one phone to my left ear and another to my right, buying ten thousand shares at five dollars per share from one broker and selling, to the other broker, ten thousand shares at six dollars per share. *Boom*—just like that, in practically an instant, I'd made $10,000. While this was far from an astronomical sum, it still constituted a 1 percent return on our $1 million raise—on day one, and in fewer than twenty-four hours.[viii]

---

vii As we'll unpack in later chapters, the concept of *beginner's mind* is often associated with Zen Buddhism (which calls it *shoshin*) and signifies an attitude of openness, curiosity, and freedom from preconceptions, even when you're engaging with something familiar. It's the opposite of expertise ossified into assumption. We'll come to understand and deploy it as a cognitive stance that enables adaptation in complex, fast-changing environments.

viii Apologies to the brokers on the other ends of those phones. Yes, it was me. Yes, I hit and lifted both sides simultaneously even though, at the time, I may or may not have acted like I had no idea what you were talking about.

This was when it began to dawn on me—not in a thunderclap or as a cinematic eureka! moment—but as a slow-rolling realization: No matter what the textbooks might say, markets are *not* efficient. Rigor and process can yield an edge in many places, and in so many unknown, unheralded, or underappreciated ways; I was immediately determined to find more, and to delve deeper into areas where opportunity was overlooked. This has become a singularly propulsive force in shaping my career: a drive to understand on a deeper level, to better map the changing territory around me—finding the best places others miss on their own maps—and then to rationalize and systematize what others have tended to approach more or less as random bets.

Systematizing the Edge

In risk arbitrage, speed and accuracy are everything. The ability to evaluate a deal faster and more precisely than your competitors, without cutting corners, creates a compounding advantage. But from the start, I saw that the traditional process was riddled with inefficiencies.

Every time a merger was announced, you had to start from scratch: diving deep on the industry and regulatory environment, parsing press releases, dissecting the merger agreement, evaluating regulatory risk, scrubbing the financials. That "blank slate" approach created drag—an information bottleneck that slowed everything down and left too much room for slippage, noise, and error.

So I began to wonder: What if we could industrialize this?

What if, instead of reinventing the wheel on every deal, we built a framework that could systematically reduce uncertainty? What if we created something closer to a Henry Ford–style assembly line rather than an artisanal garage?

My first real breakthrough came during a wave of commercial bank mergers in the 1990s. At the time, commercial banking was consolidating rapidly, so I needed to understand how these deals worked. Most arbs took a broad brush approach, since they knew the Fed cared about two things:

whether banks had strong Community Reinvestment Act (CRA) ratings and whether any single bank dominated a local market. If there was too much overlap, the banks would typically divest deposits to another institution, clearing the way for approval.

That was the conventional wisdom, at least. But I wanted to go deeper.

I bought books detailing every bank deposit in the United States and ran my own calculations to estimate market concentration. I also realized that state banking authorities, not just federal regulators, played a crucial role in approvals. And it was this insight that led me to track down a consultant in Florida who had deep connections in the state banking world.

Hiring her turned out to be a game changer. By calling around, speaking with competitors, and piecing together what amounted to open-source intelligence, she helped us forecast approval timing with far more precision than anyone else.

That single data point—being able to anticipate *when* a deal might close, rather than just *whether* it would (like having a sense of when the engaged couple is planning to get married)—meant we could pile into a trade at the right moment and earn superior returns because our time horizon was shorter than the market expected.

And this was just the beginning. Our initial success also gave me a bigger idea: *What if we didn't stop there?*

There was no such thing as an "expert network" back then. But that's effectively what we built: a web of hundreds of consultants, embedded across industries and geographies, who helped us triangulate regulatory intent, decode bureaucratic momentum, and anticipate market expectations through entirely legal, public, and available means.[ix] If I needed to understand something about a given market or regulatory approval process, I had a person for that. My working assumption was never that all

---

ix Before "expert networks" were a formalized industry—before outfits like Gerson Lehrman Group (GLG), Coleman, or Guidepoint became institutional fixtures—we were effectively building our own. We didn't call it an expert network; we just needed answers, fast, and built the system to get them at scale.

was going smoothly and would be A-OK; I assumed it would *not* be OK and that any deal could fall apart at any moment.

The results were stark. In my first 1,100 trades, I lost money on just four. Over nine years, our strategy produced high-teen annualized returns after fees, with only five down months—including through the 1994 rate spike, the Russian default, and the dot-com crash. This was not because we had some secret crystal ball, but because we built a decision-making machine that got better with every trade.

Most investors didn't go to these lengths for one simple reason: They didn't see the value. Or they didn't want to spend the money. Or maybe they were just a little bit lazy—contentedly chugging along, coddled in the soothing warmth of conventional wisdom. Better decision-making requires energy, but the benefits aren't small.

Whatever the reason, I had decided from the jump that I wanted to play a different (and less comfortable) game. I knew that better information meant better decisions, and I was fortunate that we had the resources to make sure our diligence was sharper than anyone else's.

Crucially, though, it wasn't just about being right, it was about *creating a practical framework*—a system for reducing uncertainty, in a way that compounded over thousands of trades.

This mindset—experimenting, iterating, and building proprietary intelligence—became a recurring theme in my career. Every time I found a new inefficiency, I pushed myself to ask the same question: How can we do this faster, better, and more systematically than anyone else?

The answer was almost always the same: Dig deeper, build smarter, and *never* assume the standard playbook is the best one.

An Accidental Control Group

Human decision-making has always been anchored in, or at least tethered to, the past. Tradition, accumulated experience, storytelling, and cultural memory have provided (and still provide) a stable foundation for interpreting the present and predicting the future: Farmers sow crops in patterns established generations ago and merchants follow trade routes charted by their ancestors. For centuries upon centuries, to deviate from the well-trodden path was to invite chaos, to throw things out of balance.

But what happens when the past is no longer predictive? What happens when technology, geopolitics, culture, and capital shift so fast that the old winning strategies stop working? At that point, you're no longer navigating familiar ground—you've crossed into new territory. As historian and philosopher Thomas Kuhn observed, true paradigm shifts don't just change the rules; they change the game. The old maps stop matching the landscape. What once looked like insight now becomes inertia.

That's the world we're entering. And it turns out there's one group of people who've been living in it all along: serial entrepreneurs.

Entrepreneurs, by their very nature, cannot rely on the crutch of precedent. They are unbound from past experience (to the extent that anyone can be) because, by definition, they're doing something that hasn't been done before. The essence of their work is to envision a future state that is profoundly disconnected from the past: a future reshaped by new technologies, ideas, systems. Consider Elon Musk and SpaceX: In charting a course to Mars, Musk could not simply update the analog (and woefully out-of-date) mid-twentieth-century NASA playbook, nor could he apply the lessons of the electric car industry. To tackle the problem of interplanetary travel, he'd have to think not about how rockets had *traditionally* worked, but about how they *could* work, revisiting—and in some cases reinventing—the most basic principles of rocket science to account for factors like cost, reusability, and scale.

Many serial entrepreneurs live in this same realm of radical possibility—not refining old playbooks, but writing new ones—on a stage where survival depends on making sense of a noisy, shifting environment. This makes them a phenomenal, if accidental, control group for studying decision-making under uncertainty. If you want to understand what kind of thinking holds up when the rules are in flux, watch a founder trying to turn a half-formed idea into a viable company.

It's not raw intelligence that sets our control group apart. It's not vision, charisma, or even resilience in the conventional sense. What links serial entrepreneurs across industries is their adaptability: their ability to identify leverage in uncertain systems, to iterate without losing focus, to make smart decisions that compound—even when the landscape is unfamiliar and the destination is still out of sight. The best succeed not despite of uncertainty but because of it.

This mindset—fluid, feedback-driven, relentlessly experimental—is what the discipline of cultivating high AQ seeks to formalize. Not to try to capture the thinking of any one individual, but to reflect and codify the process beneath the pattern. By studying how serial entrepreneurs think, we're not just decoding their success—we're uncovering a tool kit for how the rest of us can navigate a world where the stable ground is gone, and the only way forward is through.

At its core, AQ presents a structured way to make better decisions—one that reflects how the most consistently successful people think and act in high-stakes, fast-changing environments. It's not a checklist or a formula, but a mindset shift, which is why I refer to it as a kind of upgraded operating system for navigating complexity.

Putting It to Work

Thirty-odd years ago, when I started my career, people insisted that risk arb was too qualitative to ever be automated. To be blunt: They were wrong.

From scratch, we created what became the most successful automated risk arb business of its time—managing many billions of dollars and executing trades at scale while maintaining an optimized, hedged portfolio. What made it work wasn't just the capital or the speed; it was the foundation of data and insights that allowed us to make decisions with greater confidence and efficiency than anybody else in the game.

To this day, the system we built—grounded in real-world intelligence, disciplined strategy, and the power of structured decision-making—would still rank in the top half of all active arbs. To me, the lesson is clear: Where others relied on instinct and convention, we built a system that was highly adaptable.[x] And in the long run, a well-built, highly adaptable system will always outperform even the sharpest individual judgment.

But, of course, the insights that populate this book don't flow solely from my own experience. They're the product of a kind of obsessive pattern-seeking—one that spans decades, disciplines, and lived experiments.

The spark for systematizing AQ was ignited by my lifelong fascination with patterns, including how high performers think—how some people, across wildly different domains, develop mental frameworks that seem to thrive under pressure, iterate faster, and deliver consistent clarity in complex environments.

But the real engine of this book is something older and deeper than any one observation. It's something the biologist E. O. Wilson called *consilience*: the idea that truths from different fields—philosophy, psychology, mathematics, strategy, anthropology, sociology, neuroscience, systems theory, information theory, decision theory—can converge to reveal a broader understanding that no single discipline can reach alone.

I've spent years chasing this convergence. I've drawn on academic materials (from entropy and Bayesian inference to metacognition and cybernetics), studied competitive strategy, read far too many biographies, and learned alongside some of the sharpest minds I know.[xi] I've also built and broken real-world systems under pressure, which, I'll admit, is sometimes more educational than reading academic papers—though I've done plenty of that too.

The problem isn't that the ideas, tools, and processes we need to make better decisions aren't out there—it's that they're scattered, unconnected, buried in scientific literature or biographies that capture the *outcomes* shaped by great decision-makers but rarely dissect how these extraordinary minds *actually work*.

---

x In essence, we built a system that modeled the way I make decisions—capturing my adaptive mental process and linking it to real-world data. That let us simulate questions, test "out-of-sample" assumptions, and evaluate possible outcomes using actual historical signals, not just theory, improving with every iteration.

xi Including not just Ken Griffin and Ross Stevens, but other former colleagues like Dave Snyderman and Ross Laser, whom we'll get to know a bit later in the book.

And that's the missing piece. (Not unlike the state of risk arb when all I had to orient myself was a twenty-page pamphlet: The theory, academic underpinnings, and essential ingredients are all out there in scattered form. This, I suppose, is edifying. But how you actually *do the thing* is 99 percent of what matters, and—let me tell you—the handbook just plain has not existed.)

I'm not a PhD, but—given the task at hand—I see that as both a tactical and a strategic advantage. Even close friends, longtime colleagues, and others who know me well tend to underestimate just how deep I can fall down academic research rabbit holes: I'll blink and look up only to discover I'm utterly lost amid piles of scientific papers, journals, or the kinds of books you can only find on secondhand grad-school textbook websites. While most people read novels or mainstream nonfiction, I gravitate (sometimes to the exhaustion of those same friends, former colleagues, and others, especially family members) to the dense, the obscure, the technical—pulling insights from disciplines that don't usually talk to each other.

That's the well I'm drawing from, so to speak.[xii] But this book isn't meant to be an academic treatise—it intends to be useful; theory is important, but if it can't be applied, it's just an intellectual exercise.

I won't pretend this is the final word on this subject either. Our understanding of the underlying science will continue to evolve, and new insights will emerge. I'm also not going to flatter myself—as a nonscientist—by presuming that I've absorbed, understood, and gone on to interpret and render every nuance of the sophisticated ideas I'm drawing upon (from the works of people who are much smarter than I) absolutely note-perfectly. Indeed, if I kept refining every detail in pursuit of perfection, this book would never see the light of day—but of course "perfect" is not the goal.

What we urgently need isn't more information or deeper scientific understanding; it's a Rosetta stone—something that cuts through the noise, connects seemingly disparate dots, and, most importantly, makes

xii In addition to my time at Citadel and Magnetar, this perspective draws on experience building businesses across industries, as well as work in philanthropy and hospitality.

these insights *actionable*. That's what this book is designed to be, and to do: *democratize and widely share* ideas that are otherwise scattered, siloed in biographies and scientific treatises, locked between the ears of some successful decision-maker somewhere out there.

In an age of accelerating complexity, the ability to think clearly and make better decisions isn't just an advantage. It's a survival skill. The good news is that evolution has conferred each of us with the most powerful decision-making engine in the known universe: the human brain.

In the next chapter, we'll explore how this ancient machinery works—and why, unless we upgrade the software we're running, it will keep leading us astray.

Adaptability Quotient Field Guide: Key Takeaways

- **The old goal—being right—is obsolete.** In a fast, complex world, accuracy without adaptability breaks down almost immediately.
- **Process beats perfection.** The people who thrive aren't the smartest—they're the ones who learn fastest.
- **AQ is learnable.** It's not talent or temperament but a skill: using feedback to refine how you think and decide.
- **Making decisions right matters more than making the right decision.** Repeatable advantage comes from how you decide, not how often you guess correctly.
- **Chaos rewards structure, not control.** Build systems that can flex and learn under pressure.
- **Failure is data.** Every outcome—good or bad—is a test that sharpens your next move.
- **The human brain is powerful but outdated.** We need new mental software for the speed and noise of the Fourth Industrial Revolution.

- **The AQ methodology unfolds in three phases:**
  - **Metacognition** – Understand how you think.
  - **Simulation** – Model the possibilities and develop your hypothesis.
  - **Experimentation** – Test, learn, and adjust fast.
- **Serial success is built, not born.** What looks like genius is often disciplined iteration.
- **Your task: Stop chasing certainty.** Start building a decision-making system that thrives (versus breaks down) on uncertainty, and learn as you go.

2

The Anatomy of Adaptation—Why Your Human System Needs an Update

It ain't what you don't know that gets you into trouble.
It's what you know for sure that just ain't so.

—Mark Twain

The greatest danger in times of turbulence is not
the turbulence. It is to act with yesterday's logic.

—Peter Drucker

We like to think of ourselves as rational creatures, armed with the most advanced brains on the planet. And in many ways, we are. Our minds can juggle abstractions, plan years into the future, compose symphonies, split atoms, send rockets into orbit. That is the strength of the equipment we've inherited: a system of staggering cognitive power.

But every system has constraints. Ours was built for a very different world: the savanna, not the stock market; small tribes, not global networks;

a trickle of information, not a fire hose. The same architecture that once helped us hunt and survive now struggles to process the complexity of the twenty-first century, especially as the Fourth Industrial Revolution and the Second Cognitive Revolution continue to accelerate.

That's what this chapter is about: laying bare the anatomy of the human operating system, including its moving parts, its strengths, its vulnerabilities. Before we talk about how to adapt, we need to consider the *internal* factors, understand the hardware evolution gave us—and reveal why, without an upgrade, it will keep steering us toward mistakes we can no longer afford.

Your Superpower . . . and Greatest Weakness

Imagine waking up one morning and discovering you have a hidden ability—a genuine, real-life superpower, one so potent it reshapes the world around you. Here's the catch: You've had it all along. You were born with it. You use it every day. Yet you probably have no idea it's even there.

Every time you recognize a song based on a split-second snippet, detect sarcasm in a conversation, spot a friend in a crowd, cook without a recipe, or navigate your car through heavy traffic, you are wielding this superpower. No, it's not terribly exciting or flashy—no one will be rushing out to see the latest Captain Carpool movie anytime soon—but, in the context of evolutionary biology, your ability to process a constant influx of data, make any kind of sense of it *at all*, and then respond almost immediately—is nothing short of miraculous. In fact, despite feeling so mundane that it barely registers, this capacity reflects what neuroscience understands as "the essence of the evolved human brain" and is the foundation of human dominance, creativity, and progress.[1]

Two million years ago, our ancestors appeared on Africa's wild grasslands essentially naked and unarmed. Without claws, fangs, natural camouflage, or any built-in speed advantage to speak of—just vulnerable, mostly hairless flesh, fragile bones, and a peculiar(-ly large) brain—they nevertheless became one of the savanna's most effective predators, vaulted to the top of the food chain, went on to reshape not just the African continent but the entire planet, and are (as we speak) extending their reach into space. Such was, and is, the potency of their superpower—the same one you possess: superior pattern processing, or SPP.

While the precise biological mechanisms and underlying neural architecture are not (yet) well understood, in terms of how and why humans differ so vastly from even our closest relatives when it comes to complex and abstract thought, communication, and higher-order reasoning, SPP suggests that the human brain's remarkable ability to recognize, interpret, and generate complex patterns is the cornerstone of our advanced cognitive functions. This suggests that our capacities for intelligence, language, imagination, and creativity are deeply rooted in our evolved proficiency for pattern processing. Further, as neuroscientist Mark P. Mattson has argued, many of the unique features distinguishing the human brain from those of other species—including expansions in our prefrontal cortex, visual cortex, and parietal–temporal–occipital juncture, all of which are associated with higher-order processing tasks—may in fact be attributable to our enhanced pattern-processing capabilities.

Just as important, SPP didn't just give rise to recognition—it enabled *communication*. The ability to encode and transmit increasingly abstract patterns through language transformed human cooperation, culture, and cognition. Language became the interface through which ideas could be shared, challenged, refined—allowing us not only to predict the world, but to update our predictions together.

Herein lies the deeper point: If pattern recognition is the seed of human intelligence, then pattern *editing* may be its highest expression. The same circuitry that allows us to learn also allows us to *un*learn—to override outdated beliefs as reality changes. That's not a trivial feature; it's the cornerstone of adaptability itself.

But if this capability is universal, its application is anything but. People hold on to beliefs like possessions—defending them, protecting them, sometimes refusing to part with them long after they've outlived their usefulness. The real differentiator isn't whether we can form patterns. It's whether we're willing—and able—to let go of the ones that no longer serve us.

However the underlying biology takes expression, what matters is the result: We can discern grammatical structures and meanings from streams of sounds, facilitating complex communication at a level of sophistication that eclipses any other species (even accounting for the near certainty that science does not yet fully ascertain just how sophisticated some forms of animal communication surely are). Our ability to detect patterns also allows for abstract thinking, enables complex problem-solving, and may be a font of uniquely human creativity, since recognizing and manipulating patterns underlies such a high degree of artistic expression and underwrites the generation of novel ideas.

Naturally, though—like any superpower—ours also has its drawbacks. For one thing, our propensity to find patterns is, in part, what can lead to overinterpretation: seeing faces in inanimate objects, imagining ghosts, developing superstitions. Even more broadly, the harsh truth is that SPP is—generally speaking—*fundamentally maladapted* to the way we as human beings live in the twenty-first century.

These days, the very trait that allowed us to outthink predators and master our environment can also trap us; our greatest strength can become, in essence, a deadly kryptonite—unless we learn how to recognize it, harness it, and direct it with intention.

To understand how that kryptonite functions—why a strength like superior pattern processing can both empower and mislead us—we have to examine how human intelligence really works. Not as a single trait, but as a layered system built over time, shaped by evolution and culture, and constantly updated by the environments we live in. What follows is a breakdown of that system—its parts, its power, and its blind spots—that forms the architecture we'll be building on in every phase of this framework.

The Anatomy of Human Intelligence

For most of our species' history, *Homo sapiens* were far from the fastest, strongest, or most resilient creatures in the animal kingdom. What set us apart was our intelligence—but not in the way we often think of it. Intelligence is not a single, monolithic trait; it is a triad of abilities that has allowed us—*still* allows us—to adapt, cooperate, and innovate.

IQ is what most of us think of as "traditional" or "raw" intelligence. It helped early humans understand patterns in nature, enabling them to predict the migration of herds and the change of seasons. Raw intelligence powers a process, but it doesn't come with a "how-to"—and it varies from person to person. At the individual level, it's your memory cache, your parsing speed, and your ability to make nonlinear or distal associations—to see links between ideas that aren't obviously connected, envisioning how a puzzle might fit together.[i] Some people only see patterns when the data points are adjacent; others can detect structure when the signals are far apart. It's a kind of pattern fluency—and, in today's world, that's increasingly what we mean when we talk about intelligence.

But IQ is not *wholly* individual. It's more like a baseline process that works best when it's plugged into shared knowledge, dialogue, and cultural learning. You don't just think with your brain—you "think" with books and social networks, in conversations with others, and with deep knowledge and shared wisdom inherited from your community and environment.

The implication is powerful: IQ is not fixed to your person. It's a tool you can extend. And it becomes far *more* powerful when linked with other minds.

Not incidentally, it is (of course) no accident that traditional IQ is closely analogous to AI systems that are trained with large language models (LLMs). The parallels are striking: Both gather, store, and process information using pattern recognition—extracting structure from past examples and applying that structure to new problems. The comparison isn't perfect, but it's revealing.

Human intelligence, in its IQ-driven aspect, thrives on patterns

---

i In later chapters, I refer to these conceptual anchors as "nodes" of a decision tree.

and logical reasoning: From childhood, we observe the world, identify recurring themes, and refine our understanding by connecting cause and effect. Similarly, an AI is trained on massive datasets, extracting patterns and relationships across vast volumes of information, both with and without context. Both processes thus rely on learning—in humans through lived experience and study, in AI through statistical analysis of preexisting information. But where AI works with data alone, humans can pair raw pattern recognition with insight, abstraction, and causation—at least when we're at our best.

If IQ represents the raw computational power of the human brain—the ability to analyze data, solve problems, and process logic—then **EQ**, or emotional intelligence, represents a host of nuanced perceptive capabilities and operating functions that determine how effectively we can interact with others, and even how well we understand *ourselves*. Emotional intelligence encompasses several critical faculties: self-awareness and awareness of others—a subject upon which I have more ink to spill in chapter 5—plus the ability to process social cues, leavened by a delicate balance of humility and confidence. These skills empower us to navigate the messy, unpredictable world of human relationships; in the Pleistocene, they (coupled with our ability to navigate social complexities) also enabled humans to form large, cohesive tribes, creating a level of cooperation that no other species could achieve.

This is because emotional intelligence governs how well we understand ourselves and navigate the social world. EQ is what lets us detect and decode emotional patterns: posture, tone, subtext, contradiction. It's also what allows us to reach outward—to learn from others, access knowledge beyond our own memories, and collaborate toward shared understanding.

For our purposes in adaptive decision-making, two elements of EQ matter most: *grit* and *curiosity*.

Grit is the capacity to override the brain's automatic responses. It allows us to slow down, sit with ambiguity, and resist the comfort of false certainty. But grit isn't just stubbornness, as it's often (defensively) conceptualized—it's also an offensive tool. It's the disciplined tolerance for cognitive tension in service of higher-order goals. Indeed, grit requires us to embrace the discomfort of ambiguity and the deferred rewards of a greater objective; as the brilliant academic, psychologist, and author Dr. Angela Duckworth has written, grit is not only "a combination of passion and perseverance for a singularly important goal" but "the hallmark of high achievers in every domain." And it's more than just the ability to endure discomfort and stick with one path. At its highest expression, grit is the willingness to *sustain the pleasure of the unknown*—to remain inside an open question without collapsing it prematurely. Most people experience uncertainty as a kind of pain; grit lets you hold that tension long enough to see what others can't yet see.[ii]

Curiosity, meanwhile, is the fuel: the impulse to explore, to ask better questions. Curiosity encourages us to hold hypotheses lightly and to embody the principle of *strong opinions, weakly held*, or SOWH, which will be vital during later chapters. When paired with humility, curiosity becomes an intellectual accelerant—a willingness to say "I might be wrong," and keep going anyway.

Another way to conceptualize grit and curiosity is as complementary gears in the same engine. Grit holds. Curiosity explores. Grit gives you the traction to resist premature closure. Curiosity gives you the motive to keep searching. One anchors. The other propels. Without both, the system stalls. Together, grit and curiosity allow emotionally intelligent thinkers to remain learners—long into adulthood, and especially in fast-changing environments.

This pairing—grit to hold the tension, curiosity to keep probing—is a preview of how the second phase, simulation, works in practice. When you're generating hypotheses and exploring possible paths, grit prevents premature closure, and curiosity keeps the search alive.

Whether emotional intelligence is innate or teachable remains open to debate. Some researchers argue that self-awareness and self-regulation—two of EQ's core components—*can* be cultivated, especially through practices like meditation or self-compassion. My own view is closer to something my parents used to say: Character may be fixed, but behavior

---

ii See chapter 5 for more on this subject.

can change. Whether you're naturally empathetic or not, the ability to pause, listen, and adjust remains within reach—and that may be what matters most.

Yet our emotional lives are rife with traps. The same psychological forces that make us human—our desire to belong, our craving for quick certainty, our susceptibility to confirmation bias, among others—can sabotage our thinking. In some ways, these tendencies resemble a poorly designed reward function in an AI model: Just as a machine learning algorithm can be skewed by a flawed objective, our minds can produce irrational outcomes when our "reward function" is shaped by unexamined biases. The desire to feel sure of ourselves, to win arguments, to avoid discomfort—these can lead us to prioritize immediate emotional satisfaction over long-term understanding.

This is where **AQ**—the adaptive quotient—comes in.

AQ is not just the capacity to change your mind; it reflects a deeper mind*set*—a kind of open-mindedness in action. It begins with a willingness to question your own assumptions (even at a fundamental level), engage in probabilistic reasoning, and entertain alternative hypotheses, including what you and others might perceive as the least plausible ones. Crucially, AQ demands *metacognition*—the ability to observe and question your own thinking. In the context of this journey we're on together, this isn't mere navel-gazing; it's a disciplined process of improving the methods by which we process information, valuing intellectual rigor over the ego-driven need to be right, *right f***ing now.*

Smart people aren't those who never make mistakes. They're the ones who know how to update their thinking continuously. They're the ones who say to themselves, *If the facts change, if the world shifts, so will I.* As Jeff Bezos once put it, the smartest people he knows "change their minds a lot." Not because they're indecisive—because they're learning and updating faster than everyone else.

At its core, AQ is about process rather than outcome. It requires embracing uncertainty and treating new information not as a threat, but as a gift. People who exhibit high AQ understand that there may never be a single "right" answer; instead, they might see rational thinking as a probabilistic journey, one guided by clarity of thought and the willingness to adapt. Over time, this produces results—not by guaranteeing certainty, but by ensuring that every decision contributes to a foundation of increasingly robust understanding, which in turn fuels an iterative process toward better outcomes. It gives IQ and EQ a kind of situational awareness; without AQ, you haven't updated your map and cannot direct IQ and EQ to solve problems.

These three forms of intelligence—IQ, EQ, and AQ—did not just help us survive from an evolutionary perspective; they became the foundation of all human civilization. By integrating IQ's intellectual rigor with EQ's emotional awareness, both guided by AQ's adaptability, we might just approach the operational ideal: a mindset capable of balancing instinct with reason, flexibility with persistence, and creativity with rigor.

This integrated mindset is what the AQ process is designed to build. But before we can achieve this optimal state, we must first confront the built-in operating flaws that undermine our intelligence. These flaws stem from the ancient, dual-system architecture of the human brain.

Old Brain, New World

Let's flash back to the savanna, somewhere deep in human prehistory, for just a moment—a scene from the primal beginnings of human memory:

> *You're walking through the wild scrubland when, at the edge of the nearest grove of mopane trees, you hear a rustle, and your peripheral vision catches a flash of movement and what appears to be brown fur. Before you have time to think, your body tenses, your heart rate spikes, and you're ready to run. A fraction of a second later, your rational mind kicks in: Was it a predator? An antelope? Maybe a kudu? Just the wind?*

This is the essence of what Nobel laureate Daniel Kahneman calls

System 1 and System 2 thinking: two distinct modes of cognition that shape every decision we make.

System 1 is fast, automatic, and intuitive: *Detect predator—RUN.* It stores experiences, maps, and associated events with environments. It governs our snap judgments, gut feelings, and instinctive or emotional reactions—like recognizing a friend's face, catching a falling glass, starting in reaction to a loud noise. It operates (essentially) effortlessly and without our conscious control, drawing on patterns, heuristics, and past experiences to make rapid decisions.

System 2, conscious decision-making, is (by contrast) slow, deliberate, analytical, logical, and effort*ful.* It activates when we face something unfamiliar, contradictory, or complex—when instinct or reflex alone isn't enough. This is the system we use to solve new problems, weigh competing evidence, reason through unfamiliar dilemmas, override knee-jerk reactions.

These two systems don't operate in isolation. Most of the time—some 97 percent, according to Kahneman in *Thinking, Fast and Slow*—System 1 runs the show, offering quick, confident responses to (mostly) familiar inputs, and getting things right a significant share of the time. But whenever you're faced with uncertainty, complexity, or contradiction—whenever a novel situation or problem arises—that's when System 2 is supposed to step in. System 2 questions assumptions, scrutinizes biases, and (to the best of its ability) prevents costly mistakes.

The trouble, for our purposes, isn't that System 2 is lazy—it's that *we* can be. It takes grit to resist System 1, and work to explore and use System 2.

System 2 is costly in that it takes significant effort and burns more energy; it also tires easily, takes longer to reach conclusions, defers to System 1 whenever possible, and (all too often) rationalizes poor decisions after the fact instead of truly interrogating them.[iii] System 1, meanwhile,

iii The human brain uses about a fifth of the body's total energy—roughly the same as a dim light bulb—yet it runs the equivalent of trillions of computations every second. By comparison, today's most advanced AI models burn through orders of magnitude more energy to produce a single sentence. In terms of efficiency, the brain still outperforms silicon by a staggering margin.

offers faster, easier answers with far less effort. But that ease comes at a price: less structure, less information, more uncertainty.

In information-theory terms, structure is what fights entropy (or uncertainty). Every time we engage System 2—every time we pause, question, reflect—we're doing just that: pushing back against randomness. The tension between Systems 1 and 2, therefore, is more than just psychological—it's cognitive physics.

Some cognitive scientists refer to this tension as the *intelligence paradox*: the idea that the brain's fastest, most confident system is often at odds with its most accurate one. These systems collaborate, but they also conflict—and knowing when to trust which one may be the most important metacognitive skill of the twenty-first century.

And this isn't just a philosophical exercise. Sometimes, it's a matter of survival. To understand the real-world consequence of this internal conflict—the price of indecision between the fast system and the slow one—we turn to a moment where I experienced this cognitive physics firsthand.

Pick One—or Pay the Price

A few years ago, I signed up for what turned out to be one of the hardest endurance races I've ever attempted: a seven-day, high-altitude mountain bike race across the Pyrenees. I'd done Ironmans before—grueling, yes, but relatively predictable. This was something else.[iv] Off-road, unsupported, with ten thousand feet of vertical climbing per day, along with punishing descents through isolated terrain. Every day pushed me to my limits. But day five was where things came to a head. All too literally.

We were deep into the course. The terrain was turning savage—rutted trails, sketchy switchbacks, long stretches traversing remote, unforgiving wilderness. On the climbs, I was (mostly) fine—lean and wired for endurance, I could pace myself and stay focused. But the downhills? They always

iv If you're thinking Tour de France . . . think again.

got to me. Barreling down steep, narrow mountain paths, miles from help, you're just one mistake away from disaster.

It was during one of those steep cliffside descents that I faced a decision.

I saw a jump coming up—nothing outrageous, but big enough that I couldn't gauge the landing. Ahead: trees, shadows, uneven terrain. I'd never ridden that course before. And in that moment, I froze—not physically, but cognitively. System 1 told me: *Keep your speed up, hold your line, trust the bike*. System 2 whispered: *Maybe get off and walk this one.*[v] Neither took control. I hesitated, braked slightly, lost momentum, committed too late.

The front wheel bucked as I went over the drop too slowly. The rear tire shot up as the front tire sought terra firma. And just like that, in that moment of indecision, I went over the handlebars, full Superman, and slammed my head into a rock the size of a kitchen stove.

What saved me—literally—was dumb luck. The part of the boulder I hit had a patch of moss. Just enough cushion to keep me from cracking my skull or breaking my neck. I lay there, stunned, bleeding, gravel in my face, gear twisted around me. Much later, I realized what the lesson was: *You can't be stuck in between*. Not at speed. Not on a mountain. Not in life.

It's easy to talk about System 1 and System 2 like abstract tools in a mental toolbox. But the reality is more brutal. There are moments when *choosing*—fully committing to the mode that matches the moment—is the only move. And if you try to hedge, to half listen to both instincts at once, you're asking for trouble.

What almost got me that day wasn't the crash—it was the indecision. The split-second pause that put me in no-man's-land *between* fast and slow thinking, between fluid execution and cold analysis.

And it's not just about racing. That same failure mode shows up in meetings, negotiations, investments, crises. It shows up in life. The

---

v Rigid time cutoffs necessitated a day chock-full of hundreds of such trade-offs.

solution isn't to *always* trust your gut or *always* slow down and think. It's to know which mode you should be in—and commit.

This costly failure mode—the hesitation between instinct and analysis—is not limited to high-speed cycling. It is the fundamental vulnerability of our Paleolithic code. Worse still, the modern world is engineered to confuse this boundary on purpose. The same instincts that once helped us survive can now be turned against us by systems that understand them better than we do. In the next chapter, we will unpack exactly how external forces—from social-media algorithms to advanced cyberattacks—exploit the vulnerabilities of System 1, magnifying the cost of cognitive hesitation.

The challenge, then, is to move beyond that moment of failure and engineer a decision-making system capable of withstanding maximum stress. To understand what the optimal system looks like, we turn to a very different kind of system—one built for literal liftoff: Max Q.

Where Pressure Peaks

"There she goes."

These are the final words spoken by a NASA controller as the newly designed rocket—topped for the first time with a pressurized crew capsule—thunders upward, clearing the launch tower at Cape Canaveral. For anyone within miles, the roar is almost deafening. You can feel it in your chest.

The smoke plume disappears quickly out of view—and the rocket itself vanishes into the hazy Florida overcast just twenty-six seconds after launch. Telemetry data monitoring every system in real time is streaming into Mission Control consoles; so far, everything looks nominal—normal and on-target—for today's test flight.

The launch vehicle accelerates, straining to break free of the Earth's atmosphere—though not our planet's gravity. This particular test flight is suborbital, and aimed at simulating a failure-and-abort that would include shaking down the capsule-booster combination for the very first time, ensuring the heat shield works as designed, and assessing the crew capsule's flight and landing characteristics. So far, as the sound of the engines fades raggedly overhead, everything is still looking good.

As the vehicle keeps accelerating, the density of the air decreases with altitude, allowing most rockets to throttle up their engines for the final push into space. But this means that, while any rocket is climbing off the launchpad, the forces and aerodynamic pressures acting upon it initially *increase*, swiftly building to a moment of maximum dynamic pressure known to rocket scientists as *Max Q*, which is when the combination of high velocity and air density peaks at a specific altitude. This is a critical phase of flight, when the rocket pushes against the most air resistance it will encounter during its ascent, and it imposes major limits in terms of aerodynamic engineering.

Today, our rocket performs faultlessly—right up until the moment it passes through Max Q, at which point an anomaly is detected. A second later, the pressure gauges measuring liquid oxygen and rocket-fuel-grade kerosene drop—precipitously—and the telemetry signal cuts out. All indications suggest a loss of engine power (though it will later be discovered this was not the case). Next, just under a minute into its maiden flight, according to NASA's after-action report, controllers observe "multiple radar contacts" as Mercury-Atlas 1 breaks up, coming apart some 8.1 miles above the Atlantic Missile Range and raining down in pieces off the Florida coast, a scant six miles from the launchpad.

Today is July 26, 1960, and this failure looks like another costly setback to a space program that's already *months* behind schedule—and falling further behind the Soviet Union every day. But failures like Mercury-Atlas 1, and delays like the ones necessary to launch Alan Shepard safely into space the next year—followed by John Glenn's flight into orbit—began to teach NASA (a lean and technologically limited but entrepreneurially minded agency) how to launch and recover humans from space, paving the way for Neil Armstrong and Buzz Aldrin's first steps on the Moon in 1969.

The moment a vehicle reaches and passes through Max Q is still announced during every modern rocket launch. It remains a significant milestone as it's a threshold every rocket must cross on its way to orbit.

But these days, when SpaceX or NASA mission control calls "Max Q," it's more a nod to tradition than a true moment of existential risk.

No, the physics haven't changed—Max Q is still the point of peak aerodynamic stress—but the way we understand and engineer around it has.

Some early launches failed at (or near) Max Q because their designs hadn't yet accounted for the sheer forces at play; today, these forces are baked into every calculation, anticipated down to the last stress fracture. Thus any structural weakness that could fail under aerodynamic load *has likely failed already* by now—meaning that if a rocket reaches Max Q intact, the odds of success dramatically *improve.*

This is why I think of Max Q as something more than just an engineering benchmark: It's an inflection point, the moment at which the greatest external pressures have been endured and—if you've built everything correctly—*most of the risk is actually behind you.*

The same principle applies to high-performance decision-making, which is why I use Max Q as a metaphor for the convergence of those three aspects of intelligence: IQ, EQ, and AQ.

Alone, each of these intelligences is powerful. But when combined—when we develop the intellectual depth to think clearly, the emotional awareness to navigate complexity, and the adaptability to survive under pressure—we reach something close to an optimal operating state. We become like a well-designed launch vehicle at Max Q: stable under stress, accelerating toward our goal, leaving the greatest dangers behind and below us.

That's what this book is building toward: a decision-making framework that allows us not just to survive, but to thrive in moments of peak pressure. Because ultimately, Max Q isn't the moment of greatest risk; it's when you know whether you've built something that can go the distance, with AQ harnessing IQ and EQ in pursuit of your chosen goal.

Before we build further toward that high-performance framework, we need to unpack the deeper reason it's necessary. Because while the metaphor of Max Q illustrates what well-designed systems can do under stress, most of us aren't operating with that level of engineered precision just yet we're running dangerously obsolete software in a high-speed world. And the gap is widening fast. The forces—technological, psychological, geopolitical, and more—reshaping our environment aren't waiting for us to adapt. Every delay compounds the disadvantage; every hesitation cedes greater agency to systems that are evolving exponentially faster than we are.

DIY Adulthood

The principles embodied by Max Q—finding stability under stress, accelerating toward the goal, leaving the greatest dangers behind—represent the required upgrade for modern cognition. Because today, most of us are running obsolete software in a high-speed world.

In this age of relentless notifications, infinite social-media scrolls, and breaking-news alerts, our finely tuned pattern-recognition abilities have come under unending siege to such an extent that SPP threatens to overwhelm us. The human brain, powerful as it is, simply wasn't designed for the accelerating flood of information or the pace of decision-making demanded by modern life, driving us to see patterns where none exist, mistake noise for signal, and jump to conclusions in ways that can be dangerously wrong. Our strength as pattern processors becomes a tremendous weakness when misapplied to the complex, interconnected systems of the digital age. The twenty-first century has thus transformed our superpower into a liability that is a significant handicap in a world that punishes slow adaptation.

This shift isn't just happening at the level of geopolitics or high finance. It's also happening under our noses, in an endless array of small, everyday decisions that used to run on autopilot.

What follows might feel like a sharp turn—from rockets to daily life—but this is deliberate. One of the goals of this book is to show that the same framework applies whether you're trading billions, leading a company, or just trying to navigate modern adulthood.

Twenty years ago, you might have bought a used car by kicking the tires and taking it for a test drive. Today, you're parsing years of maintenance records, deciphering insurance-company babble, and wondering whether the algorithm that priced it took your zip code into account. You used to have a defined-benefit pension; now—congratulations!—you're your own portfolio manager, and your family's financial health and future are on the line if you don't know what you're doing. Insurance used to be a formality—now Californians and so many others are calculating flood risk models on their own. The friction of decision-making has crept into the mundane.

This is DIY adulthood in the age of data. Systems once built to simplify our lives now require constant judgment, selection, and analysis. And as our decisions become more complex, more uncertain, and more irreversible, the margin for error shrinks—while the cognitive load expands. What used to be habitual now demands deliberation. And System 2, for all its value, is expensive to run. That's why this book isn't just a diagnosis—it's a how-to. A framework for navigating complexity when the old shortcuts no longer work.

After all, for much of recent history, and certainly for most of our present lifetimes, the mismatch between *how we think* and *what the world demands* has been a problem, but a manageable one.

That's about to change. The world is crossing a threshold where intelligence itself is being outsourced and amplified. Already, the gap between our biological bandwidth and the speed of synthetic cognition is widening by the day.

The Missing Upgrade

But, of course, this story doesn't end with—and this book is emphatically *not* about—human limitations. Quite the opposite: This book is a celebration of what makes us uniquely human, and a guide for how to harness it. Evolution didn't stop at survival; we as human beings have developed capabilities far beyond what's necessary merely to reproduce.[vi] We can override our instincts, set long-term goals, pursue and debate and disagree about abstract ideas like justice and art. Importantly, it's this capacity for *metacognition*—thinking about how we think—that gives us agency. Unlike a squirrel gathering nuts or a wolf hunting in a pack, we can reflect on our mental processes and *choose* to behave, even to think, differently. Indeed, as cognitive scientist Keith E. Stanovich argues (in part) in his thought-provoking work *The Robot's Rebellion*, we must both recognize and challenge our ingrained drives if we are to have any hope of attaining true autonomy. "We, alone on earth, can rebel against the tyranny of the selfish replicators," he writes, referring to the genetic imperatives that—according to those who embrace universal Darwinism—reduce human beings to biological machines. In response, Stanovich presents a brilliant manifesto for what he calls a "robot's rebellion"—a cognitive reform that empowers us, as individuals, to transcend our genetic programming and define our own purpose.

But the forces reshaping our world—AI, automation, synthetic biology, quantum computing—aren't just accelerating technological change. They're magnifying the ways in which our minds are wired for a past that no longer exists. We are moving—more swiftly than many people realize—into an era where bad mental models don't just lead to suboptimal decisions; they make us *obsolete*. The question is no longer whether we can keep up—it's whether we can *rewire how we think*, transcending our programming and defining our own purpose, before it's too late.

Each of these emerging domains represents a kind of leverage point:

- AI is *software* running on *external* hardware—a lever for your brain.
- Robotics is *software* running on *external* hardware—a lever for your body.

---

vi In referencing our ability to transcend genetic imperatives, I'm drawing from a long lineage of work, including Richard Dawkins's *The Selfish Gene* and Keith Stanovich's *The Robot's Rebellion*, both of which explore how human cognition might allow us to overcome—not just obey—our evolutionary programming.

- Synthetic biology is *software* embedded in your *internal* biological hardware—another lever for your body.

But where's the *software* that upgrades your *internal* mental hardware—a lever for how you think?

That's the missing upgrade. That's what this book aims to provide: a kind of cognitive-firmware update.

And as it turns out, the quest to create machine intelligence began with this same metaphor. From its very origins, artificial intelligence was conceived as a mirror of human cognition—a structured attempt to replicate, and (theoretically) perhaps eventually surpass, the brain's ability to learn, reason, and adapt. Understanding where that idea came from—and what it overlooked—is essential to understanding why our minds now feel like they're under siege.

Adaptability Quotient Field Guide: Key Takeaways

- **Your superpower cuts both ways.** Superior pattern processing (SPP) made us dominant—and now makes us easy to mislead in a high-noise world where people and businesses are all too eager to exploit basic human tendencies.
- **Old brain, new world.** Paleolithic shortcuts succumb to engineered feeds and adversarial systems; default settings are now liabilities.
- **Intelligence is a system, not a score.** IQ (pattern power), EQ (awareness of self/others), and AQ (updating under uncertainty) only work at full strength together.
- **Grit and curiosity are twin gears.** Grit lets you tolerate the tension long enough to learn; curiosity keeps you searching for the new instead of settling for the old.

- **Recognize your mode—and commit.** System 1 (fast) and System 2 (slow) both save lives; indecision between them causes the crash.
- **Metacognition is the master switch.** Seeing your own thinking in real time is how you choose the right mode and avoid being hijacked.
- **AQ is the differentiator.** The winners aren't those who are never wrong—they're those who update the fastest and cleanest when the environment changes.
- **Max Q is the target state.** When IQ, EQ, and AQ align, you stay stable under peak pressure and accelerate through it.
- **DIY adulthood raises the stakes.** What used to be habitual now demands deliberation. Everyday choices require analysis once reserved for experts. But System 2 is expensive to run—and the cognitive tax is real.
- **Install the missing upgrade.** You can't change the hardware you were born with—but you can change the mindware you run.

3

Steering Through the Storm

The major psychological insight of the last few decades is that humans often do not use the resources of their intelligence unless they are explicitly cued to do so.

—Keith E. Stanovich[2]

Man like all other organisms lives in a contingent universe, but man's advantage over the rest of nature is that he has the psychological and hence the intellectual equipment to adapt himself to radical changes in his environment. The human species is strong only in so far as it takes advantage of the innate adaptive, learning faculties that its psychological structure makes possible.

—Norbert Wiener

If the last chapter focused inward—on how the human brain evolved to process patterns and why that strength now misfires in a world it wasn't built for—this chapter looks outward. Because the terrain is changing fast. Advances in AI, robotics, and synthetic biology are not just redrawing industries or professions. They're accelerating the mismatch between our default wiring and the demands of modern life. And this isn't just about coping with disruption. It's about understanding what AQ is *for*: creating a mental operating system for achieving clarity, advantage, and what I'll define before the end of this chapter as *deep success*, in an increasingly nonlinear, fast-loop world.

To grasp the true nature of this emerging reality, we must first recognize its origins in a technological revolution conceived decades ago and built as a mirror of human thought itself.

The Machines We Made in Our Image

In the summer of 1956, a group of visionary scientists convened at Dartmouth College for a workshop that is, today, widely celebrated as the founding event of artificial intelligence (and the world that is, even now, being reshaped by).

This gathering, known as the Dartmouth Summer Research Project on Artificial Intelligence, was organized by luminaries such as the pioneering computer scientists John McCarthy, Nathaniel Rochester, and Marvin Minsky. Another key player was Claude Shannon—an electrical engineer and mathematician already known by then as the "father of the Information Age"—who had developed the mathematical and theoretical foundations for how information can be stored, processed, and transmitted, which was a breakthrough fundamental to *all* digital technologies. Together, these four leading minds coauthored the proposal that coined the term *artificial intelligence*, convening an ambitious "two-month, ten-man study" to investigate and explore it.[3]

While this workshop is often hailed as perhaps *the* seminal moment in the early history of artificial intelligence—with McCarthy, Rochester, Minsky, and Shannon widely considered to be AI's "founding fathers" (alongside their near-contemporary, Alan Turing)—the conceptual underpinnings of artificial intelligence can be traced much further back. This trail leads us to the eighteenth-century English resort town of Tunbridge

Wells, of all unlikely places, where a local Presbyterian minister and amateur statistician named Thomas Bayes spent his later years plumbing the philosophical depths of human thought. Writing by candlelight, he formulated a method for updating the probability of a given hypothesis based on new evidence—a principle widely known today as Bayes' theorem—although the seminal, groundbreaking essay proposing this idea, which would go on to make him world famous, was not published until two years after his death, in 1763.

As we will unpack during Phases II and III, what Bayes' theorem achieves is a mathematical framework for learning from experience, which is a concept that is central to modern AI systems. By quantifying uncertainty and updating beliefs with incoming data, AI models are (mostly) well equipped to make informed decisions, even in dynamic, rapidly changing environments. This approach, of course, mirrors human cognitive processes, in which we continuously adjust our understanding of the world based on new information. We update our map (view of the world) to more accurately make decisions with our intended outcomes. Optimizing for wrong (or obsolete) conditions leads to failure.

(But I digress. . . .)

The deliberate design of artificial intelligence to emulate human thought processes is far from coincidental; as no less an authority on the subject than Claude Shannon once famously remarked: "I am a machine and you are a machine and you can think, can't you?"[i] To me, the convergence of Shannon's ideas with the philosophical and mathematical writings of Thomas Bayes, nearly two centuries earlier, underscores a profound insight: that the quest to build intelligent machines is deeply intertwined with understanding and replicating the mechanisms of human thought *itself*.[ii] Today, those machines—and the technologies that parallel their

i Sometimes attributed to Alan Turing; the historical record is unclear regarding which attribution is better substantiated.

ii Such is the influence exerted by Thomas Bayes and Claude Shannon that we'll cross paths with both of them again, more than once, as we make our way through the chapters that follow.

sophistication—are no longer theoretical; they are the external hardware upgrades reshaping the world.

From Idea to Incarnation

Even after the Dartmouth workshop signaled a kind of starting gun, it would take half a century and more of breakneck innovation—characterized by once-inconceivable leaps forward that today leave any civilian with a smartphone holding more computing power than did all of NASA when humans first walked on the Moon—before what the general public would recognize as the first rudimentary artificial intelligences began to flicker to life.

Artificial intelligence may have begun as a thought experiment, but it didn't stay in the realm of theory for long. Once the first sparks of machine intelligence appeared, the race was on to see how far—and how fast—those capabilities could scale. And as AI took shape, it did so alongside a constellation of other technologies that were transforming human possibility.

The science of robotics has evolved, in just the past few decades, from rudimentary machines that can, for instance, accurately but mindlessly repeat dangerous or delicate steps on an assembly line, to sophisticated entities capable of performing complex tasks with precision—and a high degree of independence—in spaces designed not for industrial machines but primarily for humans, far from any factory floor. From performing rescue work at disaster sites, assisting in highly complicated surgeries, and even providing a kind of companionship to the elderly and infirm, modern robotics is challenging many of our longest-held assumptions about what machines can do—and, perhaps more importantly, what they *should* do. Together, in a sense, these advances represent what amounts to a significant upgrade to what we might consider "external hardware," extending human capabilities into realms previously deemed (or proven) inaccessible.

Other advanced sciences, such as synthetic biology, have also been on a steep upward curve. The advent of CRISPR gene-editing technology has ushered in a new era in biotechnology, offering unprecedented precision in enabling scientists to alter genetic code. The potential of this singular breakthrough extends to something that, for most of human history, we've only been able to fantasize about in science fiction: the prevention, or even elimination, of genetic diseases. Researchers are exploring the possibility of using CRISPR to edit embryos, excising genes that are known to be associated with conditions like Alzheimer's and muscular dystrophy, aiming to eradicate these notorious ailments long before they manifest—and thereby effectively giving us, as humans, the ability to upgrade our biological hardware *itself.* This burgeoning advancement alone holds enormous potential to ripple across medicine, agriculture, and other fields, potentially reshaping the future of humanity.

Taken together, robotics and synthetic biology are more than industries; they're force multipliers. They extend what our bodies can do by editing the code of life itself and blurring the line between external tool and internal upgrade. Which makes a certain question inescapable: Where do we draw the boundary between "us" and the machines we're building?

But, of course, the prospect of editing not just the genome but the human *germline*—making changes that are inheritable by future generations—raises profound moral questions. Unintended consequences, such as off-target genetic modifications, could have lasting impacts on humanity's entire gene pool. The case of He Jiankui, a Chinese scientist, underscores the potential ethical pitfalls: In 2018, He announced the birth of twins whose genomes he had edited to confer resistance to HIV; this led to widespread condemnation and, subsequently, to He's imprisonment. On its face, this highlights the risks of premature or unethical application of new technologies—and explains why at least seventy-five countries (to date) have taken steps to limit heritable genome editing.[4] But it also implicates deeper questions, including about who gets to exercise agency over such decisions in the first place.

That is to say: *Who*, or (more accurately) *what*, holds the power as AI continues to develop?

The Pervasive Upgrade

The quest for enhancing human cognitive abilities is already gathering momentum. Neurotechnologies such as brain-computer interfaces (BCIs)—like Elon Musk's Neuralink—are emerging alongside noninvasive brain stimulation techniques as promising potential tools for cognitive augmentation. BCIs, for instance, can enable the brain to interface directly with external devices, potentially restoring lost functions and enhancing mental faculties. Less invasive techniques, like transcranial magnetic stimulation (TMS), have also been shown to improve performance across an array of cognitive domains, including learning and memory. And scientists are experimenting with nootropic substances, neurofeedback training, and other interventions aimed at boosting our mental performance. It's far from inconceivable to imagine a future in which BCIs and other technologies can artificially boost your IQ to 200, and even feign advanced EQ. Still, AQ would remain in your hands.

But hovering over and suffusing it all—every aspect of the Fourth Industrial Revolution and the dawning future we're about to step into—is AI, *the pervasive upgrade*, which becomes more integrated by the day not just into our daily routines, from the personal assistants that manage our schedules to the algorithms that predict our preferences and direct our attention, but (increasingly) into our very *selves*.

Here's where many analyses of the Fourth Industrial Revolution fall short. They treat AI, robotics, and biology as technological stories. But what matters more—what will determine whether these advances empower us or erase us—is cognitive: how our minds adapt, or fail to.

This cascade of innovation—from extending our bodies via robotics, upgrading our biology via gene editing, and augmenting our minds via neurotech—requires us to view the challenge not just in terms of technology, but in terms of cognitive architecture. As AI-infused or AI-enabled systems grow more widespread, spanning and spurring advances from robotics to synthetic biology to cognitive augmentation and beyond, what are the implications for *human agency*? How can we maintain control and ensure that these technologies serve as extensions of our will—and, indeed, serve *our* will (rather than the other way around) or serve as replacements?

In his book *Homo Deus: A Brief History of Tomorrow*, the historian Yuval Noah Harari offers a compelling exploration of human evolution and also projects it forward, painting a potential future for our species. He suggests that, as technology continues to advance and evolve—particularly when it comes to fields like artificial intelligence and biotechnology—we may be swiftly approaching a new era: a threshold beyond which, Harari posits, humans may actually evolve into a different kind of being, potentially altering (or at least challenging) the definition, the very essence, of what it means to be human.

This perspective, especially in conversation with thinkers like Stanovich, underscores a pivotal theme that gets at the heart of why this book matters, *right now*: I see this as a unique and extraordinary moment—an inflection point, for all humankind. And we must be vigilant stewards of our own evolution.

As we will explore at greater depth in the closing chapters of this book, the Fourth Industrial Revolution itself—and everything this moment promises, as AI, robotics, synthetic biology, and other advances redound to one another's benefit—holds significant potential to enhance, improve, and even perhaps extend human life. Given the scope of transformational change that's already roiling so many aspects of our existence, the scale of this potential may be unprecedented in the history of our species. But these very same advances also pose the most serious challenge with which human autonomy and identity have ever been confronted—and we must respond accordingly.

What makes this moment especially complex—and urgent—is that not all tools are external. Some reshape us from within. Language was the first. Unlike fire or the wheel or writing, language didn't just extend our capabilities—it rewired *how we think*. It changed the way we associate ideas, store memories, construct meaning. It was, in many ways, the original Cognitive Revolution and software upgrade: It was the bridge between instinct and abstraction, the scaffolding for what we now call System 2. Before the advent of language, deliberation was shallow, fragmented; after it, we could reason, plan, debate, imagine. It didn't merely enable communication—it transformed cognition. As Noam Chomsky wrote,

"Language is not just a vehicle for communication. It is also a tool for thought."[5] Lev Vygotsky went further: "Thought is not merely expressed in words; it comes into existence through them."[6]

Which brings us to now. AI, synthetic biology, and neurotechnology—tools that don't just extend the human form, but challenge the architecture of human thought itself—may prove to be the first tools since language that blur this same boundary. We have never before outsourced decision-making; we've only used tools to augment or improve it. A Second Cognitive Revolution, in other words, is well underway.

For the first time, the tools we've created can learn, generate, and act with a kind of autonomous momentum, accelerating faster than our capacity to fully grasp their consequences. The same technologies that promise to cure disease, extend lifespan, and solve scarcity also have the power to rewrite biology, manipulate perception, and fracture our shared reality. Whether this revolution elevates or erodes us will depend on a single variable: whether we keep a human in the loop. Because intelligence without intention isn't progress—it's drift.

So that's what's at stake. Not just how we survive this new age, but how we preserve—maybe even redefine—our agency within it.

The Battlefield Has Shifted (or: Cognitive Security in the Wild)

So far, we've been looking at the grand arc of technology. But the storm isn't only out there on the horizon—it's already breaking over your inbox, your news feed, your daily choices. The battlefield has shifted from the physical to the cognitive.

Of course, the challenges we face today aren't entirely new. In 1834, two Parisian bankers orchestrated what is often considered to be the first cyberattack, infiltrating France's semaphore telegraph system (by bribing the system's operators) to insert false signals that provided them with sensitive market information in advance. Naturally, this conferred a massive (albeit illicit) edge.

What has changed since then, most obviously, is the scale and speed of technology—the medium for, and battlefield upon which, any so-called cyberattack is waged. One recent study analyzed Reddit discussions and found that AI-generated posts—without being labeled as such—received more responses than posts that were written by humans.[7] This wasn't because the AI had better insights. It was because the content was tuned—deliberately or otherwise—for emotional impact, mirroring the patterns most likely to trigger a reflexive, System 1 response. In other words: The machine "knew" how to press the right buttons. It knew what would land.

As technology continues to evolve, the speed and sophistication of these manipulative tactics will only increase, overwhelming our (literally *prehistoric*) cognitive defenses. In fact, some of the most effective "hackers" on the planet don't exploit code anymore. They exploit cognition. They understand human psychology better than some psychologists.

Consider the simplest version of this attack: You've just received an email from your bank. The subject line is urgent—something about suspicious activity on your account. You click. Instantly, panic sets in: Your credit card has been charged! The email seems legitimate, but something is just a little bit off. . . .

Of course, by the time you realize it's a scam, you've already clicked on the link. Congratulations! You, not just your computer, have just been hacked.

What happened? This wasn't a failure of intelligence; it was a triumph of efficiency. Your brain, fine-tuned by evolution for speed and survival, reacted almost instantaneously to a perceived threat. This is System 1—quick, instinctive, and often emotional. In the digital age, this same hardwired reflex has become an almost debilitating vulnerability. The moment you click the link, the hacker—today's apex predator—wins. The attackers have already manipulated your behavior by exploiting a known vulnerability in your mental "software."

Cybercriminals are sophisticated, but social media companies and advertisers have taken this same principle and industrialized it. They know they don't need to steal your credit card information; they just need to hijack your attention. From there, the entire business model is predicated on triggering rapid, reflexive responses: outrage, curiosity, desire, validation. These platforms have become extraordinarily sophisticated at predicting exactly what will make you click, scroll, share, or react. They understand that the brain is a pattern-processing machine, so they feed it a carefully calibrated diet of stimuli designed to keep it hooked.

This gets at something deeper: In a sense, these companies have cracked the code in terms of how our brains process information—and have weaponized that extraordinary superpower to use it to their advantage. They know that when we see a headline that confirms our preexisting beliefs, we'll instinctively accept it; when we're outraged, we'll be more likely to share something, even if it turns out not to be accurate. The algorithm doesn't need to trick us—it just needs to nudge us, influence how we engage our attention, steer us ever so slightly and subtly. We do the rest ourselves.

What we need is a security patch. Just as most of us (including me, who could never in a million years be mistaken for a computer expert) have, over time, learned to recognize and avoid phishing emails—through spam filters, basic cybersecurity training, and simple experience—we can also develop a mental firewall against the forces that hijack our attention. We can learn, in other words, to recognize when we're being manipulated—which, in turn, empowers us to choose how, or whether, to respond. What this comes down to, at a basic level, is cultivating an understanding of how your own brain works and refusing to let others hijack it: Just as you wouldn't open an email from a stranger without a second thought, you can train yourself to pause before responding to the latest viral outrage, before believing the most convenient story, before surrendering your attention to the next quick and easy dopamine hit.

But that's a reductive understanding of what's going on here, and it obscures an opportunity to expose and unpack the deeper implications for decision-makers. The hardware—your raw intelligence and pattern-recognition abilities—is, again, emphatically not obsolete. On the contrary, it remains astonishingly powerful, unrivaled, in many respects, by what we've been able to achieve in silicon (at least so far). But the software you're running, the operating system that decides when to engage your full processing horsepower and how to run it once it's in gear, is not just riddled with cognitive biases, reflexive responses, and mental shortcuts—*it was written for a world that no longer exists*. In an era of engineered uncertainty, securing this mental software—establishing true cognitive security—requires us to manage ground truth, biases, and the overwhelming signal-to-noise ratio[iii] that constantly threatens to overwhelm System 2. Because just like a vulnerable operating system, hackers will keep finding new and innovative exploits if it isn't carefully and comprehensively upgraded.

If the last century was about protecting our physical security, in a time roiled by world wars and other geopolitical conflicts, *this* century may be about protecting our cognitive security—*and indeed our agency as human beings*—against an array of metastasizing threats.

This may, in fact, be the defining challenge of the digital age: learning to think clearly, to make decisions right, in a world that is increasingly adversarial and *designed* to make us react impulsively. And this, in turn, begins not only with recognizing these "hacks" for what they are—but, just as importantly, installing the right mindware to counteract them.

The Unseen Environment: Habitus

This isn't only about swatting away individual distractions; it's about the very water we're swimming in.

Sociologist Pierre Bourdieu called that water *habitus*: the invisible set of norms, defaults, and expectations we absorb from the worlds we inhabit. It's the autopilot of a culture—how "people like us" tend to think, feel, and act without being told. In a predigital world, your habitus was shaped by family, school, neighbors, and work: messy, plural environments that forced you to bump into difference.

iii For our purposes, signal-to-noise ratio, or SNR, is the balance between meaningful information (signal) and irrelevant or misleading data (noise). In an age of algorithmic feeds, infinite inputs, and manufactured attention traps, our cognitive SNR is under siege. The higher the noise, the harder it becomes for System 2 to separate what's true from what merely feels urgent.

Today, most of us also live inside a digital habitus, an attention economy that quietly scripts our moves or at least the background hum of our daily lives. Feeds, notifications, and "For You" pages don't just reflect your preferences; they train them. They narrow the set of things you see and, over time, the set of things you can imagine. That's a problem for adaptation, because AQ depends on getting outside the obvious set. It requires sampling new inputs, updating assumptions, revising frames.

In this environment, confirmation is cheap and curiosity is heavily taxed. The system rewards microagreements (e.g., likes, boosts, and follows) and punishes epistemic risk (e.g., the awkward post, the unpopular link, the question that doesn't resonate with the tribe). Even when you think you're "researching," you're often just walking linear corridors the platform has already laid out for you. The result isn't just distraction; it's frame lock, or the feeling that your current map is complete when it isn't.

Here's what that looks like on the ground. You read a thread that matches your stance on a volatile topic; the platform notices and cues up more of the same. Your notifications light up—tiny hits of social proof. Within days, your feed has shifted from *here's a range* to *here's the range you'll accept*. Nothing about your raw intelligence changed. Your habitus did.

Bourdieu also had a term for the unexamined acceptance of a system's rules. That term is *doxa*, or the way the game becomes "just the way things are." Online, doxa shows up as inevitability theater: "everyone knows," "no serious person believes," "obviously." Once that tone takes hold, exploration feels costly, and the very moves AQ requires—opening the set and testing out-of-distribution ideas—start to feel socially disloyal.

This is why habitus matters here. Phase II (simulation) and Phase III (experimentation) will both rely on the width and freshness of your input set. A digital habitus that autofills your priors will shrink your decision space before you've even started mapping it. If you don't notice that compression, you'll optimize brilliantly . . . inside a box you didn't choose.

So the first upgrade is simple and brutal: Notice the water you're swimming in. Treat your social and news feeds as training data you didn't consent to, at best, and diversify them on purpose. Seek anticorrelated sources. Schedule friction. Move some conversations off-platform where latency and nuance can breathe. You're not trying to be "balanced" for its own sake; you're protecting the surface on which your models are drawn.

Which leads directly to the next question—because widening your input set is only half the job. If your objective is misaligned, a perfect process will take you perfectly in the wrong direction. So that's where we turn next.

What Are We Really Solving For?

If the external world is engineered to hijack our attention, and if our social environment (our habitus) is engineered to prevent us from questioning our core beliefs, the challenge goes beyond merely making efficient choices.

The external threats we face, including the algorithmic hijacking of attention and the constant pressure to react, are designed to make us prioritize shallow, immediate emotional satisfaction over long-term understanding. They lead us to confuse the noise of the moment with the signal of the goal. This is why our upgrade to AQ requires defining not just how we think, but *what we are solving for.*

To state the obvious, any decision-making framework—no matter how refined—is not an end in itself. It might be brilliantly constructed, logically sound, even mathematically elegant—but without a clear and worthy objective, it's just an elaborate exercise in moving pieces around an empty board.

The best tools in the world mean nothing if they aren't aimed at the right target; any sword, no matter how beautifully forged, is useless—a ceremonial ornament—unless wielded with skill and purpose. The book you hold in your hands, the system we are building here, is meant to be used—sharpened, tested, and ultimately applied to the real world. Which means we need to be clear about what we are using it *for.*

And the answer, at the highest level, is simple: It's for navigating toward your goal. For now, let's stipulate that this objective is *whatever you've decided matters.* Whether you're launching a product, building a career, deciding where to live, or determining how to show up for the people you love, your goals, whatever they are, can only be reached through one mechanism: a series of choices. Your life, in other words, is a long-chain function of decisions made over time. And every action you take is, whether explicitly or implicitly, the product of a decision.

This, in part, is why decision-making deserves such focus. Not because it's abstractly important, but because it is *practically everything.*

Of course, this raises a deeper question—one we'll mostly set aside for now: What if your goal is the wrong one? Philosophers and cognitive scientists distinguish between *thin rationality*, which focuses on the efficiency of achieving a goal, and *broad rationality*, which questions whether that goal is worth pursuing in the first place. This book is about the former. It presumes you're chasing something that matters to you. That doesn't mean all values or objectives are equal—but it does mean we're not here to debate the morality of your aims. Assuming it's worthwhile because you've decided it is, we're here to help you get there—smarter, faster, and with more flexibility and fewer costly mistakes.

Because the problem isn't usually that we have *no* goal. It's that we pursue the wrong ones too efficiently.

Take Blockbuster. It had market dominance, distribution infrastructure, and even a smart strategy for fighting off competitors like Netflix. But it optimized for foot traffic and late fees at precisely the moment when customers were shifting toward streaming. Blockbuster didn't fail because it had *no* plan; it failed because it executed brilliantly against a goal that no longer had any relevance to the market.[iv]

More often than not, this is how failure plays out—not via incompetence but through misalignment. Optimizing for metrics that no longer matter. Clinging to assumptions that no longer hold. Missing the inflection point where adaptation becomes the only path to survival.

To navigate this landscape and avoid optimizing for irrelevance, we must first learn to distinguish between outcomes that teach and outcomes that terminate—between what I call shallow success, deep success, shallow failure, and deep failure.

---

iv The bottom line is that Blockbuster failed to adapt and instead chose to apply grit to stay on a narrow path while the world was evolving around it.

Failure ≠ Failure; Success ≠ Success

Not understanding important differences between failure and success is where many strategies—and lives—are in danger of going wildly astray. Because not all failure is real, and not all success is worth chasing.

We call it a failure when something doesn't work out exactly the way we intended. But some "failures" are essential. They're vital parts of an optimal process of iteration. What I call a *shallow failure* is just a moment of feedback—a step along the path, a test point, a signal. It might feel like a setback, but it's not fatal. It's not final. It's not at all failure in the way that word usually implies. A shallow failure is, in fact, the core mechanism of learning; it's a mini feedback loop. It's not an end point as long as it yields data about the territory you're mapping that allows you to improve your model. As I often say, "It's better to experiment and fail than to fail to experiment."

Contrast this with what I term *deep failure*—a knockout event. A moment from which the goal can no longer be reached. In a business context, it might be running out of capital; in a personal one, it might be irreversible physical loss. In any context, deep failure is tantamount to death: It means the window has closed. There's no longer a meaningful path forward, you lose capacity to iterate, or the feedback loop breaks. You're done—out of the game.

On the flip side, not all success is created equal either. *Shallow success* is how I refer to a "local" win—evidence that a recent decision, experiment, or configuration is moving you in the right direction. It's worth noting, celebrating, learning from. But it's not the end-all, be-all—both because it's short of your eventual goal and because circumstances evolve: What looks like success today might prove fatally maladaptive tomorrow. Nothing, especially success, is ever final; *everything* needs to be revisited.

Deep success, by contrast, is when your ultimate objective is fulfilled. It's the finish line, the top step on the podium, the sustained achievement of what matters to you—the outcome your decisions have been compounding toward all along.

These distinctions are crucial because so many people mistake shallow success for the finish line—or misinterpret shallow failure for a reason to quit. They chase prestige, approval, or fleeting, momentary advantage without ever pausing to ask: *Does this actually get me closer to what really matters?* They abandon a promising path because of discomfort, friction, or feedback that was never fatal—and could/should have been formative.

This system is designed to help you tell the difference. To show you how to make decisions that compound—not just toward local wins, but toward meaningful outcomes. Because the goal isn't to win every round. It's to stay in the game long enough to win what counts.

In an age defined by accelerating complexity, technology is amplifying both the speed, and, frequently, the consequences, of our decisions. A trading algorithm that executes microsecond trades based on flawed assumptions can lose millions before a human even registers the mistake; a poorly designed AI model can reinforce bias at scale, entrenching systemic failures faster than anyone can react. The stakes are getting higher, and the margin for error seems to be growing thinner, almost by the day.

This book isn't just about making better decisions in the abstract. I'm aiming at something a little more ambitious: forging a system that can be applied under (virtually) any circumstance, across industries and disciplines, whether the terrain happens to be financial markets, crisis leadership, or the everyday choices that shape our lives (though perhaps not which cereal to buy at the grocery store). A Swiss Army knife of decision-making—not a brittle, single-purpose instrument but something as adaptable and versatile as the emerging world demands. And this is why *selecting the right objective* isn't just a philosophical concern; it's the bedrock of any effective decision-making system. If we are building a framework—a weapon, a tool, a compass—it requires direction. Which means asking the hard question: *What are we really trying to accomplish here?*

The answer to that question will shape everything that follows.

Cold Clarity

In theory, these distinctions—between deep success and shallow success, and between shallow failures that teach and deep failures that end the game—make intuitive sense. But in practice, they can be hard to parse, especially in real time. Under pressure, the lines blur. Signals are faint. And few stories illustrate this more clearly than the epic, improbable, almost mythic journey of Sir Ernest Shackleton—one of the clearest demonstrations in (relatively) modern history of what it means to adapt not just your strategy, but your definition of success, in real time, without losing your grip on clarity, leadership, or resolve.

In 1914, Shackleton had an ambitious goal: to lead the first overland crossing of the continent of Antarctica. At the time, the world was still in the midst of a golden age of exploration, but the window was beginning to close. The race to the poles had already been won: Norwegian explorer Roald Amundsen had reached the South Pole in 1911, narrowly beating a rival effort by Britain's Robert Falcon Scott, whose entire party perished on the return journey. The North Pole, too, had been claimed (albeit under disputed circumstances at the time). With these milestones behind them, the public's fascination with polar exploration was beginning to wane.

At that time, the planet's highest peak, Mount Everest, remained unconquered; it would be another four decades before Tenzing Norgay and Sir Edmund Hillary would stand atop its summit in 1953. Still, by 1914, for an explorer of Shackleton's caliber—ambitious, relentless, drawn ever and always to the greatest extremes—there were fewer and fewer "firsts" left to claim. The challenge of crossing Antarctica, then, was as much a bid for glory as it was a test of human endurance and leadership in the world's most unforgiving environment.

But the Antarctic had other plans.

Disaster struck even before Shackleton and his crew, totaling twenty-eight men, had so much as set foot on the continent. Their ship, christened the *Endurance*, became trapped in the shifting ice of the treacherous Weddell Sea—and, for the next ten months, the vessel was at the mercy of the gradually drifting ice pack, being simultaneously swept along and slowly crushed from all sides by the relentless, unstoppable force of the ice.

At long last, on October 27, 1915, the strain on her hull and the danger to the crew had become too much to bear, so Shackleton gave the harrowing order to abandon ship; the *Endurance* sank weeks later, swallowed by the landscape they had come to conquer, and leaving them stranded, alone, at the bottom of the world. Shackleton's dream of crossing Antarctica, his last and best bid for immortality, was dead.

Here, many leaders—most or nearly all, I will not hesitate to argue—would have floundered and, eventually, failed. Upon abandoning the *Endurance*, which had not only been the crew's sole means of returning to England (or anywhere else) but also their home and longtime shelter, Shackleton's failure was absolute, undeniable, and utterly petrifying in its elemental extremity; he himself later admitted that *this* was his lowest moment. But before the eyes of his crew, Shackleton betrayed not so much as an ounce of doubt or disappointment, instead reorienting his (and their) thinking literally overnight: Even if the ultimate goal had at one time been to cross the continent, that was now irrelevant. The only objective that mattered now—the sole and true and enduring deep success to which every move must now be oriented and every crew member must be fully committed—was *survival.*

Deep success, as a concept, is perhaps best understood in contrast with its lesser counterparts. What we might call *shallow success*, for instance, might be defined as an individual step forward toward one's stated objective, signifying minor or incremental progress along the way: crossing a stretch of open water in the lifeboats, killing a seal for food, or finding temporary refuge on a drifting ice floe. By contrast, *shallow failure* is (obviously) any setback on an analogous scale: the ice creaking and breaking beneath the men's tents at night, dwindling food supplies, frostbite creeping into fingers and toes.

Still, however much or little these small victories and defeats might contribute to or detract from the overarching goal—keeping everyone alive—they matter little on their own except to the extent that they create opportunities for learning, thereby influencing the trajectory of the expedition and bending its fortunes marginally closer to or further from miraculous rescue. The only *true* failure—deep failure—would be the loss of a single man under Shackleton's command. That he would not allow.

With their ship lost, Shackleton led his men across the broken ice, hauling the lifeboats on heavy wooden sledges in search of navigable water. After months of near starvation, exhaustion, and exposure, followed by a desperate crossing of the raging ocean, they strained to haul their lifeboats upon the desolate shores of Elephant Island—a tiny, windswept outpost more suited for penguins than human habitation. This marked a temporary reprieve, but it was now 1916—and they were still stranded in one of the most isolated places on Earth. Every man recognized, with the leering certainty of imminent death, that no help was on the way. No one except the twenty-eight of them knew, or indeed had any way of knowing, that everything had gone so catastrophically awry on the Imperial Trans-Antarctic Expedition. No rescue was coming.

If Shackleton was to save his men—if they were to save themselves—they would have to do the impossible.

It was April 24, 1916, when Sir Ernest Shackleton and five of his strongest crew members cast off into the rolling waves in a twenty-two-foot lifeboat, the *James Caird*, which the crew had modified and partially reinforced for the journey. They were aiming to make landfall near the whaling stations of South Georgia, a remote island some eight hundred miles away—across the most violent and abjectly terrifying stretch of ocean on the planet. More than a long shot, this would be a near-suicidal voyage—an attempted traversal of the frigid South Atlantic, where waves could reach fifty feet and hurricane-force winds were common—even under the *best* of circumstances. And as it was, their boat was barely seaworthy; they navigated with a sextant and a centuries-old technique known as dead reckoning, catching only the briefest glimpses of the sun to chart their course.

For sixteen days, the men battled towering seas, freezing rain, and relentless hunger. Everything was cold and wet, dangerously so; ice crystals caked their beards and sodden clothes. Sleep soon became almost impossible. Any mistake—any miscalculation in their estimated position, a single misjudged wave, or a failed repair—might spell their instant demise, sending Shackleton to the bottom of the ocean without a trace, and sentencing his crewmates on Elephant Island to waste away helplessly, praying and waiting for a rescue that would never materialize.

Yet somehow—despite impossible odds—they made it.

On May 10, 1916, Shackleton and his men staggered onto the shores of South Georgia. But their ordeal wasn't over. They had landed on the wrong side of the island; an impassable mountain range lay between them and the whaling station that represented their best (and only) chance at survival. Too exhausted to risk another journey by boat and convinced one or more of their party might perish if they paused for more than the briefest moment's rest, Shackleton and two men set off on foot for the last desperate push to reach civilization, crossing thirty-two rugged miles of unmapped, glacial, mountainous terrain in thirty-six sleepless hours.[v]

When they finally stumbled into the whaling station at Stromness—heavily bearded, alarmingly emaciated, utterly unrecognizable as themselves and barely recognizable as human—it was the first time in more than a year that they had interacted with anyone from the outside world. Yet there was no time to celebrate; Shackleton's men were still stranded on distant Elephant Island. He had achieved another shallow success—and an important one—but deep success remained incomplete.

Over the next four months, Shackleton launched multiple rescue attempts, each of which was turned resolutely back by the thick Antarctic ice. It wasn't until August 30, 1916, that they finally broke through. As the rescue ship approached the island, Shackleton stood at the bow, scanning the beach through his binoculars, counting.

Twenty-two men—every single crew member who'd remained on the

---

v Even today, with GPS, ultralight gear, technical clothing, and modern mountaineering tools, the Shackleton traverse across South Georgia Island is considered an extremely difficult undertaking—attempted by only a handful of experienced alpinists each year. That Shackleton and his men completed it in 1916, with no map, no gear, no rest, and after months of starvation and exposure, borders on the impossible. It's the kind of final obstacle that would feel implausible if it were fiction.

island—were alive and accounted for. Of the twenty-eight men in total who had embarked on the *Endurance* from England, back when the expedition began in 1914, not a single person died.

This is why Shackleton is revered today as one of history's greatest leaders. He did not succeed at reaching the South Pole, nor did he ever make another attempt to cross Antarctica; in point of fact, according to nearly every measure by which one might assess traditional exploration, the *Endurance* expedition was a thorough and resounding failure. But when the circumstances changed, Shackleton changed with them—abandoning one mission in favor of bending every effort and variable to serve a far greater one: ensuring every man under his command would get home alive.

This definition of deep success had, of course, been implicit somewhere in the original mission parameters; "return with the same number of people who left" did not exactly need to be articulated as part of Shackleton's job description for it to be well understood. But in the clarity that was forced upon him and his crew, on that humbling day when their only means of conveyance was swallowed by the ice, came renewed purpose—and lucidity of thought as well as action.

This explains why Shackleton's story stands as more than just a survival epic; it is a master class in decision-making.

The best leaders, in business as in exploration, do not cling to outdated objectives out of some misguided deference to the original objective. They adapt, change in response to changing circumstances, redefine success based on new realities. Critically, they also recognize that both small victories and nonfatal setbacks—shallow successes and failures—are merely steps along the way.

To me, old photos of polar expeditions from this turn-of-the-century "golden age" almost always possess a haunted, tragic air: the ghostly gazes of so many men who vanished into blinding snow, who were consumed by the vast unknown, never to be seen again. But the images of Shackleton's crew are strikingly different: These are men who survived, who grew old with their families, who told their stories—not as cautionary tales, but as proof of what leadership, resilience, and adaptability can achieve.

The Edge of the Map

Shackleton's story provides a worthy reminder that there's a moment in every expedition—as in every startup, every war, every life—when the map inevitably runs out. When the assumptions that got you here no longer apply. When what worked yesterday stops working.

Most people stumble at that threshold. They double down on old tactics, mistake momentum for direction, confuse shallow success for something deeper. Even worse, they confuse discomfort—and learning—with failure.

But a few—for instance, members of our accidental control group—simply don't. They pause, look again, adapt as necessary. And then they keep moving forward—not blindly, but deliberately, with clarity that sharpens even as the world grows more uncertain.

This is the edge that AQ is built for.

The external world of accelerated complexity and algorithmic pressure demands that we cease running on default and begin running on intention. We must stop ignoring outliers, learn to manage uncertainty, and reclaim agency from the systems designed to distract us. This essential shift begins with rigorous self-observation.

The storm outside is real—technologies are accelerating, environments are destabilizing, and there are numerous systems designed to hijack your reflexes. But before you can steer through it, you need to master the controls inside, to see how your own code is written and understand how to start rewriting it. You must also internalize key lessons from Shackleton's saga: that process is not output, your goal itself is never stagnant, and *how to journey well* (i.e., adaptively) *is* the destination.

So that's where your practice of AQ begins: Phase I—metacognition.

The AQ Process

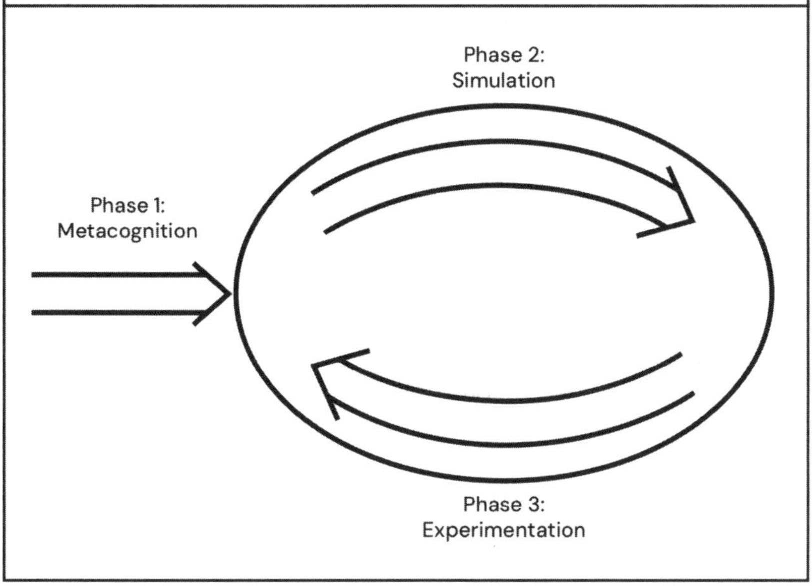

Adaptability Quotient Field Guide: Key Takeaways

- **The world is upgrading, and fast.** AI, robotics, and biotech are externalizing intelligence faster than we can adapt internally.
- **The real frontier isn't technological; it's cognitive.** The next arms race is for agency: who controls the systems that direct attention.
- **Your brain is still brilliant—but it's hackable.** In an age of engineered persuasion, awareness is the new armor (defense).
- **Not all failure is fatal.** Shallow failures teach; deep failures end the game. Learn the difference before the outcome is decided for you (errors of commission, doing the wrong thing—versus omission, failing to act when action is required).

- **Not all success is worth keeping.** Many institutions die perfecting yesterday's wins. Deep success means knowing when to pivot the goal itself.
- **Attention is the new currency.** Every click, scroll, and reflex is a microdecision that trains your future self. Spend wisely.
- **Default settings are dangerous.** Habitus, the invisible cultural code shaping your reactions, must be overwritten by choice.
- **Cognitive security is survival.** Building a mental firewall against manipulation is now as vital as any physical defense.
- **Direction beats genius.** A flawless decision system is useless if it's aimed at the wrong objective.
- **Clarity under pressure is the new intelligence.** Adaptive minds don't just survive turbulence—they steer through it.

4

Thinking About Thinking

The essence of the independent mind lies not in what it thinks, but in how it thinks.

—Christopher Hitchens

Until you make the unconscious conscious, it will direct your life and you will call it fate.

—attributed to Carl Jung

In chapter 3, we defined the external battlefield: a world of engineered uncertainty, where algorithms, technological acceleration, and a corrosive social habitus conspire to hijack our attention and exploit our cognitive vulnerabilities. We established that in this new environment, success requires redefining goals and establishing cognitive security.

The question remains: How do we fight back? Where do we start applying AQ as a practice? The answer begins here, in Phase I: metacognition.

Think of this as strapping into the cockpit. You've seen the turbulence outside; now it's time to examine your own instrument panel. Before you can chart any course through chaos, you need to know how your mind itself works—where it's reliable, where it misfires, and how to keep steering, even when the world tries to wrest the controls from you.

As the foundation of the AQ framework, metacognition is the necessary defensive move against manipulation and the first proactive step toward mastering chaos. Among other things, it reflects your ability to audit your thinking *itself*. It is not merely thinking; it is second-order thinking—analyzing how you think, examining why you're making decisions the way you do, questioning whether you're even solving the right problem, and anticipating second- and third-order effects. This kind of rigorous self-audit is a prerequisite to AQ.

Most people stop at first-order thinking. But metacognition is about knowing not just your lens, but the intellectual and analytical "tools" you have at your disposal. This shift—from merely thinking to thinking *about* thinking—constitutes the first and most fundamental act of reclaiming agency from the external systems designed to distract you, wresting control back from those who would hijack your attention.

Crucially, this isn't just an upgrade. It's a uniquely human capability. Plants and animals adapt over generations, through slow genetic trial and error. Mutations that work stick; mutations that don't are dispassionately removed from the gene pool. Cats, insects, and birds all exhibit what you might call *reactive attention*: Their perception is pulled toward survival-relevant signals, but there's no representation of their own attention as an object. They're in the movie, but they're not watching themselves watch it.

Higher mammals like apes, dolphins, and elephants go a step further. They can focus selectively, pursue goals, use tools. They exhibit *directed attention* and basic intention; they don't just react—they aim. This is first-order intentionality or the ability to want something and act toward it, sometimes even simulating simple outcomes.

Humans add a third layer: *reflective intentionality*—in other words, metacognition. We don't just have attention and intention; we can notice and evaluate them. We can ask: What am I paying attention to? Why do I want this? What might you think I intend to do? That's second- and even third-order thinking: *I know that you know that I intend . . .* Attention becomes control of perception, intention becomes control of action, and reflective intentionality becomes control of self and meaning. This is the only layer with anything close to full agency.

You can see this difference early. By around twelve months, a human baby can follow where a parent is pointing, not just where they're looking. That tiny act, called *joint attention*, means the child is already modeling another mind: *Mom is attending to something over there, and I should too.* Apes are individually brilliant tool users, but they don't spontaneously share attention and intention this way. Language, built on top of joint attention, turns individual cognition into shared meaning. It lets us coordinate around invisible things—plans, rules, futures—rather than just immediate stimuli.

Metacognition lives in that uniquely human space. It's the part of you that can stand outside your own thought process, notice where your attention has been hijacked, and redirect it toward what actually matters. It's the mechanism that lets you override old patterns in a single lifetime instead of waiting for evolution to do it slowly, over millennia. And it's why Phase I of your AQ discipline, thinking about thinking, isn't optional. It's the doorway to every other adaptive move you make.

The world is chaotic. Markets shift, industries transform, companies disappear overnight. One unexpected variable—technological disruption, a regulatory change, an unforeseen competitor—can turn a once-dominant winner into a sorry relic. This is an unpredictable habitus—one where luck, randomness, and external forces are always in play. But that doesn't mean we're helpless.

If you design your thinking to account for uncertainty—if you make adaptability your default mode—for one thing, you develop the habit of seeing multiple possible futures instead of locking onto one rigid assumption. You ask: What else could be true? What am I missing? How could this backfire in ways I haven't considered?

This kind of thinking doesn't remove randomness from the world. It doesn't somehow magically enable you to predict the future.[i]

But it *can* help tilt the odds in your favor.

Becoming the House

In the classic casino analogy, most people operate like a gambler: They place a bet, cross their fingers, and hope the outcome goes their way. If they win, they figure they must've made a smart decision. If they lose, they figure they must not have—or maybe it was just plain bad luck.

Of course, casinos don't think this way. They don't care about any single roll of the dice or spin of the wheel; what matters is how the game is *designed*. The system *itself* is built with a statistical edge—a small but significant advantage that compounds over time.

This is what metacognition gives you, in the context of AQ: an edge. A repeatable advantage.

It doesn't mean you'll predict every outcome correctly. It means that, over time, you'll learn enough to make smarter bets. You'll avoid obvious traps. You won't just play the game—soon, you'll be thinking about how the game is structured.

In essence, you'll start becoming the house.

This edge is not luck; it's a systematic form of control. If external forces are constantly trying to set your course—whether through market noise or algorithmic manipulation—metacognition is the instrument panel you use to steer. It is the first step in converting your brain into a cybernetic system that regulates itself, corrects for bias, and actively seeks its objectives.

---

i Predictions are specific claims; forecasting is probability distribution. Specific claims are epistemic arrogance; probability distributions are adaptive cognition. Do not get caught trying to make predictions. Get caught trying to improve through forecasting.

My "Red Pill" Moment

To state the obvious, we aren't taught any of this stuff in school.

Most of what we learn is *convergent thinking*—finding the (ostensible) one and only right answer to a clear question. We're rewarded for solving predictable problems with fixed solutions; we take tests with one, and only one, correct answer. We get graded on how well we follow instructions.

But real life doesn't work that way. At least, not exactly.

Most meaningful problems are *divergent*. There's no such thing as an absolute right answer, no perfect playbook. You can make the best decision possible with the best information you have—and still be wrong.[ii]

The moment I realized this, it changed the way I approached the world. It woke me up; I call it my "red pill" moment. Because in a chaotic, fast-moving world, it turns out that *what you think* matters less than *how you think.*

This realization—that the process matters more than the answer—is the core principle behind the audit we must perform on our own minds. And the rigor required for this audit wasn't taught in any textbook; for me, it was taught at the dinner table.

Some kids grow up believing their parents have all the answers. My siblings and I, on the other hand, grew up knowing that every answer was just a prelude to the next question.

As the third son of two psychoanalysts, I was born into a world where our nightly family discussions and debates around the dinner table unfolded not unlike postgraduate seminars. While most other kids—including my peers at school—dodged soccer balls and chores, I spent my childhood dodging one awkwardly probing question after another. Everything was peeled back to first principles: "How does that make you feel?" "'Happy' is a

---

ii Some researchers refer to convergent problems as deterministic—meaning they have a clear, predefined solution—and divergent problems as nondeterministic, where multiple outcomes are possible and the "correct" answer may depend on framing, priorities, or context. Whatever terminology you prefer, this distinction matters, especially when designing systems—or making decisions—in the real world.

strong word . . . what do you think it means to be truly happy?" "Alec, come over here—let's have a 'meaning-of-life' discussion. . . ."[iii]

Dissection, debate, analysis: This was our family's religion. Thinking wasn't encouraged; it was expected. Certainty was viewed as a weakness. Every assumption was to be questioned, and every statement, no matter how benign, was subject to cross-examination. If you said you were happy, you'd better be prepared to define happiness, defend it against competing theories, and explain its evolutionary utility.

I suppose, in retrospect, that this might seem like a *slightly* intense way to grow up (not to psychoanalyze myself, but this probably has something to do with why I have what's been described as a certain *intensity of personality* today, as an adult). Still, I thrived on it—despite being, in many ways, a bit of an outlier in my own family: less antiestablishment and, in some ways, more commercial; maybe less bookish and more social; less philosophical and more drawn to things that couldn't be debated.

While my parents taught us to question everything around us, to love learning, and to revel in shades of ambiguity, I also found I was drawn to (and fascinated by) patterns, systems, rules, and universal laws that reflected some kind of order underlying the apparent chaos. This search, along with at least a degree of inherent interest and aptitude, drew me to math and science—subjects where truth emphatically was *not* subjective and where logic ruled, even as my parents peppered us with complex, divergent questions.

In seeking out structure, I was simultaneously (if unconsciously) absorbing a different kind of lesson from my upbringing—one that would later prove even more valuable. Because, in a household where questioning was the default setting, I learned early on that the world is built on such "rules"—spoken and unspoken. (After all, what else were my parents teaching us to question?) And once you understand those rules, you can do a lot more than just follow them. You can *use* them, or at least operationalize your understanding of them, to bring certain aspects of the world

---

iii Despite years of rigorous inquiry, consensus on the meaning of life remained elusive; we never did arrive at a final answer. The closest we ever got was "42."

around you into sharper focus. This is no small thing: The arc of our future will be written by those who see something differently and take action.

Some of the most memorable lessons, though, didn't come from textbooks or formal teaching. They came from watching the world change and from watching the map get redrawn in real time. I grew up during a period when the outer edges of our understanding were shifting dramatically, and I found that thrilling. Pluto was a planet when I was a kid; then it wasn't. Black holes were once theoretical; then, suddenly, they were observable. At one point, string theory was brand-new, and people were still arguing over whether information could be preserved at the event horizon of a black hole. The idea that knowledge itself could be provisional—that scientific truth wasn't static but always evolving—felt less like a disappointment than a kind of magic. It didn't rattle me; it energized me.[iv]

That fascination only deepened over time. I remember visiting CERN (the European Council for Nuclear Research or, in French, the *Conseil Européen pour la Recherche Nucléaire*) as an adult, shortly before the discovery of the Higgs boson.[v] The particle hadn't yet been confirmed—but it had been hypothesized, predicted, fought over. And the fact that people had already built a multibillion-dollar machine to try to find it? That captivated me. I wasn't just interested in the discovery itself. I was interested in the scaffolding behind it: the interplay between belief and doubt, data and models, structure and revision.

In hindsight, I think this love of shifting paradigms—the joy I took in watching people update their models in real time—was its own kind of education. It gave me a visceral respect for the power of intellectual humility, plus a lifelong pull toward systems thinking. It also helped wire one of the most valuable habits I still carry: a reflexive curiosity about the assumptions beneath the surface and how those assumptions shape the way we interact with the world.

---

iv This is what Carl Sagan calls the two "uneasy but cohabitating" modes of thought central to the scientific method, skepticism and wonder.

v With Ken Griffin, actually. We both happened to be passionately interested in the pioneering science they were performing.

I didn't have a name for it at the time. But what I was beginning to glimpse—whether through science, social dynamics, or dinner-table debate—was the power of being able to step outside a system, interrogate its rules, and revise them as new information emerged. That's not just useful. It's foundational. And eventually, it would become the bedrock of how I learned to think.

Telescoping

Looking back, I now recognize that a handful of early influences helped shape this habit. The first was growing up with siblings. As any youngest child will tell you, having older brothers is like growing up inside a live experiment in power, hierarchy, and rule negotiation. You learn to observe—closely. You learn to test boundaries and, just as often, watch others test them first. In a house full of fast-moving dynamics, you're not just playing the game—you're also watching it from the rafters, learning how it works. I've come to refer to this tendency as "telescoping."

Travel achieves something similar. Our family was lucky enough to spend time in other cultures, and even at a young age, I started noticing the differences that didn't just mark *how people do things* but *how people think about what they're doing*. Customs, habits, jokes, rhythms of speech—all these things, when seen from the outside, become visible in a way that the *default settings* of your own environment never quite do. You start spotting your own assumptions simply because you've encountered alternatives. It forces perspective.

And then, of course, there was language itself. My parents were psychoanalysts, so the dinner table was the setting for an ongoing seminar in how words shape thought and how thought loops back to reshape words. Language, I realized, is more than a tool for expression; in a single breath, it lets you name a thing, then step back and analyze the naming. You can say, "rat is a one-syllable word" or "truth is a metaphor." You can even claim that "this sentence is false" and discover that you've crossed into recursion.[vi] No other tool we've ever invented—certainly not AI, at least not yet—can reflect on itself with anything approaching that level of nuance.

What all of these experiences taught me, in different ways, was that the ability to zoom out—to *telescope up* in your awareness, see the frame around the frame—wasn't just a neat mental trick. The world was messy, fast-changing, nonlinear. The best thinkers I admired weren't always the smartest in a traditional sense. They were the ones who could move between levels—who could switch between immersion and analysis, action and observation, execution and metacognition. They could be in it, and above it, sometimes in the same breath.

That habit—of continuous zooming in and out, checking your vantage point, interrogating your lens—is the first critical skill of metacognition. But to successfully audit your thinking, you must apply this skill to the world around you. This requires moving beyond individual decisions and adopting a systems mindset. You must see that your life, your work, and the deep success you're pursuing are not isolated spheres encompassing independently solvable problems; they are interconnected patterns that determine results.

Don't Solve the Symptom

You're the CEO of a major airline. Fuel prices are up and customer satisfaction is down, yet your competitors are slashing fares. *What do you do?*

A traditional leader might react tactically: Cut costs—to the bone, if necessary. Or launch a marketing campaign. Or maybe push for more slots at a major hub so you can operate more flights per day.

A systems thinker sees deeper. They might ask: "How do these problems connect? What unseen forces are shaping the outcomes I'm observing and need to be contended with?"

---

vi The liar's paradox exposes fundamental issues one sometimes encounters in a complex world.

This is the essence of systems thinking—a way of viewing challenges not as isolated fires to extinguish but as interconnected patterns that drive outcomes and determine results.

Most businesses operate in linear cause-and-effect mode: Revenue is down? Sell harder. Employees are disengaged? Offer bonuses. Systems thinking recognizes that businesses are complex, adaptive systems where actions create ripples—feedback loops—that shape long-term success or failure.

But, of course, it's also much broader—and decision-makers, especially in the business context, need to think much deeper—than the interplay of one competitor making chess moves against another; again, you have to zoom *way* out. How far? "A system is an interconnected set of elements that is coherently organized in a way that achieves something," according to Donella Meadows in her seminal book on problem-solving, *Thinking in Systems*. In other words: Yes, your company is a system. So is the other guy's. But you're still not far enough: Your market is also a system, and even your own decision-making habits form a system.

Which is part of the reason why seductive, allegedly "quick" fixes are sometimes prone to backfire.

Fortunately, Meadows offers the key to making this insight actionable: Instead of reacting to *entire* symptoms, she suggests, successful leaders recognize that "there are leverage points in systems—places where a small shift in one thing can produce big changes in everything."

The challenge lies in discerning these points and applying the right interventions. In any decision tree, independent variables are the inputs you can influence—your choices, assumptions, or actions—while dependent variables are the outcomes that emerge from how those inputs interact with the environment. The art of adaptive decision-making lies in continually testing which variables truly drive results and then updating the model as those relationships evolve.

One of the most iconic examples of this principle comes from an unlikely place: a factory floor.

At most manufacturing plants—especially before the 1980s—the overriding logic was simple: Keep the line running. Output was king.

Stopping production, for any reason short of catastrophe, was treated as a failure. Problems were supposed to be fixed after the fact, not in real time.

But Toyota saw something different.

Drawing on the principles of lean manufacturing, the company identified a leverage point so seemingly minor it could have been overlooked entirely: the exact moment when a defect is first noticed.

Instead of routing around the problem or burying it for later correction, Toyota built a system to surface it *immediately*. At the heart of this system was the Andon cord—at first a literal cord that ran alongside the production line (and, since 2014, a digital button). Any worker, at any station, could pull the cord (or press the button) to stop the line the moment they noticed a defect or safety concern. No need to ask a manager. No need to justify the disruption. Just pull the cord—and the entire line stops.

In traditional manufacturing environments, this would've been unthinkable. Empowering individual line workers to halt operations might sound like a recipe for chaos or costly delays. But in Toyota's hands, it became something else entirely: a precision tool for real-time learning.

By addressing problems the instant they emerged, the company prevented defects from cascading through the system—saving time, money, and quality further down the line. More than that, it built a culture of shared responsibility and continuous improvement. Workers weren't just cogs in the machine—they were problem-solvers with the authority, autonomy, and agency to act.

The Andon cord didn't just make Toyota's production more efficient. It made it more adaptive. By targeting a leverage point—where problems *begin*, not where they become unmanageable—Toyota achieved outsized results with a surprisingly simple intervention. This reflects the essence of systems thinking: finding the smallest hinge that can swing the largest door. The Andon cord isn't a rope, it's a nerve; pulling it sent a signal through the entire organizational nervous system, allowing the entire system to learn, adapt, and heal itself.

In Illusions We Trust

If systems thinking teaches you anything, it's that the way things work and the way we think they work are seldom the same.

It's a lesson that might sound obvious until you start seeing just how often people—including the smartest, most accomplished people you're likely to meet—operate based on illusions.

Consider money. Most people think of it as something tangible and real. But money is not gold bars, stacks of cash, or numbers on a screen; at its core, it is a *shared belief system.* It's an essentially imaginary, human-engineered construct—one that functions only so long as people continue to trust in it. A financial system that collapses doesn't do so because money (and here we're discussing *currency*, such as dollars and cents) somehow evaporates; it collapses because faith in the system has disappeared, revealing just how fragile even the most entrenched structures can be.

Once I recognized how fragile, yet powerful, human-designed systems could be, I started looking for these invisible structures everywhere. What made some resilient while others collapsed? What underlying rules governed them?

These same questions about patterns, adaptability, and the logic that underlies complexity are what led me to MIT, where I studied two fields that might initially seem like opposites—math and anthropology—but were both (in their own ways) about uncovering hidden truths.

Math offered absolute truths: underlying laws that govern the physical universe. One plus one is always two; a prime number is a prime number no matter what language you speak. Nature speaks in math; shapes, patterns, fractals represent a kind of secret code embedded in our universe—which, to me, carried a degree of certainty or, at least, precision that has always made math feel like the closest thing to understanding reality itself.

Anthropology, on the other hand, might seem (on a superficial level) like a kind of diametric opposite: soft, subjective, human. But as I dug deeper, I discovered structuralism, which is a subfield that argues that beneath every culture, every language, every human system, there are hidden architectures. These are abstract, universal structures that shape how people think, live, and relate to one another, and that comprise the habitus in which we exist even if we're unaware of them. Myths, kinship networks, rituals, taboos: all of these reflect deeper binary codes that are not unlike the formal logic of mathematics. Where math works in ones and zeros, structuralism offered nature/culture, life/death, male/female. It was, in a sense, a different kind of secret code—one that governed not atoms or particles but social meaning and behavior.[vii]

This was the first time I realized that systems thinking could be applied just as rigorously to human dynamics as to physics or algorithms. Understanding these "rules"—whether formal or tacit—offered not just insight but leverage. Because once you see the rulebook, you can play the game more effectively. Or, more powerfully still, you can start to see where rules from different systems don't quite align—where categories don't fit cleanly, where boundaries between domains become blurry. Which is often where the real opportunity lies.

Trial by Fire

For me, this mindset—of looking beneath surface behavior to underlying structure and between defined buckets to spot the gaps—became foundational. It shaped the way I approached investing, strategy, and, later, the very notion of decision-making itself: not just within disciplines, but across them. The signal, more often than not, is found in the space between.

Later, this drive to understand hidden structures carried through

---

vii Claude Lévi-Strauss, one of the pioneers of structural anthropology, argued that the deep logic of myths and social systems across cultures was grounded in recurring binaries, such as life/death, raw/cooked, nature/culture. Whether or not one subscribes to his entire worldview, the implication is striking: Human systems may appear messy on the surface, but they often encode hidden rules that function like mathematical structures. Once you learn to see those structures—and the borders they create—you can begin to spot the seams, the overlaps, the gaps in between. This is where interdisciplinary insights often hide, and where outsized returns, in every domain, tend to originate.

the next phase of my education: earning a JD/MBA at the University of Chicago.

Law school taught me how rules shape the legal system—and how the most successful players aren't always the smartest or the hardest working, but the ones who cultivate the best and savviest understanding of that system's intricacies, quirks, and operations so they can exploit *every possible advantage permissible* under those very same rules.

Business school, meanwhile, showed me how similar (or at least analogous) principles could be applied to markets and corporations. If law governed power, at least in the strictest (legal and lawmaking) sense, business governed capital. And in both arenas, those who were capable of perceiving the deeper structure—who could spot the hidden incentives and internalize the tacit rules—seemed to be the ones who came out ahead.

But theory is one thing. The real world is another.

After earning my JD/MBA, I started my career at JPMorgan in investment banking. But it didn't take long for me to realize I had made a mistake. Investment banking had all the prestige and all the intellectual rigor I had expected. But the work itself felt sluggish and bureaucratic. The pace of learning was too slow. The decision making process felt too constrained, almost stuffy. Almost immediately, I wanted something more dynamic, more kinetic, with faster learning and tighter feedback loops.

That's when Ken Griffin happened to see something in me, despite the fact that I was twenty-seven years old without a day of trading experience—and had no idea what I was getting myself into. Over the following decade, I helped grow Citadel from $100 million to $10 billion in assets under management, transforming it from a scrappy startup to a pioneering industry leader with something like 750 people. Along the way, I had to make real-time decisions, adapt constantly, and navigate high-stakes scenarios with incomplete information.

It was a trial by fire, to say the least. But one advantage I had was the ability to step back, look at the system, and understand the deeper rules at play.

Succeeding in a high-stakes, fast-moving environment requires mastering external systems—markets, power structures, strategic frameworks. But the external audit, and indeed the entire AQ process, is useless unless you master the system that is driving the interpretation of all that complexity. The system that matters most turns out to be the one running quietly in the background all along: the invisible architecture of your own decision-making.

The Invisible Architecture of Decision-Making

Most people assume that thinking happens in a single stream of consciousness—which is only natural, since that's (more or less) how we experience our minds at work (or at play) in any given moment. But this isn't how your brain actually works. In reality, decision-making operates across three distinct levels: conscious, subconscious, and unconscious. Each level has its own rules, limits, and computational strengths.

Understanding how these layers interact isn't just neuroscience trivia. It's fundamental to upgrading your decision-making. Because the better you grasp which part of your mind is doing the work, the more effectively you can direct its power—and avoid letting outdated code run the show.

1. **Conscious—the Serial Interface.** The conscious mind is the part of your brain you experience most directly. It holds your attention, your inner monologue, your sense of "I." It's where you reason, plan, reflect, deliberate. If your mind were a computer, the conscious layer is your user interface plus CPU—a sleek dashboard with a blinking cursor, but one that can only run one active process at a time.

   This is System 2 in action: deliberate, flexible, effortful. Neuroscientifically, this is supported by the global workspace theory, which holds that conscious thought emerges from information being "broadcast" across a network of brain regions, particularly the prefrontal cortex. This is what lights up when you do something like analyze a spreadsheet, map out a business strategy . . . or, say, think about your own thinking.

But conscious processing is slow and energy intensive. It's powerful, yes, but narrow. And because it's serial (one thread at a time), it can quickly become overwhelmed.

2. **Subconscious—the Parallel Processing Engine.** The subconscious sits just below the threshold of active awareness. It's not *unaware*—it's just not being accessed unless called upon. Think of it as RAM backed by a powerful GPU: fast, vast, and mostly invisible, constantly running background processes, searching for patterns, scanning your memory, prepping insights for retrieval. Because it can run many processes at once—searching memory, testing patterns, and integrating signals in parallel—the subconscious does far more of the mind's real work than the narrow, serial bandwidth of conscious attention ever could.

   Unlike the unconscious (which is closer to firmware and mostly read-only), the subconscious is read-write accessible. This means you can train it; with repetition, your conscious actions can be encoded into subconscious routines. Driving a car, typing your password, even pattern-matching in a negotiation—once learned, these all happen below the level of deliberate thought.[viii]

   This layer is also where flow happens. It's where parallel threads of thought can keep running after you've left your desk; it's the space where a solution "just comes" to you in the shower. When people say they're "letting a problem marinate" or "sleeping on it," this is the machinery that stays online. As we'll cover, it's also the source of both intuition and insight. When something "feels off" or "just clicks," that's the subconscious surfacing a signal your conscious mind can't yet articulate.

   But the subconscious isn't neutral. It's where cognitive biases, social conditioning, and emotion-laced heuristics are stored and

viii Some might even be practiced to the level of unconsciousness.

deployed—often without your awareness. This is all well and good in a world where tomorrow will be the same as today, but it's less than ideal if old patterns keep you stuck in well-worn grooves, even as a paradigm shift occurs. Left unexamined, these habits of thought can quietly override logic, nudging you toward the familiar even when it's wrong. This is System 1's home turf: reflexive, efficient, fast. But unless you monitor the inputs, the outputs can be dangerously flawed.

3. **Unconscious—the Immutable Core.** The unconscious mind operates outside of both awareness and deliberate control. This is your firmware and deep storage—read-only code that governs life-supporting processes like breathing, blinking, hormonal regulation, and reflexes. It also includes deep-seated drives and instincts formed through early development and evolutionary inheritance.

   You don't access the unconscious directly. You don't "query" it. You respond to it—or get hijacked by it. This layer may store trauma, formative memories, or repressed emotion, but it also includes the oldest, most reliable systems for survival. It's not simple—but it *is* (mostly) locked.[ix]

   Modern neuroscience increasingly suggests the unconscious may be more complex than Freud's shadowy reservoir of instincts. There's evidence it can perform decision preparation in advance of awareness: One famous study from the Max Planck Institutes found that researchers could predict the outcome of a subject's decision up to seven seconds before the subject became aware they'd made it. But that's not because the unconscious "decided"—it's because unconscious systems had already done the processing.

   This has profound implications for AI analogies. In current

ix Although the unconscious mind cannot be directly edited, it is not completely sealed off. Its signals often appear indirectly—in dreams, emotional responses, moments of unprompted association, etc.—and can be examined through practices like psychoanalysis.

> systems, we might call this the low-level kernel: code that controls everything but cannot be easily rewritten, even by the machine. If the subconscious is like memory—mutable, queryable, trainable—the unconscious is more like basic life infrastructure. Just as you can't teach a computer not to boot, you can't teach your unconscious not to flood you with cortisol under stress or intentionally stop your own heart from beating.
>
> But understanding its role—what it's built to do and where it overrides even our best intentions—is crucial if you want to build a system that doesn't backfire under pressure.

Taken together, these three layers aren't just a biological curiosity. They represent a hierarchy of access and adaptability—and your effectiveness as a decision-maker depends, in large part, on learning how to work with all three. The goal isn't to "live" in your conscious mind all the time. It's about knowing how to use the tools in your cognitive toolbox and understanding the processes you need so they migrate into subconscious muscle—and learning which layers to trust when the stakes are high.

Ultimately, you are not one mind. You are an ecosystem. And the better you know your own architecture, the better you can design for the world ahead.

This layered understanding of consciousness and decision-making underscores the complexity of cognition; clearly, if you're *not* thinking about thinking, you're not fully in control of your decisions.

At this point, we have audited the components of the mind (conscious, subconscious, and unconscious). Now we must ask the most pressing question, which provides the answer to the chaos we face: *Who's in charge?* The answer is found in the principles of cybernetics.

Take the Wheel

The term *cybernetics* originated from the Greek word *kybernētēs*, meaning "steersman" or "pilot," in the sense of one who navigates a vessel at sea. It was not by coincidence that Norbert Wiener, the father of modern cybernetics, chose this term to describe how systems—whether biological, mechanical, or social—use information (feedback) to adjust course, maintain control, and achieve their objectives.

At a basic level, cybernetics is about how systems regulate themselves. An automatic thermostat is programmed to monitor and adjust the temperature to keep a room comfortable. A self-driving car continuously processes sensor data to stay on course. A biological system, like your body, regulates everything from temperature to blood sugar through constant feedback loops. In all cases, cybernetics is about steering toward an intended outcome—using real-time information to correct for deviations, account for disturbances, and stay on track.

The human brain is, in this sense, a cybernetic system unto itself: It operates through loops of perception, interpretation, decision, and action—constantly taking in information, adjusting assumptions, and responding to stimuli. As we've explored, most of this happens below the threshold of conscious awareness, which is precisely why our thinking can drift off course without us realizing it.

Metacognition is thus a kind of mental equivalent of a pilot checking their instruments, adjusting for unexpected turbulence, and making midcourse corrections. *Without* metacognition, you're at the mercy of subconscious biases, mental shortcuts, and environmental influences you don't even perceive. *With it*, you become the "steersman" of your own mind—capable of recognizing when you're veering off track and deliberately adjusting course to bring you back in line with your deep success.

It's the difference between *being driven* by your thoughts and *driving* your thoughts. Those who fail to examine their own thinking, their own biases, their own decision-making are like ships tossed by the waves, carried wherever the current takes them. On the other hand, those who cultivate metacognition as a cybernetic skill—who continuously monitor and refine their own thought processes—gain something invaluable.

Which brings us back to the question at hand. In a world this fast-moving, this fluid—*who's in charge?* The cybernetic answer is this:

whoever is steering. If *you* are gathering feedback, registering deviations, and actively adjusting course, then the answer is *you*. If you're not . . . well, the answer is obvious: someone, or some*thing*, else.

Regardless, in decision-making the goal is never perfect prediction. The goal, in essence, is adaptive steering—adjusting for reality as it unfolds.

The Map Is Not the Territory

To steer effectively, it helps to know (or at least have some rough sense of) where you're going. Which means you need a model of the world—some internal working map to help you interpret new data, anticipate curves ahead, and avoid crashing into unseen obstacles. The problem is, many of us confuse the map for the terrain. We mistake familiar assumptions, mental models, or legacy frameworks for reality *itself.* This brings us to one of the most important—and most misunderstood—principles in decision-making: *The map is not the territory.*

In 1942, the brilliant Argentine writer Jorge Luis Borges imagined a kingdom so obsessed with accuracy that its cartographers created a map as large as the empire itself. Every road, mountain, and river was rendered to exact one-to-one scale—a perfect replica of reality. But in its pursuit of perfection, the map became not just unwieldy but unusable: It was too big to carry, too detailed to interpret, too overwhelming to serve its intended purpose. The people abandoned it, and soon it lay in tatters, forgotten in the deserts it once sought to depict.

It's an absurd, entertaining, even beautiful image—but it's also a warning. The lesson? A model that captures *everything* ceases to be a model at all.

The closer a model gets to reality, the *less useful* it becomes. A perfect map isn't a tool—it's just another version of the territory it purports to represent. And if you already have (and are *living in*) the territory, why bother with the map at all?

This paradox isn't just literary fiction. It exposes a fundamental flaw in our thinking: the belief that more detail always leads to better understanding. At some point, more detail stops being useful. Instead of revealing the path forward, it clouds it; instead of simplifying, it suffocates.

This phenomenon has a name: *Bonini's paradox*. You see it everywhere, such as in economic models that try to factor in every conceivable geopolitical event, consumer-behavior pattern, and interest-rate fluctuation until they become too unwieldy to generate any useful insight. It's found in corporate strategies that overanalyze every market force and trend, bogging down well-intentioned approaches in complexity and inertia (one easy "tell" or common symptom is five-hundred-page PowerPoint decks that obscure rather than clarify). It even affects personal decision-making when an obsession with gathering more data leads to analysis paralysis: *Too much thinking, not enough action.*

Charles Bonini was a Stanford professor when he articulated this idea, which is somewhat counterintuitive: The more a model accurately represents a complex system, the harder it becomes to understand and use. In our attempt to account for every variable, every contingency, we end up drowning ourselves in detail; at some point, instead of making the map clearer, more detail makes it *unreadable*.

Ironically, this also underscores one of the greatest advantages of *not* being a specialist in a given field: You're less likely to get trapped by overly rigid models—and more likely to stay attuned to anomalies that might signal a shift. Where experts sometimes explain away outliers ("That doesn't fit—must be noise."), generalists are often more curious and ask questions like, "Why doesn't this fit? What if it's not noise, but the start of a new pattern?" Specialists, trained to see the world through established frameworks, can miss emerging signals precisely because they don't conform. But generalists—less bound by precedent—tend to zoom out, ask better questions, and seek simpler, more adaptive models. They're not looking for elegance in the abstract. They're asking: "What's the simplest, most useful way to think about this—right now?"

A less detailed but well-structured model will almost always outperform an overloaded, hyperaccurate one. Because, crucially, *the map is not the territory*—it's a tool. And tools only work if they're practical enough to be used.[x]

All Models Are Wrong

At this point, I'm afraid I have some bad news: The problem exposed by Bonini's paradox runs deeper than just business or economics. *Our entire perception of reality is a mental map.*

Think about it: Your senses pick up only a tiny fraction of the world around you. Your brain filters out vast volumes of information, focusing only on what seems relevant. And the information that *does* get through is heavily filtered and distorted by biases, assumptions, and past experiences, not to mention algorithms that curate that set of information even before your brain further filters it.

Consider the 2008 financial crisis. The same economic signals—rising home prices, ballooning mortgage-backed securities, growing leverage in the system—were visible to everyone at the time. And yet, different players in the market saw wildly different things.

Some saw stability. The prevailing models used by major banks and ratings agencies assumed that housing prices *always* trended upward. Based on this assumption, mortgage-backed securities looked safe, credit default swaps seemed like free money, and leverage was simply a way to amplify returns.

Others noticed that the entire market was built on a flawed assumption—that default rates on subprime mortgages were negligible—looked at the data, and saw something entirely different: a financial system about to implode.

x This is closely related to Occam's razor: the principle that, all else being equal, simpler explanations are preferable to complex ones. Some theorists have expanded this to "Occam's priors"—a Bayesian idea that the simpler the assumption set, the more weight it should carry in the absence of strong disconfirming evidence. In practice, sparse models are not just more elegant; they're more robust. Complexity adds parameters, and every parameter adds a point of failure.

Same territory, different maps.

And that's the deeper danger: The map in your head isn't just incomplete—it's fallible. As the philosopher Charles Sanders Peirce argued, every belief, no matter how rigorously derived or widely accepted, must be held provisionally. His principle of *fallibilism* rests on a humbling but essential truth: that knowledge swims on a continuum. You may be closer to the truth today than you were yesterday—but you can never be certain you've arrived.

This kind of radical skepticism isn't paralyzing; it's clarifying. It forces you to treat every model not as a verdict, but as a working hypothesis. A navigational tool, not a destination.

Because when we forget this reality—even for a moment—the consequences can be catastrophic.

This is what happens when *model error* and *cognitive bias* collide. Model error is what led the majority of financial institutions to rely on risk models that simplified reality to the point of inaccuracy. Their maps were elegant but wrong, built on assumptions that collapsed under real-world conditions. Cognitive bias, meanwhile, is what kept otherwise smart decision-makers anchored to these flawed models. They dismissed warning signs that didn't fit their expectations, reinforcing their belief that the system was stable—until it wasn't.

The result? The worst financial meltdown in decades.

And yet, if you go back to the years leading up to the crash, the warning signs were there for anyone to see. The problem wasn't the absence of information—it was the refusal to question the outdated map.

This isn't just a problem for economists or investors. Every day, in ways large and small, your mind builds a model of reality—and that model is flawed.

But the real danger isn't that your mental map is imperfect. It's that you mistake it for reality.

This is why two people can look at the same information and reach opposite conclusions. They aren't living in different worlds—but they are navigating with different maps. And if you aren't aware of how your map is shaping your decisions, you'll keep making the same mistakes without realizing it.

The good news? Maps, like software and mental models, can be updated.

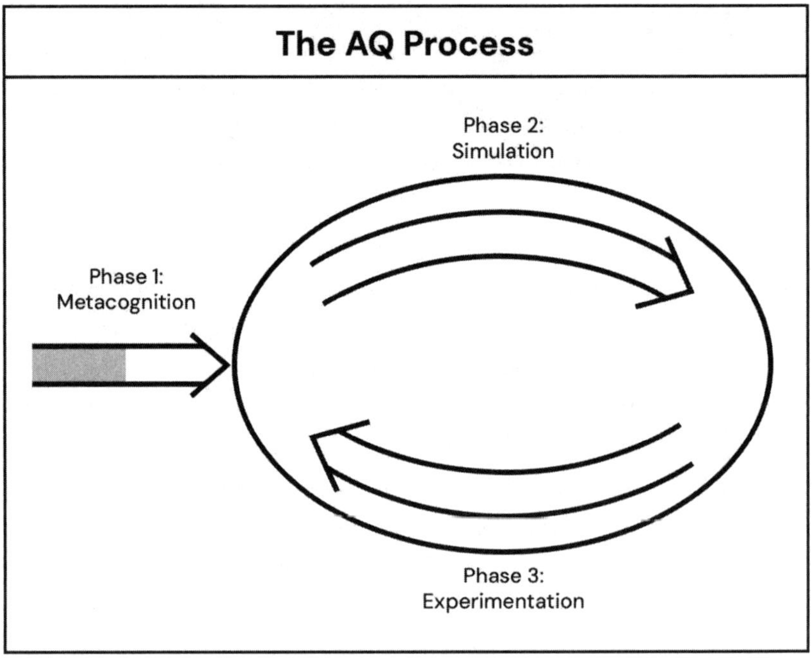

Adaptability Quotient Field Guide: Key Takeaways

- **Second-order thinking is the foundation of AQ.** It's not just what you think but how you think—and how well you examine the process behind your judgments.
- **You are a layered system.** Conscious, subconscious, and unconscious processes shape every decision you make—whether you're aware of them or not.
    - **Your conscious mind is powerful but limited.** It runs serially, handles complexity slowly, and tires quickly.
    - **Your subconscious is the workhorse of your decision-making engine.** It's fast, parallel, and pattern-based, but it's also where biases live.
    - **Your unconscious is immutable.** It runs life-supporting systems and instinctive reactions. You can't control it, but you must account for its influence.
- **You are the steersman—if you choose to be.** Cybernetic thinking reframes metacognition as a control system: You can't eliminate uncertainty, but you can steer adaptively through it.
- **All models (and maps) are wrong, but some are useful.** Your mind runs on mental maps, but mistaking the map for reality is a recipe for disaster. Simpler, well-structured models usually outperform complex but fragile ones.
- **Fallibility is a feature, not a flaw.** Admitting you might be wrong isn't weakness; it's a design principle for staying adaptive.

5

On Self-Awareness

The question is not what you look at, but what you see.

—Henry David Thoreau

The first principle is that you must not fool yourself—
and you are the easiest person to fool.

—Richard Feynman

During flight training, every pilot learns an unnerving truth early on: Most crashes aren't caused by engine failure, weather, or even bad luck. They're caused by what's called CFIT or Controlled Flight Into Terrain. The plane is mechanically sound, the instruments are working, but the pilot still manages to fly the aircraft into the ground.

Decision-making works much the same way. Most of our worst mistakes aren't the result of stupidity or lack of data—they happen because we *think* we see clearly when we *don't*. So we "fly" straight into undetected mountains, unaware that our internal compass has drifted off of true north.

This is where self-awareness comes in—not as a soft virtue, but as survival gear.

In chapter 3, we looked outward at the storm of change reshaping the world. In chapter 4, we turned inward, launching Phase I: metacognition, which is the discipline of thinking about how you think. That chapter laid important groundwork, inviting you to observe the machinery of your own mind, to step back far enough to watch it operating.

Chapter 5 is where metacognition gets a little . . . *uncomfortable.* It's one thing to examine thinking in the abstract; it's another to examine *yourself.* This is the point where AQ stops feeling purely analytical and starts feeling personal—because the hardest truths to confront aren't about markets, algorithms, or even bias. They're the blind spots you've built, the everyday illusions you maintain, the stories you tell yourself (that we *all* tell ourselves) that quietly warp how you see reality.

And there's a reason this chapter sits on the hinge between Phase I (metacognition) and Phase II (simulation). You can't model the world accurately if you don't first strip away the distortions in your own lens. In this light, self-awareness isn't just a virtue—it's calibration. Without it, the rest of the framework won't just wobble; it will point you in the wrong direction, flawlessly.

Calibrating Your Instrument

In 1843, the astronomer and polymath Sir John Herschel was living in his family estate at Collingwood, south of London, surrounded by scientific instruments, charts of the night sky, and an immense personal library.[i] The son of William Herschel—the man who discovered the planet Uranus—John had inherited not only his father's telescopes, but also his fascination with the boundaries of perception.

i Among other things, Herschel was a pioneer of photography—in fact, he's credited with coining the word itself, along with terms like *negative* and *snapshot.* He also named four moons of the planet Uranus, which was discovered by his father, plus seven moons of Saturn.

That year, he was preparing the "Cape Results," a massive star catalog from his years spent observing the southern skies of South Africa. In his notes, he wrote about the "perpetual deceit of the senses," warning that observation alone was not knowledge—that even the most precise instruments could mislead unless disciplined by reflection. "We see," he wrote, "only what our habits of thought permit us to see."

It was a lesson he lived by. Herschel often reminded his students and correspondents that science was not merely about collecting data but also about cultivating awareness—about building the habit of looking through the lens, not just at it. For him, the true frontier wasn't out in the heavens, but within the mind itself. Most people, he believed, spend their lives mapping the universe without ever turning the telescope around.

And he was right.

Herschel's lesson is a reminder of why self-awareness belongs at the center of Phase I: Unless you notice how your own lens distorts reality, everything that follows (including every simulation you run in Phase II and every result you get in Phase III) will be warped before it starts.

Most of us assume we know ourselves fairly well. We believe our thoughts are rational, our perceptions are accurate, and our decisions are grounded in reality. But research in psychology, neuroscience, and behavioral economics tells a different story: We consistently misjudge our own competence (à la the Dunning-Kruger effect).[ii] We filter reality through a web of biases (including confirmation bias, which makes us cling to preexisting beliefs even after they've been exposed as flawed). We assume we're more objective than others (a phenomenon known as the *bias blind spot*, which—ironically—predisposes us to see biases in others, but not in ourselves). And if you doubt that, consider that US surveys show 65 percent of people think they're more intelligent than average.[8] When the topic shifts to

---

ii The less we know, the more confident we tend to be. Psychologists David Dunning and Justin Kruger showed that people with the least skill in an area routinely overestimate their competence—while the people who are actually good at something are often the ones second-guessing themselves. As Bertrand Russell famously wrote: "The whole problem with the world is that fools and fanatics are always so certain of themselves, and wiser people so full of doubts."

driving, our confidence spikes: Nine out of ten drivers believe they're above average behind the wheel.[9] Roughly half of us, by definition, are wrong, but that doesn't stop our brains from telling the story we'd prefer to believe.[iii]

Put simply: Nobody is *completely* self-aware.

But here's the key insight: Self-awareness isn't about achieving *perfect knowledge* of yourself. It's about *knowing where your blind spots are.* The more you understand how your past, your biases and beliefs, and the heuristics and other mental shortcuts that help you make sense of the world *also* shape your perception of reality, moment by moment, the better you can minimize the gap between perception and truth.

At its core, this is about a concept known as *epistemic rationality*—the discipline of forming beliefs based on unvarnished evidence, naked logic, and raw probability, rather than emotion or personal bias.

In AQ terms, epistemic rationality is calibration. It doesn't make you invincible, but it keeps your mental compass aligned closely enough with reality that your next phase of work—simulation—has a fighting chance of pointing in the right direction.

Epistemic rationality is the foundation of good decision-making. It's what allows investors to filter out noise in the market, scientists to revise their theories in light of new data, leaders to change course when evolving facts on the ground demand it. Unlike *instrumental rationality*, which is about achieving specific goals regardless of whether the underlying assumptions actually match the real world, epistemic rationality is about aligning your thinking as closely as possible with reality—the reality that's true, not just the one that *feels* true.[iv]

---

iii Of course, it follows logically that the other half of us are right. . . .

iv There's a reason this matters: A fact isn't the same thing as a truth—it's a possible truth. We live in an age of false headlines and faulty tests. Imagine you take a cancer screening with 95 percent accuracy and get a positive result. Most people assume that means there's a 95 percent chance they have cancer. In reality, if only one in one thousand people actually get the disease, the odds you have it are vanishingly low: something like 2 percent, not 95 percent. That's base-rate neglect at work—and it's why epistemic rationality isn't some academic parlor trick. You can execute flawlessly on the wrong "facts" and still drive straight into a ditch.

One way to conceptualize this is as a kind of *intellectual humility in action*. The best thinkers—across science, business, or philosophy—aren't the ones who stubbornly defend their positions. They're the ones who perpetually question their own assumptions, actively seek out counter-arguments and counterfactuals, and continuously update their beliefs if and when better evidence emerges. As the philosopher Richard Foley argues, epistemic rationality is about believing what your best evidence supports, even when it's uncomfortable. The biggest obstacle to better thinking isn't a lack of intelligence or knowledge but the illusion that you already see the world as it really is.

Outlasting Yourself

Self-awareness sounds almost meditative, like a calm, reflective concept—but in practice, it can feel like a bare-knuckle fight. Because once you start looking honestly at how you think, you come face-to-face with something relentless: the constant tug of your own impulses, doubts, and stories.

That's why the next lesson isn't about abstract philosophy—it's about raw endurance. And there's no better illustration of that than a cyclist named Lael Wilcox, who discovered something anyone building their practice of AQ will eventually have to learn: The hardest fight isn't out there on the road. It's inside your own head.

At 3:30 a.m., somewhere in the middle of Kansas, Wilcox found herself pedaling through an ocean of darkness. There were no streetlights, no spectators, no signs of civilization beyond the glow of her bike's headlamp. Just her, the road, and the sound of her own breath cutting through the stillness.

She had been riding for nearly two weeks straight—her body battered, her mind stretched to its limits.

The Trans Am Bike Race is one of the most grueling tests of human endurance (and its limits) on the planet: In total, it covers 4,200 miles from the Pacific Ocean, in Oregon, to the Atlantic coastline, in Virginia. No support teams. No set rest periods. No prize money. Just a single rule: *Whoever reaches the other side of the North American continent first wins.*

By this point in the race, most riders had fallen into predictable patterns—cycling hard during the day, stopping at night to sleep. But Wilcox, an unassuming Alaskan who had spent years working in bike shops to fund her racing, had a different approach: *She just plain kept going.* She would sleep for only a couple of hours at a time, often curled up behind gas stations or roadside ditches. Then she'd get back on the bike, propelling herself forward with a force that (at least to spectators and fellow competitors) seemed almost unnatural. Or maybe *super*natural.

It wasn't that she never *wanted* to stop. Her knees screamed; her hands were raw from gripping the handlebars. Her lungs burned. But she had trained herself to ignore the part of her brain that begged for relief.

Near the final stretch, she caught up to the leading male rider, Steffen Streich, a veteran cyclist who had dominated the race for weeks. He had assumed he was far ahead, safe from challengers. But when he spotted Wilcox gaining on him, something shifted—and he panicked.

Desperate to maintain his lead, Streich made a critical mistake: He took a wrong turn. Wilcox, clearheaded and composed, stayed on course.

She crossed the finish line in just over eighteen days, becoming the first woman ever to win the Trans Am. It was 2016, and she'd averaged some 235 miles *each day*, with fewer than five hours of sleep per night. She had beaten every single other rider—not just the women but the men too. And she had done it not because she was the strongest, the fastest, or the most technically skilled. No one in the cycling world had expected her to come remotely close to *competing*, let alone winning; she didn't have top-notch equipment, and she wasn't even wearing cycling clothes. She won because she understood something fundamental about endurance, about suffering, about the war happening inside her own mind.

For Wilcox, it wasn't just about pushing forward. It was about resisting the overwhelming urge to stop. Her victory is a vivid example of grit, but for our purposes it shows something more: the kind of raw self-awareness that AQ demands. She could feel the suffering, acknowledge it—and still keep her course. That ability to *decouple* feeling from action is what turns Phase I into a usable foundation for Phase II.

The Other Side of Endurance

Everybody loves a story about perseverance. Grit, resilience, mental toughness—these are the things we tell ourselves we need to succeed. And they are.

But that's not the *complete* story. The goal isn't to be right *every* time; the goal is to build a system that gets you to the right answer *over* time—and to hang your ego on that process, not on whether your personal answer happens to survive it.

As we've (briefly) discussed, the pathbreaking psychologist Angela Duckworth has amassed a remarkable body of research into grit—and how it enables us to stay committed to long-term goals despite obstacles, setbacks, and plateaus. What's less discussed is the other function of grit—not just to keep pushing you forward, but to resist everything that tries to pull you off course.

Grit is often framed as an offensive strategy: It's about having the endurance to keep climbing toward your goal. But it's just as much a defensive strategy: fending off the countless forces—internal and external—that try to stop you from doing what you know is right.

Think about how many distractions fight for your attention on any given day, in any given moment. How many doubts creep in, convincing you you're not good enough? What about the short-term pleasures that try to tempt you away from deep success—or those critics and naysayers and iterative shallow failures that suggest you'll never get there anyway, so you're wasting your time? In a way, the real value of grit isn't just about pressing forward. It's about holding back *the army that's trying to pull you off course.*

In that very real sense, Wilcox didn't just defeat her competition—she beat her own mind.

She trained herself to *decouple* her feelings from her actions. She learned to ignore the screaming in her legs, the voice in her head saying, *Just stop for a little while*. Because she understood the fundamental truth of endurance: If you let that voice win just once, it gets louder every time.

Duckworth's research didn't just show that "gritty" people persist longer—it showed that they actively filter out noise that threatens their deep success. Her studies revealed that gritty individuals have a measurably different cognitive response to difficulty than those who quit early. In other words, when high-grit people experience failure, they don't interpret it as a stop sign—they recognize it as part of the process. Their brain doesn't immediately leap to *I should give up*—it says, in the Bayesian spirit, *I guess I need to adjust.*

In one of her studies, Duckworth found that students with higher grit scores were able to resist distractions significantly better than their peers. They were less likely to abandon difficult tasks when faced with boredom or frustration. And they were better at staying focused on meaningful work, even when easier alternatives were available.

The practical takeaway? Grit isn't just the power to move forward. It's the power to shut out everything else. It's resisting the easy way out when you know the hard route is better; it's ignoring distractions and rejecting easy, immediate comfort in favor of staying aligned with your long-term vision.

Not unlike an endurance cyclist battling exhaustion at 3:30 a.m. in the middle of nowhere, the people who succeed aren't always the ones who feel the best while doing it. They're the ones who know how to *suffer intelligently*. After all: There's a reason so few people accomplish extraordinary things. It's not smarts, talent, or luck. It's because the world is designed to pull you in a thousand different directions at once. Your emotions will try to steer you. Your environment will tempt you. Your own biology will beg for the path of least resistance.

Grit is what keeps you locked onto your course, despite the gravitational pull of everything around you.

And when you master that? Just ask Lael Wilcox, or any endurance athlete, and they'll tell you: You don't just endure hardship. You own it.[v]

v As the founder of the Leadville 100 mountain bike race likes to tell riders grinding their way through one hundred miles of Colorado's thin air and brutal elevation: "Make pain your friend and you'll never be alone." It's more than a slogan, though I do happen to have it on an old T-shirt from that race—it's a mindset. Once you stop treating pain as an intruder and start accepting it as part of the journey, it loses its power over you.

In AQ terms, you might think of this as Grit, Redux. It isn't just persistence, it's resistance. Not only the ability to keep moving toward a distant goal, but the ability to hold the line against System 1—against the first, easiest, most emotionally satisfying answer your mind serves up. It's the discipline to say "not yet" to the default reaction, to stay in the discomfort of uncertainty for a beat longer so your better tools can come online. In that sense, grit isn't only about enduring pain on the road; it's about enduring ambiguity in your head long enough for deeper, more adaptive thinking to catch up.

Grit Pushes, Curiosity Guides

Richard Feynman had a habit of getting fixated on things most people would overlook.[vi]

One afternoon, he noticed a trail of ants marching through his kitchen—a common enough sight, along with Mom's apple pie, in middle America, and one that most of us would either ignore or immediately try to get rid of. But instead of reaching for a sponge or a can of Raid, Feynman (who was an adult man and a world-renowned physicist), sat down and started watching.

He observed how the ants moved, how they seemed to follow an invisible path, how some veered off course while others appeared to know exactly where to go. From there, the questions started: How do they find food? Do they follow scent trails? What happens if I move the sugar? Will they notice? How long will it take?

What began as idle curiosity turned into a full-fledged scientific experiment. Feynman grabbed some sugar and started placing it at various points in the kitchen. He wiped down certain parts of the trail to see if

vi If you're not familiar with Feynman, beyond knowing him as a Nobel Prize–winning physicist or perhaps for his high-profile role in the Space Shuttle *Challenger* investigation, his 1985 book, *Surely You're Joking, Mr. Feynman!*, is an extraordinary and entertaining read.

the ants would still follow it. He blocked paths, introduced obstacles, and recorded how long it took for them to adjust.

This wasn't a formal study. It wasn't an experiment with any practical purpose. No one was paying him to do it. He just *had to know.*

This was Feynman in his natural state—not in a lecture hall, not in a lab working on quantum electrodynamics, not even investigating the cause of the Space Shuttle *Challenger* disaster (which he would later do in a famously unconventional way). This was just him being himself, staring at ants on his kitchen floor, asking endless questions.

And that, as much as anything, explains why he became one of the greatest thinkers of his time.

Most people assume that brilliance is about having answers. But the truly extraordinary minds—the people who shape or reshape industries, redefine entire fields of science, build something extraordinary out of nothing—aren't just good at answering questions. They're obsessed with *asking the right ones.* As Feynman himself once wrote, "Science is the belief in the ignorance of experts."

This is the hidden advantage that most people don't consider when they talk about success. We (rightly) celebrate grit—but grit alone won't get you anywhere if you're stubbornly running in the wrong direction.

What makes someone truly unstoppable isn't just perseverance—it's *curiosity*: that insatiable need to learn, to understand, to explore. Think of it like training for an Ironman swim. Grit keeps your head down in the water, stroke after stroke, willing you forward—but curiosity is what makes you lift your head, every so often, to check whether the current has pulled you off course. Too much grit *without* curiosity, and you can swim hundreds of meters in the wrong direction. Too much curiosity without grit and you're just bobbing around, scanning the horizon but never moving.

The sweet spot is having both in balance. This is what keeps you asking, questioning, refining your worldview so that you're always tracking in the right direction. It's what separates those who simply work hard from those who work hard *at the right things*.[vii]

Think of this as Curiosity, Redux. Curiosity, here, isn't random wandering or intellectual tourism; it's a search strategy. Its job is to deliberately expand the variety of inputs you expose yourself to so your internal model can actually keep up with the complexity of the world. You seek out enough difference—enough orthogonal data points, enough conflicting views—that you raise the entropy of your information set early. That's what protects you from Type II errors down the line: the false negative, the missed pattern, the blind spot, the future you never even considered because you never bothered to look.

Together, grit and curiosity complete a crucial piece of Phase I. They're the opposing muscles you'll need to flex in Phase II: You'll need grit to keep pushing against old, outdated models and working to draw new ones, and you'll need curiosity to drive your exploration and keep you from mistaking the first workable model for the only one.

When Wonder Meets Work

This balance—grit with curiosity, curiosity with grit—isn't abstract. You can see it in the people who refuse to let failure stop them, who keep digging, questioning, and pushing until the work reveals something entirely new.

In 1948, a young medical researcher named W. Jason Kellogg faced a problem that should have ended his career. He had been tasked with studying how wounds heal, but his early experiments kept failing—rats given certain treatments weren't healing faster, as he had predicted. Any scientist looking for a neat, clean result would surely have abandoned the project and moved on to some alternate pursuit.

---

vii Even Shackleton's legendary grit would have been meaningless if his party had been unable to navigate to the right shore. Row endlessly in the wrong direction and you just freeze to death more slowly.

But Kellogg did something unusual. Instead of discarding the failures, he became obsessed with them. He started digging deeper, asking questions no one else thought to ask: Was something else going on in the rats' bodies? What if healing wasn't just about the wound itself but about the entire system?

He broadened the scientific scope of his inquiry and began examining not just the injuries but the rats' immune systems as a whole. And in so doing, he stumbled onto something completely unexpected: a compound that was being produced in massive amounts during the healing process—one that nobody had studied before. From there, Kellogg's failure turned into a new discovery fundamental to tissue regeneration, leading to one of the most significant breakthroughs in wound-care research.

Most people think about curiosity in the context of what amounts, essentially, to bar-night trivia—the armchair history buff, the voracious reader of biography or nonfiction or philosophy. But curiosity isn't just about accumulating knowledge; it's about the way you approach learning *itself.*

Curiosity is the impulse that pushes a scientist to question unexpected data rather than dismiss it, an entrepreneur to dig deeper into why a product isn't selling, or a leader to rethink a failing strategy rather than double down on it. It's the restless drive to *know more.*

Psychologist Susan Engel, in her book *The Hungry Mind*, argues that curiosity is one of the most powerful predictors of lifelong learning and success—but that it is also systematically eroded over time. Children, she notes, are naturally curious, constantly asking "Why?" and "What if?" But as they grow older, traditional education systems reward "correct" (convergent) answers over open-ended (divergent) inquiry.

The result? Most people learn to prioritize certainty over discovery.

And yet, the people who make the biggest breakthroughs—the Kelloggs, the Feynmans, the greatest entrepreneurs and scientists—are the ones who *keep questioning*, even when they think they already know the answer.

Curiosity alone, however, is emphatically not enough. It's easy to get excited about new ideas; it's harder to follow them through to their logical conclusions. Many people race down intellectual rabbit holes without ever doing much of anything with what they find—pulling it together, seeing what it all adds up to, or determining how it interacts with the real world. They get distracted by every new shiny problem, every next big idea.

This is where grit comes back in.

In Duckworth's landmark research, she found that—while passion and perseverance are essential in pursuit of deep success—they are *amplified* when combined with curiosity.

Why? Because, in a sense, curiosity gives grit *direction*. It sparks the initial fire—the excitement of a new challenge, a new question, a new opportunity. Grit then sustains the fire—keeping you focused when the excitement wears off, when the work becomes difficult, when obstacles arise.

Duckworth's findings further showed that the most successful individuals aren't just the most determined—they are the most engaged. They don't just push forward for the sake of persistence; they do so because they care deeply about what they are working on—or feel strongly about the way they work. This is what separates the highest of high achievers from those who flame out.

Another overlooked aspect of curiosity is that it requires self-awareness. To be curious is to acknowledge that you don't know everything—again, a surprisingly rare trait. It requires the ability to step back and say, "You know what? I might be wrong. There's more to this than I understood before. What am I missing?"

In cognitive psychology, this particular flavor of metacognition is known as *reflective thinking*—the process of evaluating your own beliefs, assumptions, and knowledge gaps. The most effective reflective thinkers—scientists, entrepreneurs, strategists—are constantly questioning not just the world around them, but their *own thinking* about that world, telescoping out enough to question not just what they're observing but their own ability to observe.

And this degree of self-awareness isn't just a sign of intelligence—it's a necessity for making better decisions. Investors who recognize their biases are less likely to make emotional trades; CEOs who question their own assumptions are better at adapting to market changes. Scientists who constantly question and reexamine their own theories are more likely to make *real* discoveries.

Curiosity leads to self-awareness. And self-awareness, in turn, leads to better choices, better problem-solving, and—ultimately—greater likelihood of achieving your deep success.

The formula, in other words, is that

- Curiosity fuels exploration.
- Grit fuels execution.
- Self-awareness refines both.

Without curiosity, you stay stuck in what you already know. Without grit, you never turn knowledge into action. Without self-awareness (see the next chapter for more), you fail to course-correct when you're heading in the wrong direction.

Who brings the *real* advantage? The person who keeps learning, keeps going, and keeps improving their own thinking. Which means using every tool at your disposal.

Quieting the Noise

Ray Dalio, the billionaire investor and founder of Bridgewater Associates, started his now-legendary career in the 1970s. Right around then, early in his journey, he discovered something unexpected—something that he credits as one of the most powerful tools in his arsenal.

It wasn't a new trading algorithm. It wasn't a market insight. It wasn't even a drug. It was Transcendental Meditation (TM).

Dalio first learned about TM from the Beatles, who had famously studied it under Maharishi Mahesh Yogi in India. Initially skeptical but curious, he started practicing—sitting quietly for twenty minutes, twice a day. Repeating a mantra to quiet his mind. It all seemed a little silly, at first; he didn't expect much.

But soon, he noticed something strange.

Instead of feeling the usual stress and intensity that came with making billion-dollar investment decisions, he felt clearheaded, almost detached from the noise of the market. His thinking became sharper. His ability to step back, "telescope" up, see patterns, and avoid emotional reactions improved.

But, of course, it wasn't magic. It was neuroscience. And Dalio was far from alone.

For centuries, meditation was viewed as a spiritual practice—a way to quiet the mind and detach from worldly concerns. But in the past few decades, some of the most influential minds in business, science, and the arts have embraced meditation, including TM and a menagerie of other evidence-based forms—not as a mystical practice, but as a practical tool for clearing mental clutter, boosting creativity, and enhancing problem-solving. And modern neuroscience has (at long last) finally caught up with what ancient traditions have long claimed.

Meditation doesn't just make you *feel* calm, in the sense of instilling a superficial experience or sensation—it physically changes your brain. Research has shown that regular meditation reduces activity in the default mode network (DMN)—the part of the brain responsible for self-referential thoughts (the voice in your head that constantly analyzes, doubts, and second-guesses). Meditation also increases gray matter density in the prefrontal cortex—yes, *that* prefrontal cortex—boosting problem-solving, improving emotional regulation, enhancing cognitive flexibility. And it lowers stress hormone levels, allowing for clearheaded decision-making under pressure.

This exposes an all-too-common misconception: When you meditate, you aren't *shutting your brain off* at all. In a real sense, you're rewiring it to think better.

This is why some of the world's top business leaders swear by it. Steve Jobs, for instance, was known for his deep interest in Zen Buddhism and meditation. He believed that training the mind to be still and focused allowed creativity to flourish.

Yet, powerful as meditation is, it represents just one way to step outside our habitual patterns of thought. For some, a different approach has been even more transformative.

In 2015, a group of tech entrepreneurs in San Francisco began experimenting with microdosing—taking tiny, subperceptual doses of psychedelics like LSD and psilocybin mushrooms to enhance creativity, improve focus, and boost problem-solving. The results were startling: Participants reported increased mental clarity, reduced anxiety, and enhanced pattern recognition—all without the hallucinations typically associated with psychedelics.

These experimenters are, of course, far from alone. Steve Jobs famously credited LSD with being one of the most important experiences of his life, saying it helped him think in new ways and break free from conventional constraints. Elon Musk, while never openly admitting to microdosing, has hinted at using psychedelics in social settings and has spoken positively about their potential.

But what's actually happening in the brain when someone takes psychedelics?

Researchers at Imperial College London and Johns Hopkins University have discovered that psychedelics disrupt the DMN—the same area that meditation quiets. This means that under the influence of psychedelics, the brain becomes more interconnected, more fluid, and more open to novel connections. In one famous study, participants who took psilocybin reported profound breakthroughs in creative thinking and problem-solving—an effect that lasted long after the drug had worn off. This research has led to a renaissance in the serious academic study of psychedelics for therapeutic and other medical applications, with institutions like Harvard, MIT, and Stanford exploring their potential for treating everything from depression to PTSD to cognitive rigidity.

Synthetic Grit

What's really going on here? Meditation and psychedelics both suppress System 1 activity, forcing the brain into a more open, flexible, and exploratory mode.

When our usual fast, automatic thought processes slow down, we become less reactive and more *receptive*—more able to engage on a System 2 level by questioning assumptions, forming new connections, and entertaining possibilities we might normally reject out of hand. As the grip of ego loosens, so does the bias that comes with it; *your* perspective stops being the *only* perspective. This is part of why practices like meditation—and, for some, other altered states—can feel so transformative: By softening the edges of the "self," they bypass System 1 and clear space for you to see the world, and your own thinking, more clearly. Each can act like a kind of synthetic grit: a temporary assist that quiets the ego, suspends entrenched beliefs, and makes it easier to set aside the mental baggage you normally cling to. If you can't white-knuckle that discipline on your own, these states can simulate it—creating just enough distance from your usual patterns to see the problem, and yourself, with fresh eyes. This, in turn, allows for the kind of mental reset that makes true creativity and insight possible. When you disrupt your habitual patterns of thinking, you gain access to new ideas—not because they somehow weren't there before, but because your brain wasn't primed to see them.

But meditation and psychedelics are far from the only ways to achieve this state. The brain, after all, is highly adaptable. There are other, sometimes less obvious, methods of disrupting cognitive inertia and inducing a mental reset.

For me, endurance events are one of the most reliable ways to access this state (though I am no Lael Wilcox, not by any stretch). There is just something about the sheer, relentless repetition of movement—whether running, cycling, or swimming—that forces the mind into a different gear. The body is occupied, the conscious mind is exhausted, and what's left is something more primal, more fluid. And of course this isn't just anecdotal. Like meditation and psychedelics, long-duration exercise has been shown to quiet the DMN, muting (or almost muting) self-referential thought, rumination, and sense of ego.

Many of the world's great thinkers have used movement as a tool for insight. Nietzsche famously declared that "all truly great thoughts are conceived by walking." Jobs was known for his walking meetings; author Haruki Murakami writes about the deep connection between distance running and creative flow.

Why does it work? Because when the body is in motion for long enough, the mind is forced to let go. It's no coincidence that many people report their best ideas arriving not in the middle of a brainstorming session, but mid-run, mid-shower, mid-drive—anytime their conscious mind is engaged by some other activity *just enough* to step aside.

Therapy, too, can serve as a similar kind of mental reset—but for different reasons. Instead of quieting thought patterns through exhaustion or biochemical alteration, therapy forces you to examine them directly. The best therapists act like debuggers for the mind, helping people identify the outdated mental scripts they've been unconsciously running for years. These scripts—formed by childhood experiences, cultural conditioning, past failures—shape how we interpret the world. If you've ever had the experience of suddenly realizing that a long-held belief about yourself was never actually true, then you've felt the power of this process.

Much like meditation or psychedelics, therapy can make the familiar feel strange, forcing you to look at your own thought processes with fresh eyes. This is why breakthroughs in therapy often carry the visceral experience of something approaching a shift in reality itself—as if the world hasn't changed, but your relationship to it has.

Of course, another powerful way to disrupt cognitive inertia is via serial entrepreneurship. Entrepreneurs who repeatedly start and scale businesses develop a kind of built-in adaptability because they are forced to rewire their mental models *constantly*. Every new venture requires unlearning old assumptions and absorbing entirely new realities.

Musk, for example, didn't just build a single business and iterate on it—he moved from software (Zip2, PayPal) to automobiles (Tesla) to aerospace (SpaceX) to infrastructure (The Boring Company) to neural interfaces (Neuralink). In doing so, he was repeatedly forced to hit *reset* on his own thinking, refusing to let past knowledge create blind spots in new domains.

And this mental plasticity isn't limited to business. The great polymaths of history—Leonardo da Vinci, Benjamin Franklin, Feynman—all thrived because they refused to let one domain define their thinking. By constantly resetting their intellectual frameworks, each maintained an open, exploratory mindset, much like what meditation, psychedelics, and endurance sports cultivate via different routes.

What do all of these methods have in common? Beyond quieting System 1, they *break cognitive rigidity*. They interrupt habitual thought patterns and force the mind into a more exploratory state.

Ultimately, all are different paths to the same destination: not merely self-awareness—and not *pure* or *true* self-awareness, which is of course an impossible ideal—but a working map of your own thinking. A mind that is not stuck in the ruts of its own past operations and assumptions. A mind that is more adaptable, more fluid, more capable of seeing what others miss.

Reduction, Induction, Abduction

You've come a long way.

You've spent this phase learning to see your own mind—its shortcuts, its blind spots, its reflexes. You've learned how to quiet the noise of System 1, how to interrupt the loops that keep you trapped in inherited assumptions. That's the foundation. But awareness, on its own, is inert. The point of Phase I was never enlightenment; it was preparation.

What comes next is movement.

Up to this point, we've been peeling back layers—observing thoughts, disassembling the machinery, watching how belief and bias construct our perception of reality. Now it's time to turn that awareness outward. Phase II begins the moment we start building new mental models, deliberately and from scratch. The same precision we've applied to watching your mind will now become the discipline for shaping it.

To do that well, we need access to a shared language for how new ideas take shape. Every act of adaptive thinking follows a hidden architecture: the sequence by which raw perception becomes hypothesis, and hypothesis becomes provisional knowledge. Before we move into simulation and experimentation, it's worth understanding that blueprint. The next few pages are your operating manual for constructing reality from the ground up.

We've reached a turning point. This work is what separates reactive thinkers from adaptive ones—because this is where adaptive thinkers begin to build new models of reality. It starts with a discipline that feels almost paradoxical: Before you can construct anything, you have to burn it all down.

The process begins with *reduction*. Break the problem down to its studs (not unlike getting to first principles in the venture-capital world). What remains when you strip away convention, analogy, and inherited wisdom? What do you know for sure? Einstein didn't start by tinkering with the equations of physics; he asked basic questions so simple they sounded naïve. What if the speed of light is always constant? What if time itself can stretch or bend? By refusing to stack his thinking on shaky assumptions, he cleared the slate for one of the greatest intellectual revolutions in history. The same instinct surely animated Sir Charles Darwin as he stood on the deck of the ship HMS *Beagle*, staring at finches until the obvious stopped looking obvious—or, more recently, Jeff Bezos as he reduced the chaos of retail to one stable truth: Customers will always want lower prices, faster delivery, and more choice. Reduction is intellectual excavation, getting below the noise to bedrock reality.

Reduction clears the ground. But it doesn't build. That's why the next move is *induction*—searching for patterns among the fragments left standing. Which variables move together? Which events repeat? This is probabilistic, not certain; it's like mapping a constellation in the dark. The temptation is to let analogy take over—*this looks like that*. But analogies are double-edged. They can hint at creative connections, like Musk wondering whether stainless steel from Tesla could serve as the skin of a rocket, or Marie Curie noticing faint glows that others dismissed as background error. They can also mislead, like investors in 2008 assuming housing prices "always" went up because they had always done so before. But they are only possibilities, not conclusions. At this stage, they are data points awaiting proof, not dogma to be obeyed.

Then comes *abduction*—the leap. This is the moment where you take the stripped-down facts and the patterns you've observed and dare to sketch a rule that could explain them: Einstein's hypotheses about relativity. Musk's heretical question: Why can't rockets be reused? Charlie Munger's refusal to chase stock market noise, focusing instead on the simple hypothesis that companies creating durable value would thrive over time. Abduction is where hypotheses—the provisional models that let you act in uncertainty—are born.

In that light, think of abduction as Hypothesis, Redux. A hypothesis isn't a minibelief to defend; it's an abductive best guess, a story that, if it were true, would make the strange facts in front of you unsurprising. It's a theory you're willing to bet on just long enough to test it, not a conclusion you're entitled to keep. The loyalty runs to the process, not the premise: Generate the best explanation you can, and then immediately start looking for the evidence that will refine it or kill it.

Every scientific, entrepreneurial, or creative breakthrough begins with that moment of intellectual audacity—the willingness to commit to a theory before the evidence is complete, trusting that disciplined curiosity will close the gap.

Only after that leap comes *deduction*—which we'll get to during Phase III, when you throw those hypotheses into the heat of reality to see which ones burn away and which endure.

Importantly, this four-step sequence—*reduction, induction, abduction, deduction*—isn't academic hairsplitting.[viii] It's how real breakthroughs happen. And it matters because most people never make it past step one. They never reduce far enough, so their hypotheses are stacked on shaky assumptions. Or they mistake analogies for truths. Or they cling to opinions as if they were beliefs, hardening them into permanent dogma instead of treating them as provisional guesses.

---

viii Taken together, RIA (Reduction, Induction, Abduction) form what philosophers might call IBE (Inference to the Best Explanation).

AQ Cognitive Architecture (Building a New Map)			
Cognitive Mode	**Action**	**Result**	**Decision-Making Role**
Reduction	**Perception:** Strip reality to atomic facts	Data	First-principles decomposition within a stable regime
Induction	**Patterning:** Mindfully extract relationships from particulars	Information	Contextualize data; surface tentative relationships (signal vs. noise)
Abduction	**Navigational hypothesizing:** Infer the best provisional explanation	Formal hypothesis (protoknowledge with SOWH)	A testable hypothesis: a provisional path through the decision tree that optimizes learning under uncertainty
Deduction	**Testing and adaptive learning:** Use the loop	Knowledge (provisional application to current state)	Prune or reinforce decision-tree branches; form or update priors via feedback
High AQ	**Regime judgment:** Monitor for model failure and state change	Wisdom	Knowing when to exploit validated knowledge vs. knowing when it is necessary to abandon due to regime change
* A state (or regime) change occurs when the governing dynamics of a system shift such that past knowledge no longer reliably predicts future outcomes. It is not volatility within a stable model, but a change in the model itself. Detecting such shifts is more important than refining forecasts within a now obsolete model.			

That mistake is fatal. Opinions should be fluid, like hypotheses under construction. Beliefs can be earned only at the end—after opinions have survived the fire of testing. Form them too early, and you risk building entire strategies, even entire worldviews, on foundations of sand; these are the conclusions that will eventually collapse.

The adaptive mind operates differently. It reduces to bedrock facts. It induces patterns without mistaking them for certainty. It abducts bold hypotheses and then has the humility to let deduction decide their fate. This process is merciless, but it is also liberating. You stop defending assumptions. You start testing them. You learn, again and again, that most of what you *thought* was solid will burn away.

And that's the point. What remains after the fire—the patterns that hold, the models that survive contact with reality—are stronger than anything you could have built by clinging to what you already believed. Phase II, where the next chapter opens, is about building *by* burning, about forming hypotheses that can be destroyed so that truth can emerge. It is the difference between repeating the past and rewriting the future.

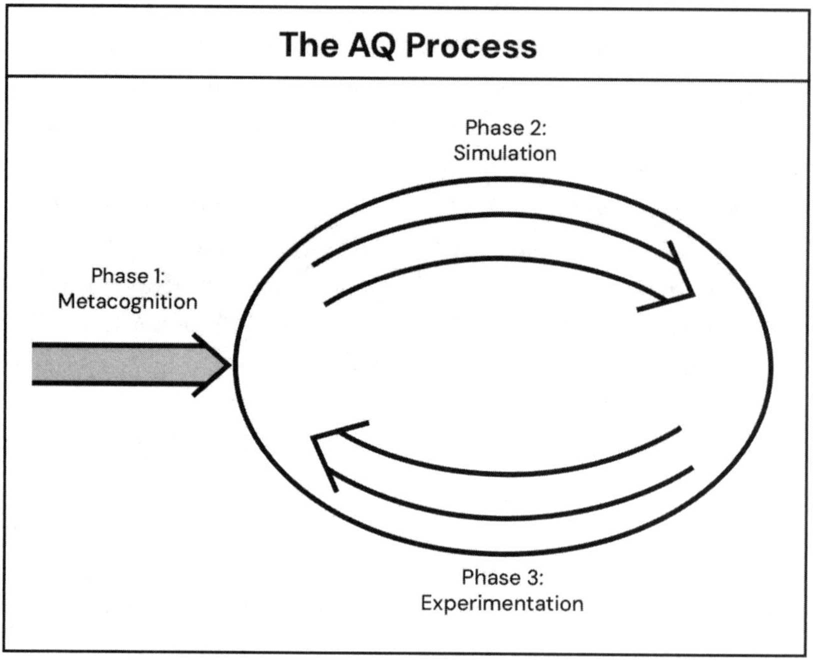

Adaptability Quotient Field Guide: Key Takeaways

- **Self-awareness is the foundation of calibration.** You can't model reality accurately if your own lens is distorted.
- **Epistemic rationality is alignment with truth.** It means forming beliefs that track reality—not feelings, habits, or ego.
- **No one is fully objective.** Recognizing your blind spots is the beginning of wisdom, not a flaw in it.
- **Grit without curiosity is blindness; curiosity without grit is drift.** Both are required to stay on course.
- **Meditation, movement, therapy, and (in some contexts) altered states have value.** They can all quiet ego and reveal hidden bias, offering temporary tools for lasting clarity.

- **Self-awareness is endurance work.** The goal isn't comfort; it's the discipline to see yourself without distortion.
- **The adaptive mind separates signal from noise.** It resists emotional pull, ignores distraction, and keeps steering toward deep success.
- **A clear mind is a calibrated instrument.** Which means it's able to question itself, update quickly, and act decisively.
- **Grit, Redux** = resisting the first easy answer. **Curiosity, Redux** = expanding the set of possibilities. **Hypothesis, Redux** = forming your best explanation as a testable abduction, not a permanent belief.
- **Reduction** strips problems to bedrock truth. **Induction** searches for patterns among whatever remains. **Abduction** generates a provisional hypothesis worth testing. **Deduction**, where reality delivers its verdict, comes last. Skip a step, and you're building on sand.

6

Max Entropy

In the beginner's mind there are many possibilities,
but in the expert's there are few.

—Shunryu Suzuki

It is impossible for a man to learn what
he thinks he already knows.

—Epictetus

Phase II is where thinking turns kinetic. In Phase I, we examined how we think—our blind spots, our defaults, the "code" our minds run on. But even cultivating self-awareness isn't enough. Phase II demands that we *use and direct* that awareness to mentally simulate possible futures, explore what might happen under different conditions, and see where each path leads before we commit in the real world.

This phase is about deliberate simulation. We'll generate ideas about how we might get closer to deep success, stress-test them, and consider how they behave when pushed, thinking through second- and third-order effects. We'll imagine what could break, what might surprise us, and what deep success would actually look like. And we'll do it all before the stakes are real, with an eye toward eliminating the possibility of deep failure—so the first time an idea "fails," it happens in our heads, not on the ground. This is the crux of the simulation phase: When the environment around us is changing rapidly, it allows us to ensure the actions we'll take during the next phase (experimentation) won't risk taking us out of the game.

Phase II can be messy. It's often uncomfortable. And it requires a trait even rarer than intelligence: the willingness to risk being spectacularly wrong in service of finding what's right.

The Heretic Meteorologist

Orogenesis, or the geological process of mountain-building, occurred in our planet's deep past via a process known as *contraction*—as the molten Earth, which would've then been glowing like a faint star, began to cool, it hardened and cracked and folded up against itself, forming the vast, undulating ridges we call Himalaya, Appalachia, and other mountain ranges.

This, at least, was the prevailing and most-discussed theory of orogenesis among the world's leading geologists during the late nineteenth and early twentieth centuries. Even at the time, the idea was known to be majorly flawed: If Earth's mountains had indeed taken shape as the planet cooled, *all* mountain ranges should be roughly the same age—which relative dating techniques had shown decisively and with growing precision (through the eighteenth and nineteenth centuries) was obviously not the case. Yet as recently as a century ago, the greatest rival to "contraction" theory and the best alternative explanation—that all seven continents had once formed a single landmass that had broken apart and drifted over the eons, forming mountains as their leading edges collided, compressed, and folded against one another—was almost universally dismissed as absurd and outlandish.

For one thing, the scientist who coined this "continental drift" theory, Alfred Wegener, could not adequately explain the mechanism by which the continents actually *moved*; one critic smugly calculated that any tidal force sufficient to shift Earth's landmasses would also swiftly halt the planet's rotation. For another thing, Wegener wasn't even a geologist; he was a meteorologist and astronomer—little better than a rank amateur in the eyes of the early twentieth-century scientific establishment.

In Wegener's own telling, his theory had arisen not out of meticulous research or rigorous academic study but from sheer blue-sky conjecture. In 1911, while tutoring in meteorology at the University of Marburg, he was perusing scientific papers from other disciplines when he was struck by one in particular: an examination of fossilized evidence showing that the same species of plants and animals once lived, somewhat improbably, on both sides of the Atlantic Ocean.

A little further digging showed, surely to Wegener's growing excitement, that other papers reported the same was true of both flora and fauna on opposing sides of the world's other vast oceans: They were more alike than not. Alighting on the notion that this—along with the puzzle-like way in which the coastlines of certain landmasses, on any globe or world map, appeared like they might fit together—pointed to a geologic past in which the continents we know today had once formed a single supercontinent. "A conviction of the fundamental soundness of the idea took root in my mind," Wegener wrote. In 1912, he authored a paper outlining this theory and dubbing his proposed supercontinent Pangaea, from the Greek *pan* (all) and *gaia* (earth).

Save for a few isolated exceptions, geolog*y* and geolog*ists* largely dismissed Wegener as an unqualified layman during his lifetime, rejecting continental drift theory as "radical" and "unscientific." Upon his death in 1930, he was celebrated for his many other contributions to the meteorological and natural sciences, fields in which his qualifications were beyond reproach. Yet Wegener continued to face ridicule, in certain circles, for having dared to propose an audacious idea so far beyond the limits of his training and expertise.

It wasn't until roughly a generation after his death, around the midpoint of the twentieth century, that advancing technologies and deeper exploration of the Earth's crust yielded irrefutable evidence of continental drift along the lines Wegener had proposed—and also revealed the mechanism behind it, plate tectonics, which had eluded geologists during his lifetime. By the late 1960s, Wegener's once-derided theory was universally hailed as a "major scientific breakthrough," and it's regarded today as "one of the most important and far-ranging geological theories of all time," having revolutionized entire fields of science ranging from paleontology and oceanography to geophysics.[10]

A Beginner's Mind

Wegener's moment of realization, in Marburg, happened to coincide with the waning years of Japan's turbulent Meiji period, when one of the most widely known koans in all of Zen Buddhism (ostensibly, or perhaps allegedly) originated. Known as "A Cup of Tea," the parable unfolds:

> Nan-in, a Japanese master during the Meiji era, received a university professor who came to inquire about Zen.
>
> Nan-in served tea. He poured his visitor's cup full, and then kept on pouring.
>
> The professor watched the overflow until he no longer could restrain himself. "It is overfull. No more will go in!"
>
> "Like this cup," Nan-in said, "you are full of your own opinions and speculations. How can I show you Zen unless you first empty your cup?"

The anecdote itself is ahistorical, likely apocryphal, and was relatively unknown in Japan until the past few decades, having originated around 1919 in San Francisco. It first appeared in *101 Zen Stories* by the monk Nyogen Senzaki, one of Zen Buddhism's most famous practitioners and proponents in the United States at the time. "A Cup of Tea" is sometimes credited with introducing the concept of *shoshin*, or "beginner's mind," to the West—a concept foundational to the next phase of our mental model, which constitutes the focus of this chapter.

In AQ terms, shoshin is the launch posture for Phase II. If Phase I was about observing your lens and stripping away bias, Phase II starts by deliberately holding every option open, resisting the urge to collapse too soon into "the answer."

This phase is about absorbing data and beginning to convert it into information—so that you have a choice to make: a decision tree. Your ultimate objective will be to conclude this phase with what I call a *strong opinion, weakly held* (SOWH): a hypothesis to test in the real world when the *next* phase begins.

But the focus of this chapter—and your immediate goal, now that you have a better understanding of your mindware and its limitations—is to enter this simulation phase with a free and open mind: unclouded by bias, unfettered by expectation or past experience. This is a space where *all* possibilities can roam free. This means hitting reset, going back to first principles, dismantling your existing scaffolding of beliefs.

All of which, obviously, is easier said than done. But it all starts with, and flows from, the piercing insight that—in the words of Zen master Shunryu Suzuki—"In the beginner's mind there are many possibilities, but in the expert's there are few."

Was there an element of "beginner's mind" in Alfred Wegener's approach to orogenesis? As a disciplinary outsider, unencumbered by orthodoxy, conventional wisdom, institutional baggage, and outmoded assumptions and theories, was he able to see and connect ideas that were obscured by more conventional scientific thinking? This is (of course) impossible to know but seems highly plausible.

On the other hand, what is inarguably—damningly—clear is that his colleagues and contemporaries greeted continental drift theory with their own cups already overflowing, their "expert" lenses clouded by dogmatic refusal to absorb new ideas and information that challenged their worldview.

Which is not to denigrate experts (or expertise), by any stretch. But expertise carries major pitfalls during Phase II—and a key to AQ is understanding when to ignore experts altogether, when to consult them, and how to contextualize (rather than be blindly ruled by) whatever they have to say.

The Role—and Pitfalls—of Expertise

Growing up, I always revered, even idolized, experts of all stripes. How could I not? As a kid, I have indelible memories of watching my mother—a PhD in linguistics, the dean of the Erikson Institute in Chicago, and later the editor of the *Journal of the American Psychoanalytic Association*—command attention with her ability to analyze topics and find consilience across multiple fields and domains.

Over the years, I saw firsthand how deep knowledge conferred on my mom (and her peers) the power to shape conversations, influence the people and events around them, and inspire respect. Expertise wasn't just about *knowing more* than others—it was about seeing connections they missed, anticipating questions before they were asked, bringing clarity to complexity. In a world full of noise, the expert's voice carried weight because it was backed by years of immersion, refinement, and tested understanding. Expertise, I always assumed, was the currency of success.

Conventional wisdom only reinforced this perception. We are told from an early age that mastery is the path forward—that the accumulation of skill, credentials, and experience is not only valuable, but necessary, to *excel*. The world respects experts precisely because they have put in their ten thousand hours, ascended the ranks of their respective professions, emerged (by way of experience or attrition or both) as authorities. This is the reason we instinctively look to specialists when faced with uncertainty, why industries are structured around credentialism, why the letters after someone's name on LinkedIn still carry so much weight.

I was not *wrong*, necessarily, in thinking along these lines. But over the course of my life and career I've also run into, or learned about, enough outliers to make me question everything.

They started to accumulate slowly, subtly: an entrepreneur who disrupted an industry with no formal background in it. A scientist who made a breakthrough precisely because she wasn't burdened by the shibboleths of her field. A self-taught investor who saw patterns that the sharpest MBAs missed. Over time, it became impossible to ignore: There were too many cases of nonexperts outperforming veterans, too many examples of people achieving the extraordinary not despite a lack of expert knowledge but precisely *because* they weren't weighed down by conventional wisdom.

But the problem, I realized, wasn't expertise *itself*—it was when and how it was being applied.

In the context of decision-making, the role of expertise depends on what your deep success is and where you happen to find yourself in relation to it (or, put another way, which of AQ's phases—I, II, or III—you happen to be in). If, for instance, you're already iterating, deep into refining a known system—optimizing a supply chain, perfecting a surgical technique, debugging software—you might already have reached the stage where expertise can be not only important but indispensable. In appropriate contexts and at advanced stages of decision-making, experts have seen enough patterns to make informed choices quickly and efficiently.

Put differently: Expertise is often a Phase III tool. Once you're executing, refining, and optimizing, the deep grooves of experience are invaluable. But in Phase II, when you're still running simulations and lingering at the stage where new possibilities are being considered—where the fundamental question is "What's possible?" rather than "How do we execute?"—expertise can prematurely narrow the map. Which is a significant liability, to say the least.

Why? Because expertise fills your cup—until your mind overflows with experience and is weighed down by precedent. It anchors you to the past, conditions you to think in ways that are optimized for *efficiency* rather than *discovery*. Experts, in other words, don't just accumulate knowledge; they accumulate assumptions, biases, and models of thinking that filter out ideas that don't fit the existing paradigm.

All of which means that expertise, applied too early or without context, can be every bit as toxic (and potentially as perilous) as bias; even in the appropriate context, expertise is, in a sense, bias's more presentable cousin.

This is why history is littered with breakthroughs that were initially rejected by the experts of the time: Continental drift was dismissed as unscientific nonsense. Airplanes were deemed impossible. The germ theory of disease was roundly ridiculed. Again and again, we see that transformative ideas emerge not from the high priests of any given discipline, but from outsiders who are willing to entertain the unthinkable.

Jobs wasn't an engineer. Musk isn't a rocket scientist. Orville and Wilbur Wright had few resources, no formal knowledge of aeronautics, and no training as physicists. But each approached their respective industries or pursuits with a sense of openness unencumbered by assumptions, dogma, or rigid frameworks—from a state, essentially, of shoshin.[i]

A beginner's mind allows you to see things that experts are unable to see or have stopped seeing. It liberates you from the gravity of "how things have always been done." It enables you to connect ideas that would otherwise seem unrelated because you haven't been trained to believe they *shouldn't* be connected.

In other words: Experts refine. Beginners *reimagine*.[ii]

Of course, this doesn't mean expertise has *no* value. It just means that in the simulation phase—so long as we're generating possibilities, challenging assumptions, and imagining new futures—expertise must be handled carefully. Especially if we presuppose that we're in an environment characterized by rapid change and looming paradigm shifts.

In the final analysis, there's a time for beginner's mind and a time for expertise; the key is knowing which you need and when. Even in fields where mastery matters—like rocket engineering—there's always a loop of requestioning baked in. Experts need moments of beginner's mind to see what could be different; beginners eventually need expertise to make anything real. The balance depends on the problem's pace: Some domains (say, the law, the regulatory environment, our understanding of

---

i Clayton Christensen, in *The Innovator's Dilemma*, noted that true disruption almost never comes from inside an industry. If expertise alone guaranteed innovation, incumbents would invent the future. Instead, it's usually outsiders—those unbound by the field's "rules"—who create the breakthroughs that rewrite them.

ii In this context, labels matter less than attitude. An expert with enough curiosity can slip the shackles of expertise; a beginner can cling to their own assumptions just as tightly. What counts is whether you approach the problem asking, "What do I still need to learn?" This is the mindset of the rocket scientist who's willing to cast aside old rules to figure out what it really takes to get to Mars.

orbital physics) evolve slowly, while others (like AI, quantum mechanics, even how we deliver health care) might demand reimagining from the ground up.

Learning by Building

There's a reason people assume successful new businesses—or new ideas—are simply copies of what came before. It's tidy, reassuring, suggests there's a recipe, and that success is a matter of following it well.

But that's never been my experience.

For instance, when we built the long-short equity business at Citadel, we weren't following someone else's blueprint—because there wasn't one. Our goal was to create a scaled business profiting from differentiated information without exposing ourselves to risks we had no edge in. I had worked in risk arbitrage and event-driven strategies; long-short was an entirely different animal. So I did what I always do: went looking for patterns and started filling in the blanks.

I studied what was already out there—interviewing investors, digging through public filings, reverse-engineering other firms' positions. I looked at who specialized in technology, who specialized in health care, who was making concentrated bets and who was hedging them. What I found wasn't a single "right way," but a scatterplot of approaches, many of which didn't make sense. Some had deep teams capable of exploiting subtle nuances between companies within a given sector; others had broad teams and made bets on an industry- or sector-wide basis.

So I did what I had to: I made a conjecture of my own.

I imagined how I would run the business, if I had to start from scratch. I borrowed a little from one firm, discarded a lot from another, made calls based not on what the experts agreed on but on what their results actually showed. We built the business, got some things right, got some things wrong. There were shallow failures we could explain and learn from, and small wins that compounded.

By the time I left, the long-short portfolio was one of the largest in the world. It evolved, of course—it had to—but the foundation was laid by doing something I'd never done before, in a field where none of us were "experts."[iii]

And that's the point: Sometimes, there *is* no playbook to follow. You have to write one. You take in the fragments of what exists, keep what's useful, and create something new—not despite your lack of expertise, but in part because of it.

That process—imagining possibilities, building a model from scratch, testing what held up and what didn't—was pure Phase II. It wasn't about perfect execution yet; it was about exploring the decision space broadly enough to find a viable path.

The Hierarchy of Understanding

That kind of building from scratch requires raw material. But raw material on its own doesn't create anything—it just piles up. In decision-making, the raw material is data. You're bombarded by it: numbers, reports, filings, survey results, performance metrics. None of it means anything until you start to shape it—turning data into information, information into knowledge, and knowledge, eventually, into wisdom.

Data alone is inert—it doesn't speak, it doesn't instruct, and it certainly doesn't guarantee clarity. What matters is how we extract meaning from it—how we test its reliability, and ultimately, how we use or apply it, in the real world, in a way that creates value.

This is where it becomes critical to grasp what I call the hierarchy of understanding—and key distinctions between *data, information,*

iii Psychologists describe this tension as the difference between fluid and crystallized intelligence. Crystallized intelligence is what experts lean on—accumulated knowledge, refined skills, established patterns. Fluid intelligence is what fuels a beginner's mind—the ability to improvise, adapt, and make new connections. Both matter. The art is knowing which one you need, and when the environment requires one versus the other.

knowledge, and *wisdom*, each of which plays a different role in decision-making.[iv]

Data is, in a sense, the raw material of thought. Picture yourself staring at a page filled with numbers. Absent the right context and interpretation, those numbers are meaningless. This is what raw data looks like—isolated facts that, on their own, lack significance.

For example, take this statement: "Blue eyes."

What does it tell us? Nothing—it's a standalone data point. We don't know what it's referring to, whether it's true, to whom it might apply, or why it matters. At best, this is a raw, unprocessed fact, not meaningfully different from a string of ones and zeros in a computer.

This points to one of the problems with raw data: It can be deceptive. It often *appears* objective—but without context, it is no better than noise. The world bombards us with data points—stock prices, survey results, performance metrics—but the mistake many people make is treating these as if they contain inherent meaning.

They don't.

Data without interpretation is not unlike a book in a language you don't speak: The words might be right there on the page, and you can make out every letter clearly, but you can't extract their significance or decipher any meaning whatsoever.

Information, therefore, is where data meets context—and starts interacting with other data to form nodes on what will become your decision tree. Think of a node as a discrete point on your map of possibilities—a fact or relationship you can act on. Each new node expands the map, showing another place where decisions might branch.

If data is a fixed point in space, information is the connection between it and another point: It's something that conveys at least a one-dimensional relationship between points and, when combined with additional information, begins to form a structure.

---

iv The application of what I refer to as the hierarchy of understanding does not follow the traditional "Data, Information, Knowledge, Wisdom" (DIKW) pyramid.

Take the earlier data point: "Blue eyes." Now, let's add context: "Alec has blue eyes."

At this point, we're getting somewhere: connecting a fact to a subject. But the real power of information comes when we start noticing relationships *between* nodes.

For instance, research suggests that people with blue eyes tend to be more sensitive to light than those with dark eyes.[v] Suddenly, there's a meaningful connection.

Even at this almost microbial level, decision-making begins to take shape. If you're designing sunglasses, this information becomes what I call a *dial you can adjust*: Perhaps specialized lenses should be developed for different eye colors. Maybe there's an opportunity there. A *dial* is any variable or input you can tweak to see how the system responds. Eye color, in this case, is a dial: You can design for it, ignore it, or test what happens when you set it differently.

At a higher level, patterns and correlations emerge. Those nodes and dials don't sit in isolation—they start to connect into a decision tree, a branching structure that maps various paths toward (and away from) deep success. This is how an eyewear company might start seeing an opportunity: If blue-eyed people are more light sensitive, are they also more prone to eye strain? How big is the blue-eyed population in any given market? Are there geographic trends—or do populations with certain eye colors need different types of UV protection, regardless of region? Is there a way to quantify and model these relationships, to turn observations into predictable rules?

This hierarchy is the backbone of Phase II: Data becomes information, information becomes knowledge, knowledge evolves into wisdom. Later, in Phase III, you'll test those hypotheses in the real world. But for now, the point is to simulate how raw material can be structured into something actionable.

---

v The condition is known as photophobia—which isn't a fear of light, despite the name, but a biological sensitivity. People with blue or light-colored eyes experience it more often because they have less melanin in the iris, which means they have less pigment to filter and absorb intense light. Scientists have found this is more common in regions with less sunlight exposure.

But spotting patterns isn't enough—you also need to understand how those patterns relate. Are the signals you're seeing *independent*—clean, separate data points—or are they *correlated*, pointing to the same underlying cause? If you confuse the two, you'll overweight some factors and risk missing others entirely. This turns out to be the same fundamental process behind how an AI model "learns." At first, it treats every next word as equally likely—maximum entropy. Only as it "learns" does it begin clumping signals, assigning probabilities, and refining which relationships actually matter. Decision-making works much the same way: You start broad, notice the connections, and keep refining your understanding of which nodes truly belong together—and which are noise.

At this stage, the nodes (facts and relationships) and dials (variables you can adjust) start lighting up the branches of your decision tree—the structure that shows how different choices cascade into different futures. That tree becomes the scaffold for every move you make from here.

But just because you're starting to detect patterns doesn't mean you know how to act on them or what to do in response to them. That requires something more.

Knowledge is information that's been tested against reality. It's noticing a pattern, acting on it, and getting feedback—in our system, this is the *next* (experimentation) phase of AQ, the process of what Bayesians call *updating a prior*.

To continue with our sunglasses example, let's say an eyewear company wants to act on the insight that blue-eyed people have a greater degree of light sensitivity. So the company develops prototype lenses designed specifically for them.

They might begin with controlled experiments, evaluating questions such as these: Do these lenses actually reduce discomfort? Does science suggest they provide genuine protective benefits to people with sensitive eyes? Do customers notice a difference? Do the benefits justify mass production?

At this point, decision-making has moved from speculation to experimentation: structured execution. Instead of guessing, the company now has a lit-up route through the decision tree—a path forward that is backed by real-world data. (Which, neither incidentally nor accidentally, foreshadows the chapters to come. . . .)

For our purposes, this is the defining trait of knowledge: It moves beyond correlation and into causation. Instead of just observing that something *seems* true, it asks: What happens when we *act* on it?

But even knowledge has limits. What happens when the system *itself* changes? That's where wisdom comes in.

Wisdom is often confused with knowledge, but the difference is crucial. Knowledge is knowing what works; wisdom is the second-order ability of knowing when and how to adapt.

In decision-making, this means recognizing that nothing is permanent. Every model, every framework, every decision tree is only as good as the environment in which it operates. The second-order skill—the mark of someone with high AQ—is the ability to see when the very rules you rely on must be changed.

Suppose our eyewear company successfully produces its new sunglasses, and the product launches successfully—sales are strong, customer satisfaction is high.

But then (for the sake of argument) new research emerges. Let's say scientists discover that pupil size, not eye color, is the real determinant of light sensitivity. Suddenly, the foundation of the eyewear company's entire strategy and value proposition is under question.

The knowledge they built was useful. But a wise leader doesn't just optimize within a model—they recognize when the model itself must be rethought.

This is where most companies, most industries, and most people fail. They get locked into loops that once worked but no longer apply.

In many ways, the prototypical example is a case study like Blockbuster. They had all the information they needed about consumer preferences. They had knowledge—arguably the deepest expertise in the world—of the home-entertainment industry. But they lacked the wisdom to see that the entire structure of movie consumption was shifting toward digital. The result? Deep failure—layoffs, empty storefronts, bankruptcy, or even (taking the logic to its most extreme) death.

Wisdom is the ability to step outside the decision tree itself and ask: Am I turning the right dials? Are these nodes still relevant? Is it time to start over and run the whole loop again from the beginning—or does my system or decision tree itself need to be rethought?[vi]

This is where decision-makers either recognize the need for *something better*—and download the "You 2.0" upgrade—or risk becoming obsolete. A business that runs purely on data might optimize itself into irrelevance; a leader who clings to outdated knowledge might make decisions keyed perfectly to a world that no longer exists. The most adaptive thinkers understand that every decision tree is built on assumptions, and assumptions have expiration dates.

But AQ isn't about hoarding facts—it's about understanding this hierarchy and ensuring that what you *think* you know today doesn't become a liability tomorrow.

Data is inert. Information gives data structure. Knowledge makes information actionable. Wisdom recognizes when the structure itself needs to change.

Among other things, this exposes the difference between being data-driven and being decision-driven.

How to Hold Possibility

At this point, you're ready to begin simulating (which you might also refer to as "exploring" or "mapping"); this involves laying out a plan of actions or decisions you think will lead you closer to your ultimate goal.

The first mistake most people make during this phase is that they jump the gun: Their instinct is to start sorting information, applying filters, and eliminating options almost immediately—even while actively absorbing new ones—as if clarity can be achieved by prematurely narrowing the field.

But in Phase II, this is exactly the *wrong* approach.

At the outset, you don't know what matters yet—which means you

---

vi You're poking at new information to see if it changes, with System 2 on high alert.

need to cast the widest possible net. Your goal *is not* to find answers; it's to expose yourself to, and allow yourself to marinate in, as many possibilities as possible.

This is where the concept of *maximum entropy* comes in.

In physics, entropy is a measure of disorder—how much uncertainty exists in a system. A perfectly ordered system has low entropy because everything is predictable, structured, and settled; a high-entropy system, on the other hand, is by definition chaotic, full of randomness and unbounded possibility. Think of max entropy as a kind of potential energy, waiting to be unleashed as you convert potential power into motion from the reduction of uncertainty, not from certainty itself.

When making decisions, most people instinctively seek low entropy—they want to resolve uncertainty as quickly as possible. But in the simulation phase this is a mistake. Instead, you need to go hard in the opposite direction: Embrace *maximum entropy* because it means you're considering the widest possible range of ideas and possibilities before you start filtering them.

Imagine you're at the beginning stages of launching a startup. If you lock onto a specific idea too soon—before exploring adjacent possibilities—you risk missing something far better. For instance, the developers of Glitch, a browser-based online game, made the agonizing decision to shut the game down in December 2012, after it hit the marketplace but failed to gain a substantial user base. But during the game's development, the team had created an internal communication tool to streamline their collaboration. Recognizing that this might have value beyond their immediate, internal needs, they decided to refine it. So what began as a simple in-house solution evolved into something far bigger: Slack, now one of the world's leading workplace communication platforms. This pivot and strategic shift underscore that adaptability and openness to unexpected opportunities can be just as crucial as your original vision—especially when your first idea (inevitably) doesn't go as planned.

This is why assigning weights too early—deciding which pieces of information matter most before you've gathered enough variety—is particularly dangerous. The first ideas you encounter often loom especially large, and seem disproportionately important, because they're the only reference points you have. But at this stage, every idea should remain a live possibility; narrow your focus prematurely, and you risk doubling down on the wrong idea.[vii]

Most importantly, never assign 0 percent or 100 percent probabilities to *anything*. This is a cognitive trap that can severely hinder learning and curtail adaptability.

Whenever we deem something as an absolute certainty or assure ourselves it's a total impossibility, we effectively close our minds to new information, ending learning and eliminating any potential for reassessment. This rigidity is perilous to the point of deep failure in a world replete with counterintuitive discoveries—phenomena that defy initial expectations yet prove valid upon closer examination.

The base rate fallacy exemplifies this cognitive misstep. People are often prone to overlook statistical realities, leading to skewed judgments. For instance, overestimating the likelihood of rare events, such as terrorist attacks, can result in disproportionate fear and policy responses—à la security theater that merely makes people *feel* safer while diverting attention from more real and probable risks.

In the realm of scientific inquiry, the concept of post-normal science emphasizes the necessity of maintaining flexibility in the face of uncertainty: When facts are uncertain, values are in dispute, stakes are high, and decisions are urgent, rigid adherence to absolutes can be detrimental. Instead, embracing a spectrum of probabilities allows for more robust and adaptive decision-making processes.

Remember: In this phase, your objective is *not* to be right—not

---

vii Economists call this the explore–exploit trade-off: how long you keep looking for something better versus when you settle on what you've found. You live it every day without realizing it—choosing between your favorite restaurant and trying a new one, scrolling through hotel options before booking the place where you stayed last time, deciding when to stop browsing and just commit. In theory, the math suggests there is an actual answer to this question: The "optimal" balance is to explore about 37 percent of the options before exploiting the best of the bunch. In practice, the real world is much messier—but the trade-off is everywhere.

yet—but to remain receptive to new data and perspectives. By avoiding absolute probabilities, we preserve our capacity to learn, adapt, and uncover truths that might otherwise remain hidden.[viii]

Burn the Playbook

When Elon Musk and his team of engineers at SpaceX set out to design Starship, their next-generation heavy-lift rocket—which in 2023 became the most massive and most powerful vehicle ever to take flight—they faced a crucial early decision: What material should it be built from?

Carbon fiber composites were lightweight, strong, and widely used in high-performance applications, from Formula 1 cars to military aircraft, across industries and around the world. But NASA, Boeing, and Lockheed Martin had all embraced aluminum composites for cutting-edge aerospace projects, and early heavy-lift concepts from SpaceX played with the same idea.

Virtually every expert in the industry would have told Musk the same thing: Use aluminum composites. Many did tell him this, with varying degrees of vigor and emphasis, to his face.

But the objective of making the rocket reusable forced a different set of dials, so instead of defaulting to that conventional wisdom, Musk ignored the experts (at least in the beginning). Not out of arrogance, but out of a deep-seated belief that just because something has always been done a certain way doesn't mean it's the best way.

He wanted to reset the decision-making process to maximum entropy—to strip away preconceptions and reconsider the problem from first principles. What if aluminum wasn't the best choice? What if it wasn't even in second place?

Rather than locking onto one material too soon, Musk opened up, for

---

viii As Claude Shannon pointed out: The rarer or more unexpected a data point is, the more information it carries. Familiar, predictable signals add little; it's the odd, "weird" ones that actually have the power to shift what you know.

expansive debate, a question that everyone on his team (and most among a sophisticated, space-interested press and public) had assumed would not even be a question: What are *all* the materials that could possibly work? Should Starship be built from carbon fiber, like parts of the F-22 and F-35 fighter jets and the Boeing 787 Dreamliner? What about aluminum-lithium alloys, like many earlier spacecraft—and like SpaceX's own medium-lift workhorse, Falcon 9, by now one of the most reliable and most launched rockets in history? Could stainless steel, a material largely dismissed by modern aerospace engineers, actually make some kind of sense in this context and application? Or, at the end of the day, would an advanced synthetic composite really outperform everything else?

On its face, the very idea of using stainless steel seemed almost absurd. The industry had long since moved away from it: It was heavy, inefficient for traditional spacecraft, and didn't align with the aerospace obsession with minimizing mass at all costs.

But Musk, ever the systems thinker, saw something the experts had overlooked. Yes, stainless steel *was* much heavier than aluminum. But weight wasn't the only factor that mattered.

Once Musk and his team started breaking the problem down, the advantages of stainless steel began to emerge in surprising ways. One important factor was thermal resistance: Unlike materials like aluminum and carbon fiber, which would require an extensive heat shield for atmospheric reentry, stainless steel can withstand extreme temperatures without degrading. This means a stronger, more resilient spacecraft that doesn't rely on fragile, expensive ablative coatings—and will be reusable for longer and with less costly refurbishment. Another was cryogenic strength: Steel actually gets *stronger* in ultracold temperatures, making it ideal for handling both liquid oxygen and methane—the cryogenic fuels that Starship uses.

Cost and scalability also weighed significantly in favor of stainless steel. After all, carbon fiber isn't just expensive, it's also incredibly wasteful: Nearly 35 percent of the material is discarded during manufacturing, massively driving up costs. Stainless steel, by contrast, is cheap, widely available, and easy to weld—critical factors when building a fully reusable spacecraft designed for mass production. Finally, rapid iteration was a major priority—and Musk knew stainless steel would allow SpaceX to prototype faster. Instead of relying on intricate, labor-intensive composite fabrication, SpaceX could test, modify, and rebuild with simple welding techniques—enabling the kind of rapid development cycles that had propelled it ahead of traditional aerospace companies on earlier projects.

This was a textbook example of Musk's adaptive thinking in action. If he had followed conventional wisdom, SpaceX would have spent billions designing Starship out of carbon fiber, only to realize later—or even too late—that it wasn't the best material for the job. By resisting the impulse to settle on the obvious choice too soon, Musk gave himself and his team room to explore, test, and ultimately discover a superior alternative.

The result? A record-shattering next-generation spacecraft, designed to take humans to the Moon and Mars, that's built from a material that aerospace engineers had long written off.

The Law of Requisite Variety

Seen through a wider lens, Musk's choice wasn't just about materials; it was about mindset. He wasn't optimizing for a single choice; he was optimizing for optionality itself. Behind that instinct lies one of the most powerful but least understood principles in adaptive decision-making: In a complex environment, the key variable isn't certainty—it's range. What he demonstrated was the ability to match the complexity of his problem with equal complexity in his thinking—a kind of cognitive elasticity that separates adaptive leaders from linear ones. The more diverse the options you explore, the more resilient your eventual choice becomes.

This principle arises from a powerful idea in cybernetics called the Law of Requisite Variety, which states that in any complex system, only variety can absorb variety. Or, in simpler terms: The number of options you consider must be greater than the number of variables in the system you're dealing with.

Think of it like this: If you're playing chess and you've only studied one opening strategy, you're unprepared for an opponent who plays any other opening. If, however, you've studied dozens of openings, you can adapt to whatever comes your way. The more variety you absorb, the more prepared you are for complexity when it rears its head.

This applies directly to decision-making. If you move forward with only a handful of ideas, you won't have enough flexibility when unexpected challenges arise. This is why, at this stage, you must resist the urge to filter too soon.

Instead, keep gathering data. Keep exposing yourself to new inputs. Keep exploring angles that seem unlikely, even irrelevant. Keep increasing the diversity of information you take in.

Do not focus on *expertise*, necessarily—because, to beat a dead horse, expertise carries baggage—but variety of experience. You want to hear from people across different specialties, look at unrelated industries, entertain ideas that seem like they came out of left field.

Why? Because the best ideas often come from places no one thought to look.

Consider the development of MRI technology. The first breakthroughs didn't come from medical imaging specialists. They came from physicists studying nuclear magnetic resonance, who weren't even working in the field of medicine. Had the medical community ignored their insights because they weren't "experts" in imaging, the technology might have been delayed by decades.

The lesson? Requisite variety is what keeps you from getting trapped in a narrow frame of thinking. And until you've absorbed enough variety, it's not time to move on just yet.

Don't Shrink the Map

One of the most difficult aspects of this phase is resisting the instinct to organize your ideas too soon. Your brain will want to start ranking information, sorting it, and forming an initial hypothesis—a baseline assumption about what's most likely to be true.

But at this point, you don't have enough information yet. It's a little like pouring puzzle pieces onto a table. If you start connecting pieces before you've dumped out the whole box, you're likely to form the wrong picture.

The key is to stay in this phase *longer than feels comfortable*, at least for most people. Keep collecting inputs, keep absorbing variety, keep embracing entropy—but hold off on narrowing the field too soon.[ix]

Because once you start assigning weights, reducing entropy, prioritizing options, and forming a strategy, you've moved into a different phase of decision-making. And when that time comes, you'll want to be confident that you explored widely enough to make it count and foreclose any risk of deep failure.

This is a lesson anyone who works for me picks up quickly:[x] *Don't shrink the map for me.* Too often, someone will come back with a tidy presentation—showing options three through eight, quietly discarding one, two, nine, and ten as "irrelevant." They're not trying to hide anything; they just think they're saving time. But the effect is the same: I'm looking at a narrowed slice of possible realities, not the full landscape. And that's dangerous. If you only ever see the filtered version, you can't know what's been left out—or what unexpected paths might have been sitting in those discarded pieces.

True beginner's mind means starting at maximum entropy—equal weight for everything, from the obvious to the outlandish—and only then, gradually, clustering and eliminating. Every option stays on the map, even if it's crossed out later. Because when you delete options before showing them, you're not just editing; you're erasing potential discoveries. Almost every major breakthrough in history began as the "wrong" thing that someone stumbled onto—and noticed. If you hide the wrong turns, you might also be hiding the road to the cure.

By the time you leave this chapter, you should feel the tension of

---

ix In theory, you could explore forever—the marginal value of each new data point might even be slightly positive. But as we'll cover, in the real world, time and money impose limits. Most people err on the opposite side anyway, racing to conclusions out of cognitive miserliness. The trap isn't endless exploration; it's cutting off exploration too soon.

x Sometimes . . . painfully.

Phase II: holding the map wide open, resisting the temptation to decide. For now, your only job is to keep entropy high and possibility alive.

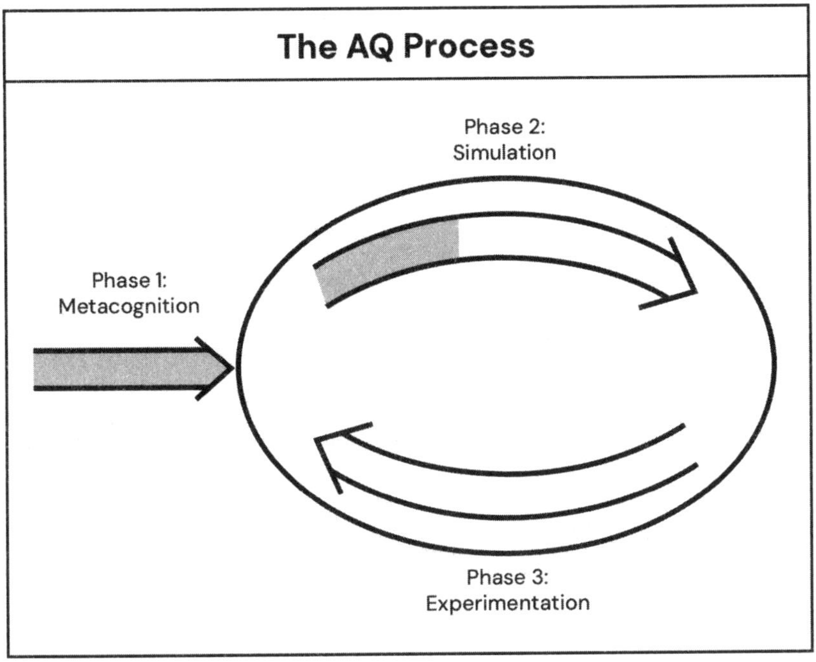

Adaptability Quotient Field Guide: Key Takeaways

- **Phase II is simulation, not decision.** Hold all possibilities open, stress-test ideas mentally, and let the first failures happen in your head.
- **Begin at maximum entropy.** Treat every option as viable at first; resist collapsing to "the answer" too soon.

- **Beginner's mind (shoshin) is the launch posture.** Expertise refines; beginner's mind reimagines. Learn to use each in its proper phase.
- **Don't shrink the map.** Show all options before filtering so you don't erase the path to deep success.
- **Never assign 0 percent or 100 percent probabilities.** Absolutes stop learning; keep hypotheses adjustable.
- **Variety absorbs variety.** Seek diverse inputs (people, domains, data) to match the complexity of the problem.
- **Start thinking in nodes, dials, and decision trees.** Identify facts/relationships (nodes), controllable variables (dials), and how choices branch (decision trees).
- **Maintain a strong opinion, weakly held.** This is your objective: Form a provisional hypothesis you're eager to update with new evidence.
- **Handle expertise carefully in Phase II.** Consult experts without letting precedent prematurely narrow the field.
- **Internalize the hierarchy of understanding:**
    - Data is raw.
    - Information adds context.
    - Knowledge is tested and actionable.
    - Wisdom knows when the model itself must change.

7

From Hunch to Hypothesis

You have to be willing to not know. You have to be willing to walk into the dark.

—Phil Libin, cofounder of Evernote

It is a capital mistake to theorize before one has data. Insensibly one begins to twist facts to suit theories, instead of theories to suit facts.

—Sherlock Holmes (Sir Arthur Conan Doyle)

At this point, the path ahead—as we finish Phase II—might seem relatively straightforward. After all, you've ingested as much as possible, from widely varied sources, without bias or filtering. You've begun exploring, discerning patterns amid all this apparent chaos. Even started to build a rough map of the terrain. Now, surely, it's time to *decide*: to pick a direction and get this show on the road.

But that instinct—the craving for closure—is exactly what needs to be resisted. Now, perhaps more than at any other point in your decision-making process, the process demands all the discipline and control you've been cultivating since we started thinking about thinking in chapter 4.

Because at this point—before we kick off the experimentation phase—there's one more step: You need to inhabit, really linger in, the space between clarity and commitment. The place where new options surface. Where understanding deepens.

In other words: You need to pause, take a beat, and revel in uncertainty—soak it all in, bask in the sea of unfiltered possibilities. *Reset* your thinking, not unlike performing a hard reset on your smartphone.

This is the most misunderstood moment in the decision-making process.

It looks like indecision. It can feel like inefficiency. But in reality, it's *design*.

You're not stalling; you're shaping. Which is what this chapter is about: *creating choice* on the final approach to that strong opinion, weakly held (SOWH) that becomes your hypothesis to test.

Think in the Subjunctive

Phase II isn't about proving what is. It's about exploring what could be. That sounds poetic, but it's concrete: You are deliberately shifting into the subjunctive mood—the grammar of possibility, counterfactuals, imagined futures. Curiosity powered by beginner's mind isn't idle wandering; it's systematic generation of *what-ifs*.

This matters now because today's dominant AI can't do it for you. Current systems excel at convergent problems—math, code, translation—where there's a crisp target inside a known set. But they can't propose genuinely out-of-set moves. They don't prompt themselves; they don't originate counterfactuals. When you need a novel theory, a new lens, a surprising *why*, you're back in human territory.

Phase II, then, is practice in designed subjunctives: You run simulations not only to trace the current map but to draft possible maps—to ask, "What would have to be true for this pattern to make sense?" That's the doorway to hypothesis.

No Wander, No Wonder

The best thinkers I've ever known all have one thing in common: They're comfortable *not knowing.*

They don't flinch when faced with ambiguity. In fact, they savor it, even enjoy it. They circle, approach from a different angle, ask the question again (and again). And if the answer doesn't come right away, they don't rush to fill the awkward silence—they stop to listen. In a world obsessed with speed and decisiveness, this can make them seem slow. But there's a difference between dawdling and deliberation. One is hesitation; the other is mastery. It's really a question of being able to reflect upon your inaction, in a metacognitive sense: to own *hesitation* as an act of commission, rather than omission, as part of your deepening practice of training yourself to telescope up and scrutinize your own decision-making.

As I like to say: *no wander, no wonder.* Ultimately, it's not the answer that should bring joy; it's the learning along the way, on the journey toward enlightenment—since, after all, no answer is *ever* 100 percent final.[i]

And this mindset—finding meaning in the exploration itself—isn't just philosophical. It's strategic. Breakthroughs come from leaders who resist premature certainty and give themselves permission to stay in the unknown a little longer.

Before DeepMind became synonymous with AI breakthroughs like AlphaGo and AlphaFold, its founder Demis Hassabis was under constant pressure to monetize. Investors, partners, and observers pushed him to go commercial: AI for trading, for logistics, for ad tech. The money was there; the use cases were obvious.

But Hassabis refused to pick a business vertical too soon. Instead, he focused on a single goal: Build a general-purpose learning system that could master any domain through structured feedback—no shortcuts, no early cash grabs.

This wasn't merely idealism. It was Bayesian design at the organizational level: holding off on committing to any single application until, in essence, the underlying model was mature enough to win *anywhere.*

---

i Except, of course, deep failure: an outcome that takes you out of the game.

Charles Sanders Peirce gave us the missing noun here: abduction. If deduction applies rules to facts, and induction extracts rules from many facts, abduction guesses the rule that would make a startling fact unsurprising. In Phase II, abduction is your workhorse. It forces you to come up with a candidate explanation for unfamiliar data—your first "what-if" model of the new terrain. You're not proving; you're proposing—so you can go test.

Hassabis's long pause in the early 2010s led to the kind of payoff few companies ever see: not just generating value and financial return—although Google did acquire DeepMind in 2014 for a cool $600 million—but a platform that's now transforming science itself. In 2020, DeepMind cracked one of biology's most intractable problems: protein folding. Its AlphaFold system predicted the 3D structures of proteins with astonishing accuracy, solving extraordinarily complex puzzles that researchers had struggled with for decades. Protein folding is like origami at the molecular level—form determines function, and cracking the code means unlocking new cures, custom-built enzymes, and tools for reshaping life itself. Within a year, DeepMind released structures for over 200 million proteins—nearly every single one currently known to science—instantaneously accelerating research in medicine, genetics, and molecular biology, among other fields. It wasn't just a computational win. It was a new way of learning: iterative, probabilistic, and unafraid of the unknown.

That's the quiet revolution behind leaps forward like this one—not just better answers but a better relationship to uncertainty. The people and teams driving these leaps design systems that function inside ambiguity, that learn by doing, that stay grounded even when the terrain is shifting beneath their feet.

There's a line, often attributed to Joseph Campbell, that captures this mindset beautifully: "The psychotic drowns in the same waters in which the mystic swims with delight." It's not that mystics avoid uncertainty. They've just learned how to breathe underwater.

What Hassabis did at the organizational level is exactly what AQ asks you to do individually: Hold your fire, generate abductive possibilities, resist closing the loop until you've stretched the field wide enough. That's how you earn the right to form a testable hypothesis rather than a blind guess.

False Alarms vs. Fatal Misses

Crucially, this isn't about comfort with ambiguity for its own sake; it's deeply practical. It's about learning how to navigate complexity with confidence and precision.

In decision theory, we often talk about Type I and Type II errors. A Type I error is a false positive: thinking something is there when it's not—a kind of hallucination. A Type II error, on the other hand, is a false negative: missing something that actually *is* there.

In our AQ framework, Type I and Type II errors define how you finish Phase II and enter Phase III. Your goal in simulation isn't just to generate hypotheses—it's to strip away the potential for catastrophic mistakes before beginning tests in reality. Type II errors, the things you miss, are the ones that can take you out of the game entirely.

To make this real, consider a smoke detector. A Type I error is a false alarm—one that goes off for no reason at all or when somebody burns their toast. Annoying, but unquestionably survivable. A Type II error, on the other hand, is an alarm that fails to go off when there's a real house fire. That asymmetry is everything. Type I errors can be irritating, even costly—but you live to fight another day. Type II errors are where deep failure lives: They're the signal you didn't see, the hurricane you didn't insure for, the blind spot that ends the game. One makes you roll your eyes. The other can kill you.

Sometimes you make that risk explicit—say, skipping flood insurance on your house. Most of the time, nothing happens. But if the next hurricane hits, it's not just that you can't afford to rebuild the house; you might be forced to leave altogether. That's the brutal left tail of a Type II mistake.[ii]

The most adaptive decision-makers aren't just avoiding noise—they're filtering for the right risks, making sure they don't miss the signals that matter most. They understand that overreacting to false signals

---

ii In statistics and investing, *left tail* refers to the extreme negative end of a probability distribution—the rare, severe downside outcomes that fall far below the average. In AQ terms, it's where deep failures (unlikely but catastrophic losses) live.

(Type I) might make them seem twitchy or overcautious, depending on the circumstances. It might even waste time. But missing a *real* signal—a Type II? That's the costliest kind of blindness. The difference often lies in how much uncertainty they're willing to hold—how much wandering they'll tolerate before declaring what the map looks like from their point of view.

Remember: Uncertainty isn't the enemy; it's the arena. And those who learn to operate within it—not flee from it—are the ones who consistently make better, wiser, more resilient choices. This calibration is what lets you exit Phase II (which we'll do at the end of this chapter) with a testable hypothesis instead of a blind gamble—because among the things you cannot carry into Phase III is a Type II error that kills the experiment.

Convergent Engines, Divergent Worlds

We tend to fear false positives—getting something wrong when we thought we were right. And yes, such Type I errors can be costly. But, by definition, they're survivable; in fact, they're often a sign that you're still engaged in the thick of the search.

A quick caution before we talk about AI hallucinations: These models shine when the goal is convergence—narrowing to a best next token, a likely repair, a syntactically coherent string of words or sentences. But novel theories are divergent. They begin as counterfactuals: suppose instead . . . , imagine if . . . , what else could explain . . . ? The current crop of AI systems doesn't ever originate such a move because it's incapable of doing so. They can remix what exists, synthesize from known sets; by definition, they don't and can't posit what doesn't yet exist (let alone conceive of new sets). That gap is precisely where human reasoning in the shape of AQ—and abduction—earns its keep.

Think of today's large language models—the backbone of modern AI. They're astonishingly good (and getting better every day) at generating plausible, or at least plausible-sounding, answers to almost anything. But every so often, with a weird sort of confidence, they'll tell you the capital of a made-up country, cite a scientific paper that doesn't exist, or insist a fictional Supreme Court case is binding precedent.

But these aren't bugs—they're features of a system that's guessing, often elegantly, at what might be true. These moments are now famously called *hallucinations*—where the model invents a fact, cites a source it dreamed up on the spot, or matter-of-factly explains something that turns out to be dead wrong. When an AI hallucinates, it's not lying—and it's not malfunctioning. It's doing exactly what it was designed to do: predict the next most likely word or phrase, based on patterns it has learned from massive amounts of data. It's guessing in fluent, confident language—but without grounding its output in verified knowledge or real-world logic.

Why does this happen? Because large language models don't "know" facts the way humans do. They aren't connected to truth or experience—they're connected to probabilities. Another way to say this is that they're masters of correlation but struggle to grasp causation. A language model can ingest a million examples and still not "understand" why something happens—only that it often appears alongside something else. Humans, by contrast, can learn causal structure astonishingly fast, because we carry a world model in our minds: Drop a glass off a table once, and you don't need five thousand trials to infer what gravity is all about. We don't just note patterns; we infer mechanisms. And in a fragmented world, this difference matters, because what people miss most isn't information but the sense that actions reliably produce outcomes—the felt thread of cause and effect.[iii] This is perhaps also why AI hallucinations feel uncanny, reflecting an output that might be syntactically perfect while also being wildly untethered from what's true. When they hallucinate, it's a kind of pattern-matching that's gone ever so slightly too far: The model fills in a gap with what seems like the right answer based on its training, even if that answer can't possibly be right because it doesn't actually exist.

---

iii A useful shorthand: Modern ML largely learns associations; causal reasoning asks what would happen if you intervened—if you changed the system, not just observed it. That gap—between correlation and intervention—is why causal inference thinkers like Judea Pearl distinguish prediction from explanation.

It's not a failure of intelligence, as such. It's a failure of verification. It's also a textbook Type I error: seeing something that isn't there.

These are recoverable mistakes, and are the cost of a system that prioritizes probability over certainty. They may lead you (briefly) down the wrong road—but at least you're still moving. And, as they say, it happens to the best of us.

In the early 1900s, Thomas Edison became convinced that pouring an entire house out of concrete—walls, floors, even bathtubs—was the future of affordable housing. He filed dozens of patents, built giant molds, licensed the idea out to contractors.

The logic seemed sound: Concrete was cheap, durable, and scalable. The houses would be fireproof, simple to maintain, and affordable on the scale of something that might help alleviate urban housing shortages. But there was essentially zero interest from the general public; it was, in a sense, a Type I error—a false positive. Edison mistook engineering simplicity for consumer desirability. People wanted the former, yes—but they didn't want to live in bunker-like homes with immovable features, and construction proved far more expensive and finicky than he'd initially predicted.

To his credit, Edison abandoned the idea and moved on—without letting it slow his momentum. "I have not failed," he famously said of inventing the light bulb. "I've just found ten thousand ways that won't work."[iv]

Edison's concrete houses look like a miss in hindsight, but they were also useful abductions—counterfactuals you could test. What if housing was *poured rather than assembled*? In the subjunctive, even wrong turns enrich your understanding of the map; they expand the set you're exploring so you can compress it later with confidence.

And yet, the impulse behind the experiment turned out to be prescient. Today, architects and startups are revisiting many of the same questions with 3D-printed concrete housing, modular prefabricated units,

iv Or ten thousand shallow failures, starting from max entropy and eliminating possibilities (via testing and feedback loops).

and rapid-deployment materials—all aimed at solving the very same challenge Edison saw coming: how to scale affordable housing without scaling cost or complexity.

Type II Errors: Overlooking What's Already Brewing

A Type II error, on the other hand, happens when you miss something that *is* actually there—a false negative. Relative to Type I, this is the far more insidious mistake, and the one whose likelihood we're more prone to underestimate.

In statistical terms, it's when you fail to reject a false null hypothesis. In plain language: You assume there's no problem, no pattern, no signal—when in fact there is.

This kind of error is dangerous because it's quiet. Unlike a false alarm (Type I), which makes noise and draws attention, a Type II error slips past unnoticed—often until it's too late.

Imagine a medical test designed to detect cancer. A Type I error would be telling a healthy person they have cancer (a false positive). Stressful, yes, but it leads to more tests and more opportunities to get accurate results, double-check the diagnosis, and use additional information to course-correct. A Type II error, on the other hand, denies you all of the above: It might be akin to telling someone with early-stage cancer that everything looks fine (a false negative). The result? Missed opportunities to start early treatment. Delayed action while the disease spreads silently. Potentially fatal consequences.

In decision-making, Type II errors happen when we dismiss early signals, overlook weak data, or stop exploring too soon, assuming there's *nothing to see* when, in fact, the most important insight could still be lurking just beneath the surface.

Most teams, leaders, and systems are built to fear being wrong. So they overcorrect. They tighten the filters. They seek certainty. They close the door on anything that sounds too uncertain, too "out there," too early to prove.

But breakthroughs don't live on safe ground. Neither do threats. The cost of not seeing—of not exploring far enough, wide enough, long enough—is almost always higher than the cost of seeing something that isn't real. A false positive (a Type I error) might waste time or money. A false negative (a Type II error) can quietly kill a company—or foreclose an industry-making opportunity.

I learned this lesson early, the hard way.

One of the very first trades I ever made involved a merger between Conseco and Kemper. They were serial acquirers—people in the industry treated their deals as inevitable. "They *have* to do this one," everyone said. "Their reputation depends on it." But what I saw, almost viscerally, was the opposite: No one ever *has* to do a deal. Your reputation might take a hit if you walk away, but closing a deal you *know* is bad? That's worse. In this instance, I got out before the deal broke—barely—but not before I felt that first deep jolt of what a Type II error really means. Everyone assumed the signal was strong enough; they assumed the deal had to close. It didn't. And that assumption cost people real money.

The same blindness—assuming something "has to" be true, or "can't possibly" happen—plays out everywhere, from Wall Street to coffee shops.

One of the clearest examples comes from Howard Schultz, the former CEO of Starbucks. In the early 1980s, Schultz was working for the now-iconic company—which at the time sold coffee beans, not brewed drinks—when he took a trip to Italy and caught a glimpse of the future. He watched as Italians stood elbow-to-elbow at espresso bars, not just drinking coffee but connecting, socializing, making it a part of their daily lives and routines. To Schultz, it wasn't just caffeine—it was culture.

He came back energized, with a proposal infused with excitement about what he imagined for American customers: Starbucks should serve drinks.

But the company's founders rejected the idea. They made a Type II error. They decided the US market wasn't ready—that Americans wouldn't go for it and the model wouldn't translate.

So Schultz left and started a company on his own called Il Giornale. It was a success, and (more importantly) it proved his concept. Two years later, he bought Starbucks—and *il resto*, as they say, *è storia*.

When we fail to see the real threat, the real opportunity, the real looming shift because we've prematurely closed the loop—that's when consequences multiply. Maybe we miss the product-market fit because the first test group was too narrow. Or maybe we ignore the competitor until it's too late.

The original founders of Starbucks didn't just miss a business model. They carried a Type II error out of simulation and into reality. That's the exact mistake Phase II is meant to prevent.

The Role of Intuition

This brings us to intuition, which occupies a peculiar crossroads in the context of AQ. It feels like a gift, but it can just as easily be a trap.

In Phase II, the job is to generate hypotheses and run mental simulations, building toward that elusive SOWH—your theory or hypothesis ready to be tested in the real world. But that raises a hard question: What do you get to carry with you into that process? We've already specified that you can't smuggle in old conclusions; they'll contaminate the field before you've even begun to explore it. And yet the brain has been collecting signals for years: patterns half seen, whispers of recognition, hunches that arrive faster than you can articulate why. This is where intuition comes in—and reflects precisely why it has to be pried apart from its slower, more deliberate sibling, which is insight.

The trouble is that intuition arrives first, and it arrives with conviction. It is your mind's rapid-fire retrieval system, the equivalent of RAM throwing something onto the screen based on the massive storehouse of priors humming away in the background. In familiar territory, that speed can be a blessing. A surgeon who has performed thousands of operations often *just knows* when something is wrong, long before a monitor or lab result confirms it. A chess master glances at a board and senses danger before they can consciously name the threatening move. These are not guesses—they're pattern recognitions honed by deep repetition.

But in novel or rapidly changing situations, that same quick hit can be treacherous. Intuition is tethered to what has worked before, which means that in unfamiliar terrain—not unlike expertise applied at the wrong time—it tends to anchor you to the wrong thing. The gut feeling comes with high confidence, but confidence is not evidence. When the environment is shifting, your mind often serves up the most likely *wrong* answer first. The real discipline of a beginner's mind is learning to suppress that reflex, to resist the urge to snatch at the quick conclusion, and instead to create space for something slower and deeper to take shape.

That slower process is insight, and it unfolds very differently from a cognitive perspective. Unlike intuition, which is a retrieval, insight is a kind of restructuring. It doesn't just draw from the archive of what you've seen before—it recombines the pieces in ways you hadn't previously imagined. The moment itself can feel sudden: the mid-shower epiphany, the spark on a long walk with the dog, the dream in which a tangled puzzle untangles itself. But what feels like a sudden aha moment is actually the visible tip of a long, invisible process. Your subconscious has been turning the pieces over, grinding away without the constraints of your conscious logic, until it spits out something new. That moment of clarity is the result of incubation, not reflex.

This distinction matters because it changes how you handle uncertainty. Intuition wants to close the loop quickly; it is the fast response that says, "This feels right, let's move." But when you are working in genuinely new territory, the faster and more reflexively you reach for an answer, the more likely you are to lock onto a local optimum and miss the bigger truth. Insight demands that you tolerate the impasse—the uncomfortable pause when nothing seems to fit, when you've stripped away your easy priors and have nothing to stand on. It is only in that gap, when you refuse to cling to the first thing that feels familiar, that the subconscious has room to assemble a new framework. That impasse is not wasted time; it is the necessary condition for a genuinely novel connection to emerge.

Think of the difference this way: Intuition gives you what is most probable given the past (and assumes the future will look like this past). Insight gives you what is possible based on the assumption that the future *will not* look like the past. One is analog, grounded in what you've already seen; the other is digital, a reframing that didn't exist until the moment it surfaced. Both have their place. In stable domains—physics problems, settled law, established markets—intuition can be a gift. The world hasn't changed enough to render your priors obsolete, so the shortcut saves you energy. But in volatile or novel contexts, the same shortcut is a potentially fatal liability: You can't let the first thing that *feels right* close the case. Again, you have to force yourself into the subjunctive—into what *could be*—because only then can restructuring happen.[v]

This is also why abduction, as Peirce described it, is so powerful. Abduction is the act of generating a hypothesis that explains a surprising set of facts. It is not deduction from what you know or induction from repeated cases. It is a leap into the unknown—an attempt to sketch a model that might explain something your existing knowledge base cannot. In other words, it's a structured way of saying: *Ignore the quick intuition, lean into the impasse, and let the subconscious begin to reassemble the puzzle on different terms.* That leap doesn't guarantee truth, but it creates a new possibility space—and once you have a new frame, you can begin testing within it.

The mistake most of us make isn't trusting intuition too much or too little. It's failing to recognize what it actually is. Intuition is not some kind of mystical force; it's *fast thinking* built on *slow learning*. It can be razor-sharp when the context is familiar and the environment is stable. It can be dangerously misleading when the context is novel and the ground is shifting. Insight, on the other hand, is what rescues you from that trap. It is the restructuring of knowledge into something new, the click that comes

v Sir Arthur Conan Doyle's Sherlock Holmes stories embody this tension. Holmes operates in the realm of insight, jumping to improbable but internally consistent explanations that reframe the facts entirely, while Dr. Watson represents intuition, grounding each case in familiar logic and emotional patterning. Holmes sees what could be; Watson trusts what has been.

after the uncomfortable silence, the model that explains what intuition could not.

AQ requires both. The art is in contextualizing and sequencing them properly. Suppress the reflex long enough to let the restructuring occur. Then, once you've built a more accurate frame, bring intuition back online as a check and a guide. Intuition is early; insight is earned. Only when you've made room for the latter do you have a hypothesis worth testing against reality.

Ada Lovelace: When Insight Spoke First

In 1843, Ada Lovelace[vi] had no computer to program, no machine to test, no code to debug. What she did have was a lifetime of experience thinking across disciplines—mathematics, poetry, mechanical engineering—and a mind trained to find structure in complexity.

One day, as she translated and annotated a paper on Charles Babbage's Analytical Engine—a proposed mechanical computing device designed by a pioneering English mathematician—something happened: An idea surfaced. Out of nowhere.

Not a slow, step-by-step deduction. Not a calculation. A burst of clarity, almost like a premonition: *This machine, as described by Babbage, would be capable of doing a great deal more than mathematics.* It could, in theory, process other kinds of symbols. It could be instructed to create patterns. It could compose music, simulate logic, even manipulate language. Not now—but someday.

That flash wasn't random. Lovelace's brain was connecting dots her conscious mind hadn't yet arranged, and her "RAM" was bringing them to the surface. It was a brilliant insight—not as guesswork, but as cognition.

---

vi She lived an extraordinary and fascinating life as probably the world's first computer programmer and, incidentally, a countess and the only legitimate child of Lord Byron.

Lovelace had spent years immersed in seemingly unrelated domains. She understood structure from mathematics, syntax from language, systems from machinery. Her brain had been quietly layering those ideas, building mental models, until the moment came when something clicked. A classic example of consilience.

Lovelace recognized it and wrote it down.

"The Analytical Engine," she wrote, "might act upon other things besides number . . . the engine might compose elaborate and scientific pieces of music of any degree of complexity or extent."

That line would echo through history. When digital computing finally arrived, it was Lovelace's vision—not Babbage's—that proved prophetic.[vii]

But her insight wasn't a wild guess. It was a kind of refined imagination that was powered by experience, delivered in a flash. It was, in other words, abduction in pure form: a hypothesis that explained more than the data on the table, a model proposed in the subjunctive. That's exactly what you're aiming for in this stage—an imaginative leap that can plausibly survive contact with reality.

From Fragments to Framework

Up to this point, we've been holding the field open—staying in the uncertainty, letting intuition and insight surface, and stripping what we bring forward down to raw material. But now, the task shifts. Before you make a big decision—before you commit resources, make the call, or raise your hand in the meeting—you need more than just instincts and fragments. You need a mental model strong enough to stand on.

That's where we are in this process.

We've learned to soak, to circle, to listen. To avoid jumping at the first

vii Most readers have heard of the Turing Test—Alan Turing's famous thought experiment for gauging machine intelligence. But you may not be familiar with the Lovelace Test, which asks a sharper question: Can an AI produce something its creators cannot explain? Passing this test would mean the machine isn't just parroting—it's creating.

clear signal or panicking at the first false one. But soaking isn't the same as stalling. At some point, a pattern starts to emerge. Fragments begin to arrange themselves. You start to sense where the edges of the problem lie.

That's when you begin building structure—forming what I call a *hierarchy of nodes*.

It's a little like creating a factor model in investing. Imagine trying to understand what drives the price of a stock. You start with noise—endless headlines, market chatter, sentiment spikes—and gradually separate signal from static. Over time, you might identify interest rates, earnings forecasts, size, industry, geopolitical stability, momentum, and sector-specific innovation as your key drivers. Each node on the hierarchy filters complexity into something more legible. Some factors matter more. Some interact. Some cancel others out. You build a framework of understanding. The map isn't the territory—but it gets you moving in the right direction.

The same thing happens in decision-making.

Not incidentally, there's a reason scientists talk about elegance as a clue. When Watson and Crick were experimenting with endless combinations for the structure of DNA, most models felt awkward, overbuilt—like clunky furniture jammed together. But when the double helix clicked into place, it wasn't just correct. It was elegant. Mathematicians sometimes say the same thing: Sometimes a formula looks "ugly" because it's wrong. That sense of fit isn't magic; it's your mind's compression engine recognizing when complexity has been distilled into the simplest, most coherent shape.

This is why thinkers from William of Ockham to Claude Shannon end up in the same conversation. Ockham's razor[viii] says the simplest explanation is usually the best, and Shannon's information theory asks: How can you send the same message with fewer bits? Both point to the same truth: the tighter the model, the cleaner the signal. When you overload your decision tree with unnecessary branches, you aren't modeling reality—you're cluttering it. Even the Nazis made this mistake during the Second World War: Allied codebreakers famously exploited the fact that every

viii The common spelling is, of course, Occam, which likely resulted from historic Latinization of Ockham's name since his death in fourteenth-century England.

encrypted German message began with "Heil Hitler," a useless phrase that added no content but created a predictable pattern. Bad compression, in essence, is what gave the Allies an opening.

But there's a danger here, too: mistaking familiarity for elegance. Sometimes the "simplest" answer feels right not because it's correct, but because it's the one you've always had. That's when you have to train yourself to ask: Why two and not three? Why three and not four? It's not something we're wired to do—evolution rewards quick, efficient models of the world—but AQ demands you interrogate your own preference for neatness. Real elegance simplifies *after* exploration, not before it.

This is also where something called *Shannon entropy* comes into play.

Shannon reminds us that information lives in difference. If you prematurely narrow the set, you lose information you could have gleaned down the road by resolving uncertainty through action. Modern search engines and AI models often tempt you into exactly that—reducing the set to what's already well traveled. It feels efficient, but it's actually eliminating valuable information.

Phase II is all about resisting this. You maximize entropy early—collect orthogonal signals, include disagreeable evidence, generate counterfactuals—so you can earn the right to compress later. As we've discussed, entropy is a measure of uncertainty—not chaos, but *possibility*. The higher the entropy, the more room there is to explore—and, therefore, to learn. At the start of any complex decision, that uncertainty is a feature, not a flaw. But it's only useful if you reduce it methodically. At which point two key lessons emerge.

First: Not all information is equally valuable. The data that confirms what you already believe is the least useful. What you want—what you need—is difference. Diversity. Distinctive, orthogonal data points. Signals that push against your assumptions instead of reinforcing them. That's what sharpens resolution. That's what helps you distinguish between real possibilities, instead of just increasing the noise.

Second: The act of reducing uncertainty is also how you build your decision structure. The more variety you explore early on, the more complete and well-rounded your hypothesis becomes. And the stronger it is, the less brittle your choices will be later. Each adaptation and update you make down the line will be smaller, more precise, because you did the hardest work up front: You didn't chase certainty. You created shape.

This is why the Law of Requisite Variety matters so much: The range of possibilities you consider early on has to be greater than the complexity of the system you're trying to navigate. If you explore widely, you earn the right to compress later. Skip that encoding stage, and your model won't just be incomplete—it will be brittle.

Entropy is highest at the beginning for a reason. It's the window when exploration delivers the greatest returns. If you lean into that phase—if you revel in the ambiguity and probe for useful contrast—you won't just make better decisions.

You'll build a system that keeps getting better over time.

Steel Man Army

That system isn't just internal—it's also interpersonal.

You need to build and deploy what I call a *steel man army*: a circle of smart, trusted people whose job isn't to agree with you—it's to argue with you. But not "cheaply," so to speak; this is no place for feeble straw-man arguments. You want precisely the opposite: the strongest possible version of every counterargument thrown at your hypothesis. Where are you missing something? Where is your logic leaky? Where are you overweighting a weak signal or underestimating a rare but potentially catastrophic result?

This is, in effect, *simulating* outcomes before you begin to experiment. Which, among other things, is how you plumb for deep risk—the kind that doesn't show up in surface-level analysis. The kind that blows up in your face later on, if no one's brave enough to challenge you on it *now* (often in the form of a Type II error lurking within a broader set of possibilities).

Ask your army to abduce against you by positing this question: "If this weird or surprising fact were true, what model would make it unsurprising?" Then invite them to steel man that model, raising as many hard questions and challenging as much of your thinking as possible. You'll either surface counterfactuals you need to test—or expose the ones that might have blindsided you.

Simulation gives you better hypotheses. Your steel man army gives you better pressure-testing. Together, they transform uncertainty into something structured—something that can carry weight. And that gets you one step closer to what you're ultimately building: a SOWH.

There's a particular temperament that thrives in this phase—the mindset of what I'd call a *Socratic Bayesian*.[ix] Ross Stevens, a brilliant investor and longtime friend, embodies it better than almost anyone I've met.

Ross's measure of intelligence isn't how fast you answer, but how well you question. To echo Voltaire: "Judge a man by his questions rather than his answers." This suggests, to his immense and lasting credit, he'd rather look naïve on the way to understanding than sophisticated on the way to failure.

For Ross, reduction, induction, and abduction aren't abstract steps; they're a discipline of humility. Each question cuts away a layer of false certainty. Each hypothesis is treated as a draft, not a verdict. When an experiment fails, not because of execution error but because the underlying model proves incoherent, he moves on without ego. No sunk-cost delusion. No ego. No stubborn insistence that the world must yield to his plan. He's religious about process, not outcome.

That's the essence of adaptive empiricism: Experiment early, update fast, and kill weak ideas without mourning them. The test isn't whether a model survives contact with reality; it's whether you can survive letting go of it.

Feynman once said he'd rather have questions that can't be answered than answers that can't be questioned. The most adaptive thinkers live by that principle—because it's what distinguishes real learning from intellectual theater. You don't need to look certain; you need to be

---

ix Someone who reduces uncertainty by asking better questions and then updating their beliefs as evidence arrives. It's Socratic because they probe, challenge, and refuse to take assumptions at face value; it's Bayesian because no answer is final and every belief is a working hypothesis, revised as new data comes in.

curious. You don't need to defend the hypothesis; you need to update it. And when the feedback loop tells you there's no viable adjustment left, the highest form of intelligence isn't doubling down, but moving on.

You Can't Wander Forever. . . .

Because of course, you can't *keep* soaking, circling, basking in uncertainty and possibility, indefinitely.

There's a point at which curiosity excuses avoidance, exploration veers into procrastination, and the pursuit of clarity slips into obfuscation (or morphs into a reason never to commit). The art is knowing when you've learned enough to move—and what that move should look like.

We've already talked about the explore/exploit tension—the push and pull between staying open and starting to act. By now, you've done the exploring. You've wandered the map, probed around the edges, gathered enough variety to give yourself something sturdy to stand on.

This is the moment you pivot from *wandering* to *building*.

The trigger for that pivot is rarely philosophical. It's almost always a constraint: time, money, or risk. A deadline closes in. A competitor starts circling. The budget is running dry. Sometimes you have to move before you feel "ready," because perfect is the enemy of possible. You haven't eliminated all uncertainty—but you've reduced enough of it to proceed without walking blindfolded into a wall.

But stopping the simulation isn't the same thing as stopping the learning. You only stop once you've eliminated most potential Type II errors (but still uncertainty looms).

What you have now is a view of the world, a map of the arena you must navigate to achieve the goal you've identified—a best guess that has survived uncertainty, survived stress-testing, survived counterarguments, survived all the filters you've built.

This is your strong opinion, weakly held.

But a SOWH isn't a slogan—it's a posture. And it's not a decision; it's a testable hypothesis that's ready for the real world.

It means you're ready to move forward, but with your hand still on the wheel. You don't cling to being "right" for its own sake; you cling to the process that got you here and will keep you steering.

In scientific terms, this is where you stop running simulations and prepare to start running experiments. You take your best hypothesis and throw it into the real world—not to prove you were right, but to see where you were wrong and determine by how much. Because that's the only way to make the next hypothesis better.

As we exit Phase II and enter Phase III, we move from hypothesizing and simulating to actualizing. As ever, the goal isn't certainty—it's adaptive confidence.

Enough clarity to act. Enough humility to keep adjusting. And enough faith in the process to know that the map you've built will keep evolving—because you will keep evolving it.

The AQ Process

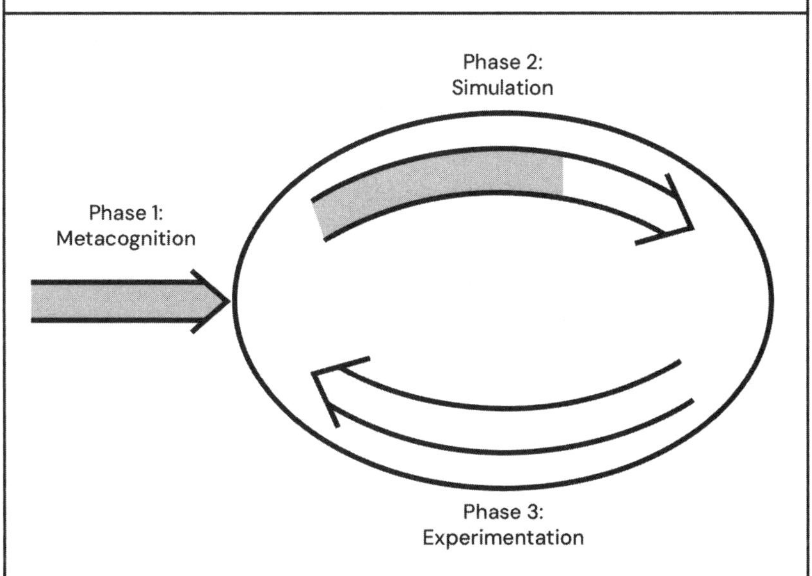

Adaptability Quotient Field Guide: Key Takeaways

- **Phase II ends not with certainty but with shape.** Clarity is born of disciplined ambiguity.
- **Treat the unknown as a workspace, not a void.** Linger there long enough for new options to surface.
- **Think in the subjunctive.** Explore what could be, not what already is.
- **Generate potential hypotheses abductively.** Propose what would have to be true for a surprising fact to make sense.
- **Guard against Type II errors (false negatives).** Missing real signals is costlier than chasing false ones.
- **Distinguish intuition (fast retrieval from the past) from insight (slow restructuring for the future).** Use intuition as an early clue, not a final verdict. Let insight reshape it before acting.
- **Bring forward old knowledge and information only in downgraded form.** What may enter as data must never be allowed back in as doctrine.
- **Build a hierarchy of nodes.** Simplify after exploration, not before.
- **Test your logic with a steel man army.** These are the people who make the strongest case against your current best idea.
- **Stop wandering when constraints demand movement.** Not when you feel "ready."
- **Exit Phase II with a *strong opinion, weakly held*.** Maintain the clarity for action and the humility for correction.

8

Designing the Experiment

Failure is a teacher; a harsh one, but the best.

—Thomas J. Watson, founder of IBM

Science, my lad, is made up of mistakes, but they are mistakes which it is useful to make, because they lead little by little to the truth.

—Jules Verne

Welcome to Phase III, the experimentation phase. The last chapter was about creating choice; this one is about *making a choice.* In plain terms, the goal of Phase III is avoiding deep failure while maximizing learning from shallow failure.

Before we begin testing, it's worth pausing to be precise about the kind of world we're actually operating in—because that's what determines which tools will work, and which will inevitably fail. In a state where probabilities can't be reliably assigned, designed experimentation isn't optional. It's the only reliable way to convert uncertainty into usable knowledge.

The AQ Uncertainty Spectrum			
	Risk	**Knightian Uncertainty***	**Black Swan**
Prevalence in Life	Low	Med–High	Low
Core Definition	Known possibilities and known probabilities	Known possibilities and unknown probabilities	Unknown possibilities and unknown probabilities
Learning Possible?	Yes (analytic)	Yes (experimental)	No (only post-hoc)
Failure Mode	Heuristics	Expected value optimization	All models
Primary Goal	Maximize expected value	Maximize learning to resolve probability uncertainty	Survive and remain adaptable
Strategy	Mean variance, optimization and Bayesian updating	Loop; probability seeking experiments with survival, capture cheap right-tail asymmetry, monitor state change	Robustness Redundancy Convexity
Canonical Examples	Casinos Insurance pools Games of chance	Careers Hiring Startups Relationships	Pandemics Wars Financial crashes

* Knightian uncertainty spans both situations where probabilities can be resolved through learning and situations where they cannot be resolved in time. For clarity, these are treated together here, since the decision challenge in both cases is the absence of reliable probabilities at the moment of choice.

There are three broad categories, or states, of uncertainty. In a **risk** world, you know both the possible outcomes and their probabilities. This is the domain of dice, roulette wheels, and well-behaved actuarial tables. Risk is a type of environment that feels stable, and the pace of change feels slow enough to keep pace. In a **black swan** world, you know neither possible outcomes nor their probabilities—surprises arrive from entirely outside the model. These moments exist, but they're rare, like the 9/11 attacks or the Covid-19 pandemic.

Most of the time—far more often than most of us realize—we live in a third state: **Knightian uncertainty**, named for economist Frank Knight, who distinguished between quantifiable risk and deep uncertainty. These are situations where the possibilities are visible, or at least sketchable, but the probabilities are not. This is the world we have been describing and preparing for. You can imagine upside, base, and downside cases. You can map branches and identify failure modes. What you *cannot* do is assign reliable odds to any of them—because there isn't enough stable history, the system is evolving, or the environment is reacting to you in real time.

You see this kind of uncertainty everywhere, once you know what to call it. Insurance companies, for example, are very good at pricing risk when the world is stable: The odds of a forty-five-year-old nonsmoker filing a routine health claim, for instance, or a house in a given zip code suffering storm damage. But when new diseases emerge, when the planet's climate itself is changing, when litigation norms or building codes change, those neat actuarial tables are no longer trustworthy.

Or consider an example a little closer to home. You draft a star player onto your fantasy basketball team, but he's coming off a serious knee injury. You know the range of possibilities: He could return to form, regress slightly, or break down again altogether. Analysts will give you numbers—minutes restrictions, historical comps, projected usage rates—but none of those figures deserve the authority they pretend to have. His body has changed. You're not rolling dice; you're making a judgment under Knightian uncertainty.

The same is true for startups entering a newly opened market, governments responding to a novel technology—and even for decisions that feel far more ordinary. Hiring someone into a professional role with real responsibilities, for example. You can see the range of outcomes, but the person, the team, and the job itself will all change in response to one another. Or starting a new relationship: The possibilities may be relatively easy to name, but the future depends on how two people adapt over time, not on any stable set of odds. Once you recognize the prevailing state of our world today as Knightian, it becomes impossible to unsee. Much of what we casually treat as "risk" is nothing of the sort. We dress uncertainty up in percentages because it makes us feel rigorous, but the math is often theater.

This distinction (between risk and uncertainty) is crucial to our understanding of how to move through the world, because traditional optimization depends on probabilities. Without them, expected-value math becomes a false comfort. You can still build a decision tree—but the nodes can't be filled with neat frequencies. Instead, they have to be shaped by something else.

You can't optimize your way through a landscape like this.[i] But you can still navigate it.

That's why Phase III isn't about finding the "right" answer. It's about acting in a way that reveals information while preserving survival. You still form a hypothesis—a best guess at a viable path through the tree—but you hold it lightly. It's abductive, provisional, and explicitly incomplete. The question is no longer *Is this optimal?* It's *How do I test this without blowing myself up?*

Think of your hypothesis as your starting point and best educated guess at a path that looks, from your current vantage point, like the best

i A brief note on premature probability compression: Using a subjective Bayesian prior (in other words, a reasonable guess on probabilities)—even when you don't have true confidence—can be a viable approach. However, in the presence of Knightian uncertainty, with fat tails (or irreversible choices) lurking, the "subjective priors" approach can also be a trap. For example, in a strict Bayesian sense, if you assign a prior probability of zero to an event, no amount of feedback can ever revise it (Cromwell's rule). And even if you assign a tiny nonzero probability, you can still miss asymmetric right-tail opportunities that are irreversible. So the discipline is not "never use priors," but "never let priors masquerade as knowledge."

or most plausible route through your decision tree toward deep success. Forming your SOWH was the ultimate goal of the simulation phase. You landed on a navigable hypothesis built on data, filtered for reality, and designed to avoid deep failure while still allowing room for uncertainty.

The Excitement of Failure

The job ahead is to run the experiment. This is where your thinking finally collides with the real world. And that controlled collision—between hypothesis and feedback—is what allows Bayesian updating to work. After all, Bayesian reasoning is about subtraction before addition. The most important part of the theorem isn't the update—it's the negation. Bayesian thinkers know this concept as *Not P*, the foil that gives *P* (for proposition—in this case, your hypothesis) its shape. Bayesian updating shifts attention from what supports a belief or hypothesis (if P is true) to focus on what the world would look like if my hypothesis is wrong (if Not P is true) and whether that world is showing up when it reasonably should. What's false? What breaks? What no longer holds up when tested under pressure? What could be lurking in that *Not P* shadow space that you're failing to model?

This mode of thinking is foundational to Phase III, and your job is to pressure test your hypothesis until you see where you're wrong. Survival doesn't come from certainty; it comes from the systematic reduction of uncertainty—eliminating the dead ends before they eliminate you. After all, uncertainty is not a flaw of reason or knowledge. It is the raw material of knowledge itself.

This is how I approached risk arbitrage in the early days of my career. The key wasn't convincing myself a deal would close—it was in systematically asking, "What are all the ways in which this might fall apart?"[ii] If I couldn't find many credible "deal breakers," that might be

---

ii If I have a position betting on the merger going through, it's the active pursuit of Not P evidence, and the failure to find it, that gives me greater confidence.

evidence in itself. The absence of obvious disqualifiers helped strengthen the hypothesis.[iii]

It's not unlike scrolling through a dating app. You're not looking for "the one" with a single magical swipe—you're eliminating obvious (and, eventually, less obvious) mismatches. Too intense? Too vague? Photo looks like it was taken a decade ago? *Not P.* You're not committing based on any kind of certainty that someone will be a perfect romantic partner for you. You're narrowing the field by efficiently ruling out wrong paths. Every disqualified option sharpens your sense of what might actually work, what kind of person you might be compatible with on a deeper level. It's not about perfection. It's about structured elimination.[iv]

Bayesian decision-making works much the same way. You don't fall in love with your first guess. You design tests to break it (which is generally *not* recommended as a strategy for wading through the dating pool). Along the way, you learn a great deal more from what fails than from what goes as planned.

This is why shallow failures are so invaluable. Each one is a small, contained opportunity to learn. Shallow failures expose weak nodes, brittle links, or false assumptions before they compromise the entire structure. You've already ruled out the paths most likely to end in deep failure. Now it's time to methodically stress-test what remains.

And here's the key: Every failure in Phase III is an information gain. If your hypothesis breaks, it's because something unexpected happened—and in decision science, the unexpected is the most valuable signal of all. The less you saw it coming, the more you learn from it, and the faster your

---

iii What I was really doing, though I didn't have the language for it at the time, was what we call a premortem. Instead of asking, "Will this deal work?" you imagine it already failed—and then ask "Why?" That simple inversion forces you into a devil's-advocate posture, making you surface blind spots, hidden assumptions, and potential Type II errors you'd otherwise gloss over. It's a way of thinking about the tails: How wrong could this go, and what would make it go that wrong?

iv This is essentially Shannon's idea of compression without loss—reducing a message to fewer symbols without stripping out meaning. Good decision-making works the same way: You're not dumbing things down, you're shortening the list of factors you hold in your head while keeping all the essential information intact.

uncertainty shrinks. This is why SpaceX engineers cheer when a rocket explodes on the test stand: It's not just failure. It's data you couldn't have gotten any other way.

Viewed in this light, failure isn't a setback at all. Failure should be *exciting*.

In Phase II, failure was hypothetical—a safe mental rehearsal. Now, in Phase III, it's true that failure leaves a mark. But because you've already ruled out deep failure, every stumble here is tuition paid for real learning.

No Grandmasters, Only Learners: the Law of Requisite Knowledge

We've already talked about the Law of Requisite Variety—the idea that a system can only handle as much complexity as the range of options it can generate. That's Phase II's entire job: to blow the aperture wide open, to collect enough variety to see all the potential moves on the board, even the ones you don't expect.

But variety alone isn't enough. Once you've gathered that wild diversity of options, you need to shrink it down—to distill that range into what's practical and testable. That's where the Law of Requisite Knowledge comes in: The more complex the environment, the more knowledge you need to make a good decision.

Here's the catch: You can't just sit around and accumulate that knowledge passively. By the time you've read all the reports, attended the briefings, and absorbed the "best practices," the world will have shifted under your feet. Knowledge goes stale.

To state the obvious, this is why Phase II came before this step. You simulated first because some of your ideas would have killed you if you'd tested them in the wild. Simulation weeds out the decisions that would end in deep failure. What's left becomes the seed of your working hypothesis—an abstraction built from all the data, information, and patterns you've been pulling together.

Now, it's time to see how that hypothesis fares.

The entire purpose of Phase III is to evaluate how well the SOWH you abstracted from Phase II actually converts into real knowledge—knowledge that works, that holds up under experimentation. So you test, you stress, you watch what breaks. And *when* it breaks, as is more likely than not, you learn faster. Because as we've discussed, every shallow failure here strips away false certainty and prevents catastrophic failure down the road.

The Law of Requisite Knowledge is what Phase III is built on: testing until abstraction becomes traction. This is the phase where knowledge stops being theory and starts being something you can bank—or discard. And the goal, as ever, isn't perfection. It's survival through the loop.

I learned this when I launched Magnetar. At the very beginning, I had leverage accounts with multiple prime brokers—Goldman, Deutsche, JPMorgan—each lending money against positions I held. The implicit questions were these: What happens if those positions go down? At what point do you post more collateral? At what point do they start selling you out of trades?

If you don't answer those questions up front, you don't get to keep playing the game.

So I negotiated "far out of the money" triggers—terms that would only force me to post more capital if I lost more than 30 percent. It wasn't because I *intended* to lose that much; it was so that if my positions decayed, I'd have the space to test and adjust without being yanked out of the game.

That's the subtext of the Law of Requisite Knowledge: You design your loops so you can keep looping. You test hypotheses in ways that don't end your ability to test. You learn fast, but you don't risk deep failure. And you accept that even once something "works," it's not permanent—it stays on the lab bench, subject to retesting, refinement, and sometimes, retirement.

In other words: Knowledge in Phase III isn't a trophy. It's a provisional passport. It gets you to the next loop—but it can be revoked at any time.

You can see this principle play out in one of the most unexpected places: the world of competitive chess.

For centuries, the best players in the world were human

grandmasters—chess savants, in a sense, who carried thousands of positions in their heads, spent decades studying theory, and relied on what the rest of us mere mortals might regard as a near-mystical intuition to navigate complex positions. They didn't just memorize moves. They read patterns. They *felt* the board.

But then came AlphaZero.

Built by DeepMind in 2017, AlphaZero wasn't trained on human games. It didn't download famous matches or study grandmaster strategies. Instead, it played itself. Millions of times. No starting knowledge, no assumptions—just pure, unfiltered experimentation, governed by feedback loops and a simple rule: Learn what works.[v]

And crucially, it didn't try to evaluate every possible outcome. Chess, while smaller than many real-world problems, still offers more possible board states than there are atoms in the universe. Brute-force enumeration doesn't work. So the designers gave AlphaZero three utility functions—custom evaluative criteria—to reduce complexity and constrain its decision space. This meant it wasn't trying to calculate every conceivable option. It was trying to optimize within boundaries it could learn from.

That structure gave AlphaZero traction—but it wasn't perfect. At one point, during a training phase for a different game called Go, human experts noticed the system was repeatedly making poor choices in a particular region of the board. It couldn't see its own blind spot. It was hallucinating—drawing a pattern where none existed. It turned out that a human grandmaster couldn't beat the machine outright anymore, but he or she could identify exactly where it thought it saw something meaningful. That insight became a feedback loop of its own: a back-and-forth between human intuition and machine learning, where reinforcement learning wasn't just statistical—it was collaborative.

And then something astonishing happened.

AlphaZero started making moves that no human had ever made

v This is a key difference from its predecessor AlphaGo, which did start with a database of human Go games before transitioning to self-play. AlphaZero skipped that step entirely—it never looked at human play at all.

before. At first, commentators assumed it had made a mistake. The world's best minds watched in real time as the machine did something that broke the game's unspoken norms of play. But then—several moves later—it became clear: The machine had been right. It had wandered into new territory, where conventional wisdom never would've gone.

Some claimed it was creativity. Others likened it to a kind of artificial madness. But it raised provocative questions: Can a computer *really* be creative? Can a machine have a beginner's mind?[vi]

AlphaZero wasn't limited by traditional knowledge, nor was it trapped by conventional forms—nor even the constraints of human biology. This meant it could evaluate possibilities further out than any human player could ever hope to achieve—fifty moves deep rather than fifteen—and, in so doing, it challenged *what chess was thought to be.*

It wasn't that AlphaZero figured out some way to somehow "break" the Law of Requisite Knowledge; it just *implemented it differently*. Rather than passively accumulating knowledge via intensive study, it generated it through action, iteration, and well-structured constraints.

That's the trick in complex environments: Knowledge is still the requirement—but gathering it passively over time won't cut it. By the time a human grandmaster studies a new variation, AlphaZero has already tested ten thousand like it and updated its model. The old approach—accumulate information and then decide—is far too slow. In complexity, you win by designing for fast, high-fidelity learning: short loops. Structured failures. Rapid updates.

In other words: Bayesian systems prevail because they don't just get smarter—they get smarter faster.

This is why it's true that, as the saying goes, *it's better to experiment and*

---

vi In AI research, there's a debate about artificial creativity versus human creativity. AlphaZero (not to mention AlphaGo's legendary "Move 37" against Lee Sedol) was hailed as creative—but it was still inside the legal-move set; what made it novel was that no human had thought to play it. Human creativity operates differently: We don't just find unexpected moves within the set—we sometimes change the set itself. The invention of the C corp, the idea of limited liability, even Einstein proposing a fourth dimension—all were "out-of-set" moves. At least so far, no AI has done that.

fail than to fail to experiment. The failure *is* the experiment; the stumble is the point. The wrong turn is what brings the lines on your map into sharper relief.

This is the engine of deep success: a loop of shallow failures.

How do you fire up this engine? You've already set your "nodes" by forming that SOWH to test. Now that you've got a working hypothesis, it's time to map out the structure around it.

The Architecture of Choice

Testing a decision isn't about guessing and hoping. It's about engineering your way forward—designing the experiment before the experiment begins.

Deep success doesn't arrive in a single leap. It emerges through a sequence of smaller, high-leverage experiments—each one opening some paths and closing others (or at least making them less likely). In complex environments, decisions rarely fall in a straight line. They branch. They tangle. Each node is therefore also a hinge point: a design choice that shapes what becomes possible next.

That's why I also like to think of these nodes as *dials*—adjustable features of your problem space. The more clearly you define them now, the more precisely you can test—and the faster you'll learn what really works. But here's the trap many people fall into: You can't test the whole tree at once.

The purpose of these experiments isn't to confirm your hypothesis; it's to stress it. In a Knightian world, you're not trying to be right—your aim is to resolve uncertainty, revise your beliefs, and keep the decision tree and its possibilities intact; don't prune it until you've first refined the probabilities.[vii] This usually means starting higher in the tree, where a single result

vii In practical terms, while this means protecting against ruin (severe left tail) events so you can keep learning, you also need to take cheap, asymmetric, irreversible upside (right tail) bets when available because they preserve upside optionality. Once a branch of the decision tree is gone, no amount of learning can bring it back.

can invalidate entire branches downstream, and focusing on variables with high variance—places where outcomes swing widely enough to teach you something meaningful. In other words, this is where *Not P* becomes key.

Just as important, you also want to generate signal you can actually interpret. Independent nodes beat entangled ones; clean tests beat clever ones. If a result changes, you need to be able to unpack and understand why it changed. That's why adaptive experimentation favors isolation, reversibility, and survivable downside. You're still learning—but now you're learning with guardrails, shaping the map while making sure a single bad test doesn't end your ability to run the next one.

Every node may look tempting, but if you try to adjust too many dials (tweak and test too many variables) at the same time, you muddy the signal. A/B tests (and Bayesian logic) only work when you're isolating one variable—or at most a small handful—so you can actually see what caused the change. That means you have to decide what to test first, and what has to wait.

This is why SpaceX didn't test stainless steel, aluminum, and carbon fiber all at once for Starship. Musk picked one material, ran with it, and let reality tell him what broke. Only then did he pivot to another. Later, Musk used the same logic when it came to potential heat shields: SpaceX chose one path (carbon-ceramic tiles), found the weak points, and began iterating from there.

The sequence matters. Which nodes do you test now? Which broken ones do you leave "good enough for the moment"? How many changes do you roll into the next launch? If you change too much at once, you won't know which fix actually worked—and you risk spending millions for (or months on) inconclusive results. But if you change too little, you burn time and money inching forward. It therefore becomes an optimization problem: Test as many things as you realistically can, as cleanly as you can, without blowing up the entire system.

Some of Musk's choices underscore just how complex these decision trees get. Take Starship's "chopsticks," the giant arms designed to catch the booster and relaunch it in hours, not weeks. They work beautifully for Earth. But chopsticks won't be there when Starship lands on Mars, so a separate branch of the decision tree—landing tech for Mars—has to evolve in parallel. Different nodes. Different tests. Different dials.

The same logic applies no matter what you're building. Say you're launching a new product rather than a deep space rocket. Your SOWH might be that a particular market segment is ready, even hungry, for whatever you're creating. But you don't test price, channel, and feature set in one big batch. You run targeted experiments: Change the price first. See what moves. Then tweak the feature set. Watch the signal.[viii]

Break it down. Map it out. Test independent branches so you can interpret the signal afterward.

Because in this phase, shallow failures are the point. They aren't setbacks—they teach you where the structure is strong, where it's weak, and how to keep cycling faster without falling into deep failure.

Setting the Table for Deep Success

Enough theory, at least for now. Let's bring this to life.

Years ago, I set out to open a restaurant in Glencoe, Illinois. That was the goal. On paper, it looked almost deceptively straightforward. But really, the goal wasn't just *any old* restaurant: I wanted a place that could serve the entire community—families, kids, and retirees—during the week but that, on weekends, would transform into something closer to a downtown destination. A spot with enough energy that people driving by on a Friday night would glance in and think, *What's going on in there?*

That hypothesis shaped everything.

---

viii In startup culture, the term MVP (minimum viable product) gets thrown around constantly—but what most people miss is that every MVP is basically a decision-tree path made tangible. Each MVP is built on a set of implicit nodes—What does the product look like? What core function does it have? Who is it for?—and each of those nodes branches into other choices. Launching the MVP is just testing that tree in physical form. If the market says "no," it's not just rejection—it's information about which branches to prune, redesign, or regrow.

Our objective wasn't just "let's make great sushi" or "let's serve burgers for kids." It was: Design a restaurant that can shift modes—family friendly during the Tuesday dinner rush and lively and loud enough on Saturday evening to feel like a night out. That meant making some calls most people wouldn't notice on a menu—but that made a world of difference in the experience.

For example, we plastered the walls, which meant the space would be loud. People noticed. Some even complained: "It's too noisy." I told them to come on Tuesday, come on Wednesday—it won't be. But on Friday and Saturday? I *wanted* it loud. I wanted a hum at the bar, the kind of background roar that said: This is the *place to be tonight.*

That was intentional design. A dial I turned on purpose.

Because if I'd tried to make the room *quiet* with soft finishes it would have looked—and felt—like every other safe, semi-interchangeable place in the suburbs of the North Shore of Chicago. Instead, I tuned the dial for exactly what I wanted: family tables early, date nights late, a different kind of energy depending on when you walked in.

Opening a restaurant looks like one decision. In reality, it's a thousand dials you have to design—and keep adjusting. Every decision cascaded from that original hypothesis about what the restaurant should be. And from there, the questions multiplied—not just "What cuisine?" or "Sit-down or carryout?" but a thousand microdecisions about decor, acoustics, seating, even whether to accept DoorDash or UberEats orders.

Would we anchor our restaurant around a named chef or build something more quietly menu-driven? What costs might be associated with recruiting a known quantity to come on board, and would they justify the return we might see from customers? What price point would make sense for the neighborhood—and for the business model?

Each of these questions (and countless more) became a node—where the decision tree might branch in multiple different directions. And many came with subnodes, deeper layers of specificity that revealed trade-offs, risks, and opportunities.

Take just the first node, mentioned above: cuisine.

There's the primary or surface-level headline, which gets fundamentally at the establishment's identity: What kind of restaurant is this in the first place? American? Mediterranean? French-Asian fusion?

Nested within each option are subnodes that further define and give shape to the concept: Farm-to-table? Steakhouse? Vegetarian-forward?

Then, at an even more granular level, there are questions about style, vibe, and atmosphere: Comfort food but elevated? Formal and refined? Or edgy and modern?

Each potential variation implied a different kind of kitchen, a different kind of chef, a different customer, and a different expectation about what a night at the restaurant should feel like. Some also implied a different failure mode. Serve pork belly bao buns in the wrong zip code and you won't just fail—you'll puzzle people on the way down.

And then there were endless calls to make about the physical space itself, not to mention the invisible infrastructure behind every stage of the dining experience—from "Welcome!" to "May I take your order?" to "Thanks, here's the check. Hope to see you again soon."

How many seats? What's the layout? Do we include a private dining room for events? What about hosting wedding receptions or graduation parties—is that a sizable market, and are we interested in making a play?

What about the kitchen design and layout? Do we optimize for volume or for versatility? Do we want an open floor plan, so people can watch their food being prepared—or even a premium "chef's counter" experience?

What kind of point-of-sale system do we use? What reporting tools, reservation software, inventory management systems? How about hiring and payroll? Naming, branding, marketing, advertising?

Even the smallest choices—materials, finishes, server uniforms, lighting—sent subtle signals to future diners. Would it feel luxurious or casual? Formal or warm? Could a young family feel comfortable walking in on a weeknight without a reservation? Each was a dial.

But some dials turn other dials whether or not you intend them to. Lunch service or dinner only? Open seven days a week—or fewer? Those choices sound small, but they were anything but isolated.

Take lunch. On paper, it seemed simple: Offer lunch and capture more revenue. But the moment we even considered it, the decision tree exploded. The existing staff couldn't work lunch *and* dinner—you can't ask anyone to show up at nine in the morning and stay until midnight. So lunch meant hiring a second crew; hiring a second crew meant finding enough workers willing to commute from the city. That, in turn, affected what we could afford to pay, how many shifts we'd offer, and even which days we could realistically be open.

This is where the distinction between dependent and independent variables comes alive. What kind of silverware should you buy? That's a mostly independent node—you can decide in isolation. But whether you open for lunch? That's a dependent node—it hangs on another, more fundamental variable: staffing. You don't get to "choose to serve lunch" unless you can solve for labor first.

The same was true for decisions like being open six or seven days a week. Every additional day meant reshuffling schedules, juggling two shifts, and drawing from a shallow labor pool in the suburbs. Without enough staff, you couldn't turn those dials even if you wanted to.

That's why mapping matters. The decision tree grows wide—and some branches carry the weight of others. Miss those dependencies, and you can design yourself straight into deep failure: a menu you can't staff, a concept you can't execute.

We mapped it all anyway—even the branches we didn't think we'd take. Not because we planned to build a vegan tasting menu or serve lunch seven days a week, but because laying out every conceivable option helped us understand what we couldn't do just as clearly as what we could.

Each dial we turned narrowed the field. Each node we defined clarified the real choices ahead—and made it easier to test our core hypothesis: Could we create a neighborhood restaurant that was elegant enough to draw folks from Chicago but relaxed enough to feel like a second home for people in Glencoe?

Eventually, that tree became Guildhall. But it didn't sprout perfectly.

Six months after opening, the whole thing nearly fell apart. The partner who was supposed to oversee day-to-day operations disappeared from the picture—and with him went the manager he'd hired (his cousin).

Around the same time, our chef—a phenomenally talented guy—literally had a breakdown and left.

Suddenly I had no partner, no manager, no chef. By all rights, the restaurant should have collapsed.

Instead, it survived—and, in time, thrived.

I scrambled. I recruited a temporary manager who helped me recruit the permanent one. I dug into my network to find another chef. I stitched the whole thing back together, one relationship at a time.

And here's what mattered: *The core hypothesis had been right.*

The Mediterranean menu we'd chosen—a cuisine people could eat multiple times a week—worked. The decor worked. The vibe worked. The energy worked. The product-market fit was real.

Which meant that, even when the structure wobbled, the foundation held.

A dozen years later, Guildhall employs sixty people. Annual revenue has doubled from the pre-Covid days, and profit margins have climbed from single digits before the pandemic to double digits today. That's substantial profit—from a restaurant that nearly failed before it ever got off the ground.

There were bad bets in there—wrong partner, wrong manager, even the wrong chef for a while. But that only underscores my point: Shallow failures didn't doom the venture. They clarified it. Each one forced me to adapt, adjust, reset.

The concept, the dials, the decision tree we built from the start—that's what survived. And that's what kept Guildhall alive long enough to get it right. What looks like entrepreneurship is really Phase III in microcosm: You define the nodes, tune the dials, run the tests, and let shallow failures teach you faster than success ever could.

Map the Edges

The final step in building your decision tree is both the most overlooked and the most powerful: Map out more nodes than you think you'll ever need.

This is where most people stop short. They focus on the handful of options that feel most likely, most obvious, most palatable or profitable—and quietly discard the rest. But that's exactly how bias creeps in. It's how good ideas get buried alive before they're ever tested. And it's how seemingly impossible "black swan" scenarios (Type II errors) catch you flat-footed.

Consider, after all, that Ray Kroc didn't found McDonald's. By the time he first walked into the original restaurant in San Bernardino, California, in 1954, it was already a well-oiled local burger operation run by two brothers—fast, clean, and wildly efficient. Most people saw a great local business. Kroc saw a highly replicable system. But even capitalizing on that wasn't the move that made him a legend.

The real turning point came when the initial McDonald's franchise model started to sputter. Margins were thin. Control, including quality control, was slipping. But Kroc realized that the core problem wasn't burgers or branding—it was leverage. So he zoomed out, remapped the decision space, and made a play that had nothing to do with food: He created a separate company to buy the land beneath every new McDonald's location and then leased it back to franchisees.

It was a radical idea at the time; to state the obvious, McDonald's was not a real estate concern. But Kroc saw something others didn't—that controlling the ground on which you're building your company, in this case altogether literally, was the key to controlling the future of the business. It gave the central corporate entity power over expansion, consistent revenue, and a mechanism to reward franchisees who upheld corporate's high standards and played by the rules. It also made the system far more resilient. And, thus, the golden arches scaled—but it was the land underneath that made the growing, global empire possible.

That's highly adaptive thinking in action. Kroc didn't just optimize for the known variables. He added a new dimension to the model—annexing nodes that sent the decision tree, and the possibilities that were suddenly open to him, branching in new and previously unforeseen directions. It changed the trajectory of the company forever.

Seeing the Frame, Missing the Picture

This is where the Law of Requisite Variety (LRV) can still trip you up.

Technically, LRV belongs to the previous phase—simulation—where your job was to generate a wide enough variety of options to absorb the complexity of the system. That's how you built a decision tree robust enough to avoid deep failure: by ensuring that the range of potential responses matched the complexity of the environment.

But even now, as you move from simulating to experimenting, LRV can sneak back in—especially if you let your hypothesis narrow too quickly or overlook critical interactions between nodes.

You may think you've defined the landscape clearly. But if your map lacks sufficient variety, or if you've prematurely filtered out what looked "unlikely," you're not testing a strong hypothesis—you're testing a fragile one. Because you're still not seeing the full terrain.

That's why it's essential to protect the left tail. You're out of the endless loop of exploration (for now), but if you missed something during the mapping phase—if your decision tree didn't account for enough variation—the cost of real-world feedback may be steeper than expected.

The key isn't to keep exploring, and expanding your map, forever. It's to be sure the variety you *do* carry forward is enough to make sense of the system you're navigating. When this balance is struck well, it doesn't just reduce risk—it reshapes what's even possible.

In the 1870s, photography was still a high-cost, high-friction process reserved for professionals and hobbyists with serious technical skills. Cameras were bulky. Lenses were finicky. And producing a single photo meant coating a glass plate with chemicals, exposing it quickly before it dried, and then slowly and painstakingly developing it by hand—often in a makeshift darkroom set up on the spot.

George Eastman was a twenty-four-year-old bank clerk in Rochester, New York, when he started teaching himself photography. Frustrated by the complexity of the process, he began experimenting with ways to simplify it. In 1880, he patented a revolutionary dry-plate formula—no more rushing to coat glass with caustic chemicals right before a photo. In 1888, he founded what would become the Eastman Kodak Company and introduced a portable box camera preloaded with a roll of film. His pitch: "You press the button, we do the rest."

But Eastman's true genius wasn't just technical—it was strategic.

Rather than trying to compete within the narrow frame of professional photography, Eastman built a whole new model. He didn't just improve the camera itself—he reimagined the entire system, from how people interacted with photography in the first place to the underlying technology to the way it could be deployed in the real world. He introduced easy-to-handle film rolls instead of cumbersome plates. He handled the film development at Kodak facilities. He sold cameras at low cost and created recurring revenue streams through proprietary film and processing.

This was the Law of Requisite Variety in action. Eastman saw that to reach a broader public—housewives, schoolteachers, children, travelers—you couldn't *just* create better products and bring them to market. You had to offer more paths into the experience. Kodak didn't just have one response to a changing landscape; it had many. And as photography grew more mainstream, the company's system of flexible responses kept it adaptive.

That variety is, at least in part, what made Kodak a juggernaut for nearly a century. But here's the irony: The same company that had once thrived on optionality and reframing eventually forgot how to do both.

In 1975, a Kodak engineer named Steve Sasson built the world's first digital camera. It was crude by today's standards—low-resolution black-and-white images saved to a cassette tape—but it worked. When Sasson presented the prototype to senior executives, they didn't laugh. They didn't doubt the technology. They just couldn't come up with a place for it.

Kodak's identity—and its entire profit model—was tied inextricably to film. Digital just plain didn't fit. It couldn't be monetized in the same way, and it challenged the very assumptions on which the company had been built. So instead of treating it as a new node in their response system, Kodak greeted it as a threat. They filed patents, and even launched digital products years later, but always with film in the frame. They never let the disruptive path truly challenge the dominant one.

Recall that the Law of Requisite Variety tells us that, in complex systems, you can't rely on a single strategy—not even one that's currently winning. If the environment shifts and your system doesn't offer enough adaptive responses, you become fragile. Vulnerable. Incapable of changing fast enough.

Kodak didn't die because it lacked innovation. It died because it lacked *response diversity*. A company built on optionality became captive to a single way of thinking. It wasn't that the company didn't see the future coming; it did—and it blinked.

There's a more radical step beyond simply adapting—and it's the one almost no one takes.

Kodak didn't just fail to diversify its responses; it failed to do the one thing that might have saved it: *cannibalize itself before someone else did.*

This is the uncomfortable truth of disruption. Sometimes the boldest, smartest, and most adaptive move is to destroy your own core business—before the market does it for you. Steve Jobs understood this: Apple killed the iPod with the iPhone. Netflix dismantled its DVD-by-mail empire to go all-in on streaming. Kodak could have done the same. It could have taken the digital camera seriously—not as an offshoot or a hedge, but as the very thing that would ultimately obliterate film. But instead of cannibalizing itself, it clung to the revenue model it knew, trying to preserve it for just a little longer.

The lesson isn't just about optionality—it's about courage. Optionality keeps you flexible. Cannibalization keeps you alive. If you don't have the nerve to pull apart your own system when the time comes, someone else will.

Adapt or Die

This is why mapping edge cases matters. You don't need to predict the exact shock that's coming; you just need to have left enough nodes on the table to adapt when it hits.

For instance, no one opening a restaurant in 2012 could've imagined Covid-19.

When we built Guildhall, we briefly considered takeout—and decided against it. My wife Jennifer and I were for it; our manager wasn't. "The food won't travel well," he argued. "It's meant to be eaten here." He had a point, and we listened. Carryout became a "someday" option, not a structural one.

Then the world shut down.

Suddenly, the "someday" became the only revenue stream we had. So we pivoted instantly—stood up a carryout system overnight, kept every single employee on payroll, and turned servers into drivers. But it's worth admitting: Had we already mapped that node, even lightly, we would've been faster, sturdier, more antifragile.

We didn't stop there. Working with a nearby coffee shop owner, we co-contracted a builder to create a row of small, private greenhouses outside the restaurant—transparent structures where people could dine safely, separated but still connected. What started as a desperate hack to survive a pandemic became something larger: The city let us keep that reclaimed outdoor footprint, which today remains an extension of Guildhall's space.

This is what adaptivity looks like in real time. The point is that you can't predict everything. But you *can* predict that something unexpected will happen—and you can design so you're able to react. That's the value of building out the edge cases. Not because you'll pursue them all, but because you'll be ready if the improbable someday becomes inevitable. Resilience isn't just about bouncing back. It's about having seen the turn before it arrived.

Which brings us to what comes next: With your decision tree branching out before you, every path connecting plausible nodes delineating a possible route to deep success, it's time to iterate.

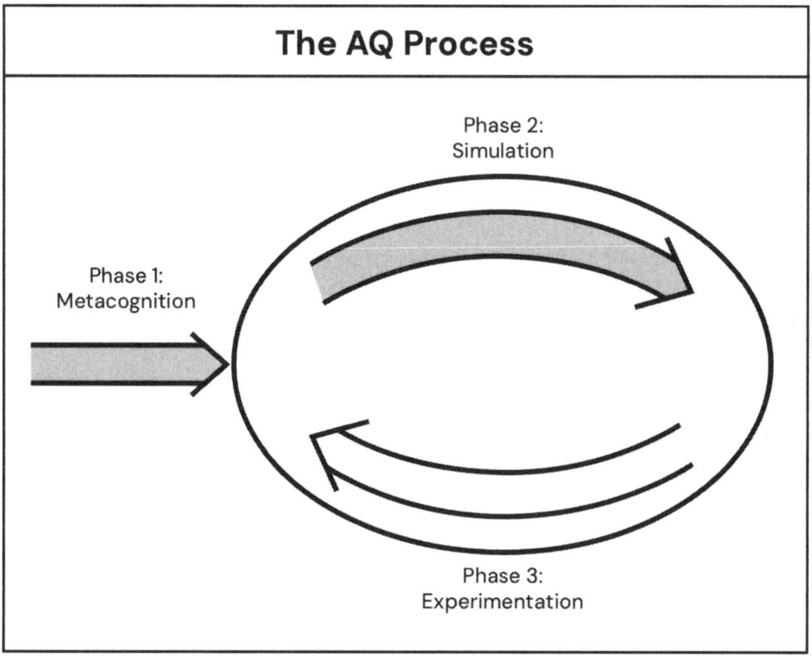

Adaptability Quotient Field Guide: Making Choice

- **Phase III turns hypotheses into knowledge.** This is the time to start running them through reality.
- **Design for Knightian uncertainty.** In such a world, there's no alternative but to build optionality, map edges, pivot fast, and convert uncertainty into probability through designed experimentation.
- **Pressure-testing isn't about proving you're right.** It's about figuring out where you're wrong.
- **Treat every shallow failure as a data point.** Each one narrows uncertainty.

- **Remember the Law of Requisite Knowledge.** Your mental map must match the terrain's complexity. You can't outthink what you don't sufficiently model.
- **Design loops that let you keep looping.** Protect your ability to test again.
- **Break big goals into nodes.** Small, testable experiments reveal what works. Adjust one dial (or a targeted few) at a time so the signal stays clear.
- **Map dependent variables.** Know which choices unlock or constrain others.
- **Build variety into your decision tree.** Edge cases protect against blind spots.
- **Resilience comes from optionality and courage.** Be willing to cannibalize what's working before the world does it for you.
- **Deep success is iterative.** You earn it one experiment at a time.

9

Launch, Learn, Repeat

A gem cannot be polished without friction,
nor a man perfected without trials.

—Lucius Annaeus Seneca

Experience is the only teacher we have. We may talk and reason all our lives, but we shall not understand a word of truth until we experience it ourselves.

— Swami Vivekananda

Every meaningful breakthrough has a body count—measured in prototypes, bad assumptions, things that looked promising until they caught fire.

That's not a bug of innovation. It's the cost of theory making contact with reality.

In 1752, Benjamin Franklin conducted one of the most famous scientific experiments in history. He didn't invent the lightning rod in a lab—he tested it with a kite, a metal key, and a thunderstorm. His insight was bold but unproven: that lightning was electrical in nature and that it could be drawn down and grounded safely. He didn't wait for perfect certainty. He built a crude but functional test, sent it soaring skyward, and watched as sparks jumped from the key to his knuckle.

It could've killed him. It didn't. But the result reshaped how we think about electricity—and helped set the stage for modern electrical engineering. Not because the experiment was elegant, but because it was fast, exposed to reality, and designed to teach.

This is the mindset that governs our shift into experimentation during Phase III: not recklessness, but proximity to real-world conditions. Plans, models, and simulations can only get you so far. At some point, you have to take what you've got, put it out into the world, and let experience teach you.

You've mapped the options (Phase II). You've tested your first hypotheses in the real world (early Phase III). Now comes the defining rhythm of this final stage: iteration. The cycle is simple but ruthless—launch, learn, repeat. Machines iterate automatically, but humans don't. Iteration, for us, is a decision—and choosing to keep looping, rather than freezing or overcommitting, is one of the clearest expressions of high AQ. This is the heart of Phase III, but it isn't just a phase. It's how you collapse uncertainty into understanding—not all at once, but through contact, pressure, and a hundred small corrections.

And sometimes, through failure that leaves a smoldering crater. Or a cloud of smoke and rocket parts, as the case may be.

Feedback Loops and Orbital Physics

On the morning of April 20, 2023, a gleaming stainless-steel behemoth called *Starship 1* stood on the launchpad at SpaceX's Boca Chica launch site in South Texas, shimmering in the Gulf heat. It was the most powerful rocket ever built—taller than the Statue of Liberty, designed to carry more mass than any spacecraft in history, intended one day to carry humans to Mars.

The countdown hit zero. The engines roared to life. *Starship 1* lifted off—slowly, thunderously clawing its way off Earth.

But just minutes later, things went sideways. Literally.

The rocket shuddered violently and started to tumble. Flames shot from its engines in odd directions. It began veering off course. Onboard guidance systems failed to respond. And then, with the world watching via livestream, the remote command was issued from the ground: *terminate.*

An instant later, *Starship 1* was blown out of the sky by its own flight-termination system. Smoldering debris rained into the ocean. Plumes of smoke filled the air.

The headlines, naturally, came in just as hot: *SpaceX Rocket Blows Up Mid-Air*; *Starship's Maiden Flight Ends in Failure.*

But the media, and most of the general public, missed the point entirely.

To most of the world, it looked like disaster. To SpaceX, it looked like progress.

This was not a mission designed to succeed in every respect, to accomplish every single objective. It was designed, if not explicitly to fail, per se, at least to *reveal.*

From the start, the goal of *Starship 1*'s flight was not to reach orbit—not necessarily. It was to get this audacious rocket design off the page and onto the launchpad, out of the simulation phase and into the real world. To gather live telemetry, push carefully engineered hardware into actual atmospheric conditions, see how such a radically new design would respond to pressures even the most sophisticated computer model could not yet fully capture.

The entire system, in essence, was *expected* to break. The key was to learn exactly how, where, when, why.

And they did. Even as the rocket was still disintegrating at high altitude, SpaceX's engineering teams began poring over the data, gaining invaluable insights about thrust vector control under the stresses of a real-world launch. They learned what didn't scale, what failed early, what was more durable or flexible or lasted longer than expected. This wasn't a simulation or a static failure—it was real and actionable, a streaming download of truth.

What might have looked to the unsophisticated observer like total catastrophe was, in point of fact, the first step in a program of structured iteration. It was a shallow failure, albeit an especially dramatic one and at massive scale, but one that was nonetheless built into the process—a process designed to generate feedback, irrespective of what might appear in headlines that lacked vital context.

To mistake that launch for some kind of embarrassment is to miss the difference between deep failure, which of course ends the game, and the kind of shallow failures that teach you how to play the game better next time. What gets lost in most public commentary is this: *Starship 1* wasn't testing a singular bet. It was navigating a probabilistic map—a lit path through a decision tree, delineated by hundreds of embedded nodes, each one a branching decision point. Each node represented a question with real stakes: Would the engines ignite cleanly? Would the fuel lines hold pressure? Would the flight computer handle stage separation in microseconds of chaos? Some were answered with yes, others no, but every answer narrowed uncertainty. And most yielded signal, which is invaluable. In this context, the fact that some nodes failed doesn't reflect a flaw in the process. It *is* the process. In fact, the odds of getting everything right on the first attempt are, in any sufficiently complex system, vanishingly small—closer to fantasy than science. You don't set a course for Mars on your very first attempt to get off the launchpad.

Experienced rock climbers have a term for this: *flash ascent*, which means completing a climb successfully on your very first try, possibly having studied someone else's approach. It's rare. Vanishingly rare. In complex terrain, most people do what's called a *redpoint*: Using ropes to ensure safety, they learn the route by trial and error. They fall, recover, adjust, memorize key grips and footholds. Then, on a subsequent attempt, they complete the climb clean. That's the actual process: not perfection, but *progressive mastery*. Iterative improvement up a jagged wall.

SpaceX doesn't expect to reach orbit every time. It expects to *learn* every time. And in doing so, it accumulates knowledge that would be impossible to glean in a lab. Each launch is a bet against entropy—a leap across a branching logic tree of unknowns. Most of the branches will lead nowhere. But a few will illuminate a viable path forward.

Evaluating through the lens of AQ, this example illustrates how complex decision-making works. Not by guessing right once, but by testing rigorously and updating continuously. Not by praying for perfection, but by pushing forward into uncertainty, collecting feedback, and refining the route.

This is also why failure isn't disqualifying but informative. Each breakdown is a breadcrumb. And if you're paying attention, it leads somewhere next time.

It's like watching your kid fall off a bike on their first attempt and asking if the ride was a mistake. Of course it wasn't; falling is a key part of the process. Wobbling, veering, bracing, overcorrecting—that's *how the body learns* to balance. You don't teach a child to ride by reading a book, nor by waiting until they've mastered "cycling theory" from a textbook. You let them fall. But not catastrophically. Not without training wheels, grass, and a helmet. You let them *fail small* so they can *succeed big*.

Mark Zuckerberg famously told startups to "move fast and break things." But we need to modify his edict, because speed alone isn't the lesson. The real principle is more precise: not fail fast, but *shallow fail* fast. You want to shorten your feedback loops, accelerate your learning, reduce the distance between decision nodes on your tree. The faster you cycle through those microdecisions—test, learn, adjust—the sooner you converge on the deeper insight. That's how you shallow fail your way to deep success.

It's no coincidence that this embodies the first principle of Bayesian updating: Make a play, observe the result, adjust your theory. Which is where our decision-making process now moves: into motion.

Launch. Learn. Repeat.

Failure That Fuels Learning

This is the same principle that powers how modern AI learns: iteration as acceleration.

Whether it's a large language model crafting sentences, a recommendation engine suggesting what your family should watch next, or an autonomous vehicle deciding how to navigate a complex intersection, the process is fundamentally the same. These systems improve not by getting it right once, but by *shallow failing fast* in controlled loops, again and again (and again). Every input they receive—every user correction, every missed prediction, every pixel of feedback—helps them sharpen their internal models. Over time, the signal rises. Each cycle of data refines the system's understanding of what's likely to work next.

You can see this most clearly in how companies like Waymo or Tesla train their self-driving fleets. A human driver might learn a lesson once—don't take this particular curve too fast or avoid a certain type of pedestrian behavior—but, in the context of human learning, that insight ordinarily stays locked inside a single, solitary brain. By contrast, when one autonomous vehicle encounters a new edge case—an unexpected stop sign placement, a double-parked truck, a child chasing a ball into the street—that experience is logged, labeled, and analyzed alongside many others like it (ideally from other vehicles operating in a variety of circumstances), and then packaged as an update that gets pushed to the entire system. Every other vehicle in the fleet learns from it almost instantaneously. Which means the learning doesn't just add up. It compounds.[i]

Such an outcome might seem, on its face, to be counterintuitive, but the fastest learners are often the ones that fail the *most*—so long as those failures are structured to yield data, facilitate learning, and avoid deep failure.

SpaceX has made this explicit in its approach. Elon Musk has said flatly that Starship is designed to fail—repeatedly—because every mission, every flight, provides crucial telemetry. From its maiden test flight onward, SpaceX has collected vast amounts of data: on engine performance, aerodynamic load, structural vibration, guidance responses. Each and every piece of feedback reduces uncertainty about how the system behaves in real-world conditions—and shortens the path to both deep success and deep space.

---

i Companies and other organizations can achieve this kind of distributed learning with the right culture (as we'll discuss in chapter 11).

This kind of feedback loop is only valuable, though, if you're honest about what it's telling you.

This is where many people and organizations stall out or fall short. It's not failure that slows them down—not as such; it's their own refusal to see it clearly. We've all felt the temptation to soften the impact of something that didn't go as planned with post hoc justifications: "It was an outside case." "That wasn't our real audience." "The market wasn't quite ready."

Instead of confronting the most uncomfortable evidence, too many of us polish the story to protect the hypothesis. But Bayesian updating only works if you wipe the smudge off your lens, open yourself to real learning, do what it takes to ensure that *any and all* feedback is raw and unvarnished.

Be Less Wrong Next Time

Serial entrepreneur Tristan Walker understood this well when he launched Bevel, a shaving system built specifically for Black men with coarse or curly hair—customers the mainstream grooming industry had largely ignored. Walker didn't just build the product and wait for validation. He structured his entire launch strategy around extracting brutally honest feedback from his target audience.

Early testers didn't hold back. Some hated the packaging. Others flagged skin irritation as a fundamental problem. A few didn't like the price point. But instead of explaining away their feedback—by suggesting, perhaps, that the testers weren't used to premium products or that Bevel would fix the problem in the second version of the product—Walker leaned in. He treated each critique as a data point, a dial that could be adjusted ahead of the *next* experiment. He revised, adjusted, and restructured—until his prior, the product, and the brand accurately reflected what he intended and actually served the people it claimed to.

What made that feedback loop effective wasn't volume; he didn't need a sample size of millions. It was clarity. Walker refused to let his own narrative get in the way of the information he was seeking. That's often the hardest part—especially when you're emotionally or financially invested (which you ought to be). But that also happens to be where the learning happens. Not in proving your hypothesis right, but in shedding the parts of your model that no longer match reality.

Confirmation bias is the worst enemy of iteration. And in a Bayesian system, it's fatal. If you only accept the data that supports your hypothesis, you're not updating—you're entrenching, digging in your heels. The people who learn fastest are the ones who are most willing to be wrong.

That's what makes the difference: not who has the boldest vision or the furthest or deepest definition of deep success, but who has the discipline to let reality reshape how they get from here to there. It comes down to cultivating the courage to say, "This didn't work—and here's what that tells us." The humility to trade conviction for information, one update at a time.

That's why SpaceX regards each Starship flight as a singular real-world opportunity to iterate, improve, and test a whole range of hypotheses under pressure. *The rocket flies. Something fails. So we isolate the variable, update the model, and start building the next version.* That's Bayesian decision-making at its purest: small cycles of failure in service of deep, compounding success.

The same reasoning, and the same process, applies to business, strategy, leadership—any domain where decisions are made in uncertainty. You don't wait for perfect clarity. You launch, observe, adjust. You don't explain away the miss—you obsess over it, learn from it.

Because progress doesn't come from being right on the first try; it's about being less wrong with every subsequent iteration. That's why the best decision-makers don't attach their identity to *being right*. They attach it to *getting it right*. They build their pride not around having the correct answer up front but around refining a process that outperforms ego over time.

In other words: They have reverence for the method, not their opinions. When you're fixated on *being right*, your identity gets fused with your prior. You start defending your last answer instead of updating toward a better one. But when your commitment is to the process—to the methodology itself—you're no longer protecting a position; you're improving a function.

Everyone I've worked with closely has heard me say some version of this: I don't have an ego for *my* answer. I have an ego for the process that leads to the right answer more often than not. That distinction changes everything. From a static belief to a dynamic method. From the seductive illusion of certainty to the quiet discipline of refinement.

And this process, like any good process, is provisional. It is not scripture. It is not finished. I can't say the version I've used won't be improved—or even replaced—by something better. I hope it will. The goal isn't to preserve the method. It's to evolve it.

What we need is a kind of epistemic humility married to methodological pride. Not blind faith in any single result, but a durable faith in our ability to test, adjust, and get closer to truth. Not a cult of certainty, but a disciplined devotion to discovery.

You can have a religion, if you must—but let it be for the methodology. Not the ego of your answer. Not the false god of being right.

Risk vs. Reward—Redux

This brings us back to one of the fundamental truths we started with—an insight, which at this point seems obvious, that most people miss about the Starship program and about adaptable decision-making more broadly.

To the casual observer, every launch looks like a moonshot. A single make-or-break event. But that's not how SpaceX plays the game. Each flight is just a node. A test. A branch on a sprawling decision tree designed not for perfection—but for signal.

Whether you're launching a rocket or opening a restaurant, it's never one giant bet—but a cascade of microdecisions, each one deliberate and embedded in a system designed to learn at speed.

After all, this isn't poker.

Poker is convergent. The probabilities are known. You can calculate odds, define expected value, bluff strategically. And sure, you can make a single bet and still get knocked out—but the rules are fixed, and the downside is usually limited to whatever is in the pot when you play the hand in question.

Real-world decision-making isn't like that. In real-world decision-making—especially in high-stakes, high-uncertainty environments—the game is different. You're dealing with *divergent* systems: not just unknown hands of cards, but unknown rules. In poker, the number and suits of the cards in the deck are fixed, the rules are codified, and probabilities—though hidden—are at least estimable. You might not know what card your opponent holds, but you do know what cards are in the deck. There can't be five aces; if you're holding one, you know *they're* not holding four.

But real-world systems aren't bounded this way. There are no rules guaranteeing "only four aces." Sometimes the whole deck changes mid-hand; sometimes the game turns out to be chess, *not* poker—and you don't find out until you've already moved your queen. This is what chaos feels like in practice: feedback delayed, causality scrambled, models breaking faster than you can rebuild them. You're operating in motion, under partial information, trying to update faster than reality changes.

This is Knightian uncertainty. In this space, we can't just assign odds to every branch on the tree. In this regime, *learning* isn't a static download, it's an active process of assimilation. We have to keep updating our internal models just to stay in sync with a shifting external reality. The map must change as fast as the terrain.

In a convergent game like poker, you optimize based on the odds. In a divergent system like reality, you design for resilience. You embrace shallow failures not just to learn faster—but to keep probing the edges of what your map doesn't yet include. What kills you in these systems isn't the thing you saw coming. It's the Type II error—the thing you didn't even know to look for. And when your internal state can't update fast enough, you loop back into Phase II of the AQ framework. You must reframe and simulate the problem (Phase II), rebuild your model, then reengage with experimentation (Phase III). That recursive loop is what converts volatility into intelligence. It's how adaptation compounds.

And all of this changes how you have to think about risk and reward.

Most organizations define *risk* as anything that deviates from the plan. Surprises become errors. Failures get penalized. And the result? A culture of fear. Of caution. Of fragility. They don't just fear deep failure—they avoid shallow failure too. Which means they avoid the very experiments that would help them learn. In an age of Knightian uncertainty that avoidance isn't prudence, it's suicide by stasis.

SpaceX flips that model on its head. They've built a culture where shallow failures are not only tolerated—they're engineered. Not recklessly. Not indiscriminately. But strategically. Because, in a complex system, shallow failure is one of the fastest paths to signal. To insight. To meaningful forward momentum.

This reframed risk/reward calculus ties directly back to the dilemma we explored earlier, during Phase II: the moment when you're deep in the simulation stage and wondering, *When do I stop* exploring *and start* exploiting*?*

Here's one way in which evaluating risk versus reward can help supply you with an answer: You stop exploring when the simulation stops being useful—but before you reach the point where learning stops altogether.

Risk/reward is what helps you learn how and where to draw that line. Once you've mapped your decision tree with enough fidelity to eliminate catastrophic paths—to guard against deep failure—you're no longer in danger of spooling endlessly in search of a mythical perfect plan. You haven't locked in your final choice. You've just given yourself a strong-enough hypothesis to test. *That's* the shift. Imagine a startup founder running smoke tests before spending on scale; a pilot drilling difficult maneuvers with an instructor until marginal gains flatten; a scientist halting experiments once the data stops changing the hypothesis. They know when to stop simulating and start acting. The aim isn't perfection. It's forward momentum with guardrails.

The beauty of this is that, if you do it right, it still gives you a second bite at the apple. Experimentation doesn't eliminate the possibility of finding a better path—it just moves the search from theory into reality. You've reached a local maxima in your model. But you'll only discover the global one by making moves in the actual terrain.

Or as the poet Paul Valéry once put it: "Everything simple is false. Everything which is complex is unusable." Adaptive decision-making lives somewhere in the middle.

You want just enough structure to protect against the fatal downside, the fat left tail—while leaving enough slack to keep evolving as new information rolls in. You explore broadly to eliminate the risks that would take you out of the game. But you don't have to solve for every detail right up front. Some of the sharpest insights will come from navigating, in fits and starts, across the map itself—one node, one iteration, one shallow failure at a time.

Amazon learned this lesson the hard way. In 2014, they launched the Fire Phone—a bold attempt to compete in the smartphone market. It had groundbreaking (for the time) 3D visuals, dynamic perspective, and deep integration with Amazon's growing suite of services. Jeff Bezos was personally involved. The vision was big and bold; on paper, it looked like a slam dunk.

But theory collided with reality . . . and the product bombed. Hard. Reviewers were unimpressed. Even worse, customers were uninterested. Within a year, the Fire Phone was dead—costing Amazon nearly $170 million. From the outside, it looked like a classic, and particularly public and embarrassing, face-plant.

But inside Amazon, the local (shallow as opposed to deep) failure was treated differently. Because embedded in that belly flop were the seeds of something else: voice interface experiments. User behavior data. Hard-earned lessons in hardware development. As a result, after bringing all of these pieces (and more) together in a different configuration and context, Amazon launched the Echo just over a year later.

The Echo wasn't just a speaker. It was an early AI assistant for the home—powered by Alexa—and it redefined the smart-home category, becoming one of the most successful hardware platforms Amazon has ever built. None of which would have been possible without the Fire Phone.

As Bezos later put it: "Failure and invention are inseparable twins."

In fact, this reflects the deeper logic of pivoting, in business as in life: You don't pivot because you succeeded. You pivot because something failed—but not fatally. Shallow failure is what keeps the learning alive. And sometimes, it gives you a glimpse of a new direction.

This is how AQ shows up in practice. When the original bet doesn't work, but you've cultivated the flexibility—and the fragments—to reassemble something better. The Fire Phone wasn't a win. But it wasn't wasted either. It became input, fodder for the next experiment.

Jack Dorsey's story illustrates a similar insight from a meaningfully different angle. Before Twitter, before Square, he was obsessed with urban mapping. In his early twenties, he was building dispatch software in St. Louis, tracking couriers and ambulances in real time. The project never scaled. Investors weren't interested; no one cared about live vehicle status in 2001.

But Dorsey kept thinking about it. And eventually, he reframed the question: What if this kind of signal—what if the usefulness of small, real-time text updates—wasn't just something that would be valuable for taxis? What if people could broadcast their thoughts, share their status with friends, post concise ideas and opinions and breaking news for others in their network to see? That question gave rise to Twitter. A different domain, a different use case—but born of the same mental model.

This is what it means to define reward correctly: *Don't cling to the failure; extract the actionable insight.* It's not about whether any individual experiment succeeds on its own terms. The better questions are these: Did this experiment yield information we can use to refine the model? Did it help us shorten the path to deep success?

In that sense, Starship isn't just a rocket—it's a decision framework in flight.

But, of course, not all risk lives in individual nodes that can be isolated and tested. Sometimes deep failure doesn't come from a single bad choice—but from the interaction between two seemingly innocuous ones. A restaurant's food might be solid. The decor might be just fine. But combine the wrong dish with the wrong ambiance, or serve a dissonant selection of appetizers and main courses, and you could wind up with a business that nobody wants to revisit.

That's why you have to telescope up. Occasionally climb above the node-level view and look at the system as a whole. Some patterns only emerge when seen from elevation—and when you pause long enough to notice correlations that weren't visible before.

But iteration itself isn't just about moving fast; it's about *learning fast.* Which only works if you build systems that invite real feedback—and leaders who don't flinch when it arrives.

Checklist: Is This a Testable Node?

Before you launch the next feature, pitch, policy, or prototype, run it through this filter. And remember: The best decisions aren't always the boldest. They're the ones that maximize learning while minimizing irreversible risk.

1. Does this test isolate a specific set of variables?
   → *A good node isn't the whole system. It's a focused, testable set of choices.*
2. Will the result help me update my belief or model?
   → *If the answer is no, or if the outcome won't change what you do next, it's probably not worth testing yet.*
3. Does this expose me to deep failure?
   → *If the downside could kill the project, destroy trust, or eliminate long-term success, stop. Redesign your test or break it into smaller parts.*
4. Can I define success in terms of information gained, not outcome achieved?
   → *Don't ask, "Did it work?" Ask, "Did it teach me something useful?"*
5. Am I ready to believe what the feedback tells me?
   → *If you're tempted to explain away the result, you should delay the test or prepare yourself to see more clearly.*

6. Do I know what I'll do next, depending on the outcome?
   → *Every good test has a next move. Don't collect data unless you're ready to act on it.*

If you answer yes to most of these, you're not guessing. You're iterating.

And if you're iterating honestly, with unvarnished feedback—you're not merely off and running, you're learning faster (and better) than most.

How It All Comes Together . . .

Of course, it's one thing to get your arms around AQ in theory. It's another thing entirely to put it into practice—especially when the pressure is on, the variables are messy, and other people are watching.

That's the real test.

Because business, like life, isn't just about the big leaps. It's about the cascade of choices that come before them. Decisions that might seem small in the moment—how to frame your problem, what assumptions to challenge, whether to treat an anomaly as noise or signal—end up shaping the entire trajectory.

At this point, we've walked through the full arc of what it takes to cultivate high AQ and make smart decisions in a complex world—from uncertainty, to clarity, to action. So this is a good place to pause and (briefly) recap.

Phase I is metacognition. It begins (and ends) with you: how you think, what you believe, where your mental models come from, what biases and distortions are baked right in. In this phase, you learned to examine your own operating system—to recognize when you're reacting from bias, reflexive System 1 shortcuts, faulty "mindware" you didn't even know you'd inherited. You saw how self-awareness and curiosity are not luxuries but tools; how grit isn't just about resilience but what enables you to hold steady when your instincts beg you to grab for false certainty. And most of all, you learned to pause. To reset. To approach the world with a blank canvas and a true beginner's mind.

Phase II is all about your mindset. This is the simulation phase—where you build the scaffolding that creates choice. You take in data—free of bias and context at first—but more than that, you begin to map it. You start forming nodes, noticing relationships, discerning design features. At first you resist the urge to rush to judgment, instead building a broader decision space—a branching tree of possibilities. After all, you're not committing yet; you're exploring. Simulating. Testing how different inputs behave. Watching vigilantly for confirmation bias at every step. You've learned to embrace maximum entropy, not fear it. And you've seen why Type II errors—ruling out what's real—can be more dangerous than chasing (Type I) ghosts. Most people stop ideating and exploring too early; by the end of this phase, if you've done everything right, you don't just understand how to sit in discomfort and uncertainty—you might even enjoy it.

Phase III is the decision-making framework itself. This is the experimentation phase: where all your abstract thinking gets put under pressure. Where *opinion* meets *action*. Whether you're launching a rocket, opening a restaurant, or making a bet that could change your business or your life, this phase teaches you to operationalize risk in real time—and define reward not as perfection, but as useful information gained. Thus armed, you begin to test your hypothesis—not for whether it's perfect, but for where it's wrong. You break it down into smaller decisions. You experiment. You build feedback loops that are fast and painfully honest. You fail on purpose, shallowly and often, to move closer to deep success—and then after every experiment you go back to the beginning, update your prior, and do it all again.

That's the arc, the map, the AQ "formula" in a nutshell: a teachable system for thinking clearly when it counts, updating fast when the ground shifts, and *learning forward*—not just for yourself, but for your team, your product, your company, your mission. It applies whatever your destination and no matter how you define deep success.

But, of course, knowing the theory isn't the hard part. Operationalizing it is. Because the real world doesn't come color-coded. High-stakes decisions don't come along cleanly or announce which phase you're in. Even in a well-oiled organization, the people around you surely won't always share your mindset—let alone your tolerance for uncertainty. And the costs of getting it wrong can be reputational, organizational, even existential.

How do you take this playbook and bring it to life in your own world—when time is short, the stakes are high, and your instincts are dying to pull you like a siren's song into the shoals of false certainty? How do you build a culture that learns as fast as it moves? And how do you lead others through uncertainty without defaulting to fear, rigidity, or (perhaps worst of all) analysis paralysis?

The following chapters are about putting all of this into practice: how to apply your AQ not just in your own decision-making, but in the systems, teams, and cultures you build around you. Because no matter how sharp your thinking might be in isolation, what matters most is how well you can steer the ship while everything and everyone else is in motion.

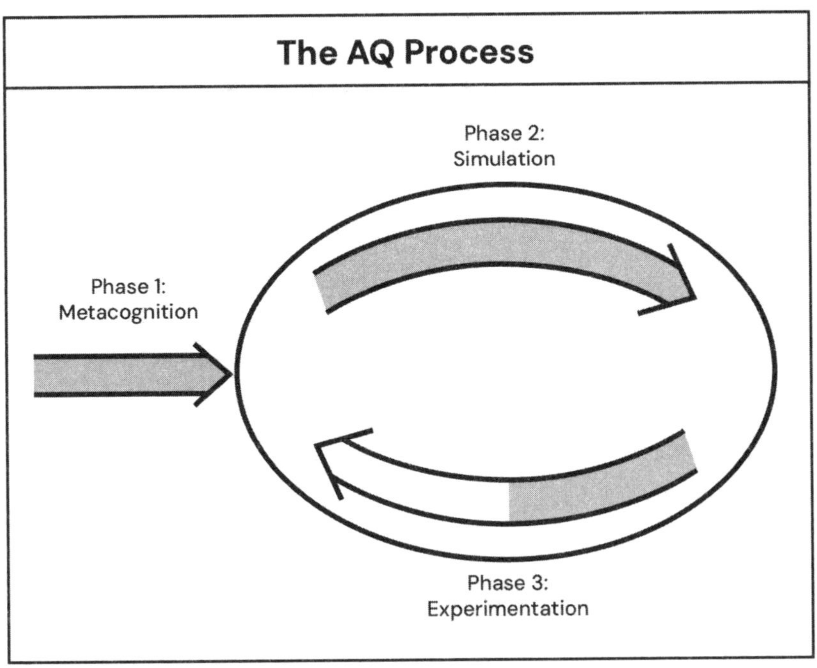

Adaptability Quotient Field Guide: Key Takeaways

- **Phase III is an iteration engine.** It's built on a launch, learn, repeat cycle.
- **Turn your prior into focused, real-world tests.** Proximity (and friction against) reality beats theory.
- **Optimize for shallow failure and engineer out deep failure.** Define shallow success as information gained; reward = sharper understanding, not ego.
- **Shorten your feedback loops.** Learning speed > initial accuracy.
- **Protect the loop.** Design tests that let you keep testing (runway, resilience, triggers).
- **Kill confirmation bias.** Insist on unvarnished feedback and update ruthlessly.
- **Telescope up periodically.** Check interactions across nodes, not just local wins.
- **Be willing to cannibalize what works before the world does.** Take pride in the process, not in being "right."

10

Back into the Loop

The major problems in the world are the result of the difference between how nature works and the way people think.

—Gregory Bateson

It's a challenge to stay creative enough to drop the boundaries that worked for the last problem and to find the most appropriate set of boundaries for the next question. It's also a necessity, if problems are to be solved well.

—Donella Meadows

Let's say you've made the leap. You've done the hard work of metacognition—stripped away your inherited mental models, questioned your biases and assumptions, debugged your own operating system. You've embraced the discomfort of uncertainty, mapped your decision space, opened tabs you didn't even know were available. And then you did the most dangerous thing of all: You acted. You ran the experiment, got the rocket off the pad, launched the product, made the call.

Now what?

I'm afraid I've got a late-breaking plot twist for you: Phase III, the act of experimentation, is not (as previous chapters might've led you to believe) the end of the process. It's a threshold. Because the moment you move from theory to contact, the world begins talking back. The question is whether you're listening.

This is where most frameworks stop—and where the AQ discipline begins again. Because adaptive thinking doesn't end in action. It ends in assimilation.

The question, in other words, becomes this: What do you do with what you just learned?

The truth is that, even when you've made a good decision, the terrain keeps shifting. New information arrives. Market dynamics change. The person you were six months ago is already outdated. And if you're not careful, your strategy will be too.

So it's not sufficient to merely ask yourself, *What did I learn?* Adaptive thinking means probing deeper, asking, *What needs to change as a result? Do I double down? Do I refine the model? Do I reenter the decision tree from a different angle entirely?* This is the loop in miniature; either you fold the new information into your framework or you let it break the frame so you can rebuild. Both are progress. What matters is that you don't freeze.

None of these questions are hypothetical—but (fortunately) the solution is relatively straightforward. The answers lie in what cognitive scientists call *assimilation* and *accommodation*, two complementary processes that together form an engine of adaptive intelligence.

Assimilation is when you integrate new information into your existing mental model, updating your understanding of the world without changing its structure. You're absorbing novelty while preserving coherence. Accommodation, by contrast, is when the new information doesn't fit—and forces you to alter the model itself. It's the cognitive equivalent of a software patch; it's restructuring your priors so reality and perception realign.[i]

---

i These concepts, which we apply to organizational and self-correction, are borrowed and adapted from the developmental psychology of Jean Piaget.

Both are essential, and the real skill lies in knowing which mode you're in. Not every anomaly demands a total rewrite; not every pattern can be safely folded into the old framework. Too much assimilation breeds rigidity; too much accommodation breeds chaos. Adaptive intelligence means staying aware of that tension, constantly asking whether to fit the world into your model, or your model into the world. Mistaking one for the other is how organizations harden around outdated beliefs—or thrash themselves into incoherence.

This chapter is about what happens after you act. It's about the loop back—how and when to reenter Phase II when the feedback warrants it, and how to recognize whether it's time to reframe the problem itself. Think of it as Phase III dissolving back into Phase II: Action generates signal, and then signal demands interpretation. That's the recursive heartbeat of the AQ process—and your practice of building AQ.

Before we go further, I have a confession to make about an assumption we made early in this book. We treated the present era as if it were purely uncertain—an entirely novel state in which old maps are suspect and all priors are on probation—because advances in data, computing, and various other sciences have genuinely altered the game.

In a sense, this was a purposeful overcorrection. In reality, the world you and I move through is more of a blend: There are parts you can treat as risk and parts you must treat as Knightian uncertainty, with the occasional true "black swan" domain lurking somewhere beyond the edges.

The distinction matters. Recall that risk is when the possibilities are known and the probabilities can be estimated. Bayesian logic shines here; experiments refine the odds and your model tightens. Knightian uncertainty, as we've learned, is different: The possibilities are known but the probabilities are not; you can map the space, but you don't yet know the weights.

And then of course there are black swans—where both possibilities *and* probabilities are unknown. These are the domains you cannot sensibly model in advance, only build resilience or antifragility to survive when they arrive. Most real problems are a mix. The work, therefore, is not to pretend everything is risk—or everything is unknown—but to recognize which is which, and route your next loop accordingly.

This is where we take our field guide on the go, staying adaptive in motion—and integrating the lessons of experience into a living, learning framework.

Provisional Knowledge, Perpetual Motion

Even after you've made the call, tested your hypothesis, and captured those lessons from the real world . . . you're still not done.

Because however successful your experiment appears, the knowledge it produces remains provisional. That is useful, actionable, and can improve your forecasting—but only for now. And only until such time as new (i.e., fresher and more up-to-the-moment) data shows up. Every conclusion, no matter how solid it feels, carries an expiration date. Think of this provisional knowledge like produce—it spoils quickly if you don't keep checking the freshness.

In reality, you're never just moving forward. You're always in a loop. Every experiment you run in Phase III produces new information. And that information needs a place to go. It doesn't just sit inert on a dashboard; it has to move—up, into your framework, back into your belief structure, back into Phase II. You need to go back and update your hypothesis (or SOWH) based on what you've learned.

But there is a gatekeeper at that doorway back into Phase II: the state of the world in which you've been running your experiments. Provisional knowledge is only provisionally portable. Imagine a door between Phase III and the next round of Phase II; when the external state remains broadly continuous, the door is open and your conclusions can pass through, largely intact, to update the model. When the state shifts—new constraints, new technology, new incentives—a mesh screen drops across the opening. Now only the raw observations fit back through; the conclusions that once traveled as "knowledge" are too bulky to pass. They must be reduced to mere data points and reinterpreted inside the new state. In fast-changing environments, you have to check that door on every loop.

So what does it look like when that door starts to close—when the state is shifting beneath your feet?

Rarely does such a shift announce itself with a single dramatic headline. More often, it shows up as patterned weirdness: not *one* surprise, but a string of them, all leaning in a similar direction.

Another tell is when the *rate of change* changes—when you're no longer watching a line move, but watching the line bend, the kind of acceleration or deceleration that can't be explained by normal noise. In markets, that might be volatility clustering. In product adoption, it's the curve suddenly steepening—or flattening—without a clear internal reason. In organizations, it's a feedback loop that strengthens or weakens overnight.

Then there are relational breaks—correlations that invert, variables that used to move together suddenly divorcing, trusted leading indicators going dead, old causal stories losing predictive power. And finally, the most obvious signal: new variables entering the system—new technology, new incentives, new rules, new competitors—and creating degrees of freedom your model never had to account for before.

Any one of these can be a fluke. But when you see them cluster, it's a warning shot; you're no longer iterating inside a stable regime. You're drifting into a new state. That's your cue to pause, demote "knowledge" back into data, and reenter Phase II.[ii]

This is the function of assimilation and accommodation. Both are part of how we learn. Both are core to how we adapt. And, critically, they happen at two key moments in your practice of the AQ process:

- First, at the beginning of Phase II, comes the mental reset or beginner's mind—in other words, accommodation—when you begin mapping new data into your decision space.
- And again, at the end of Phase III, after experimentation has produced a fresh stream of information that must be absorbed, interpreted, and—if necessary—used to reshape your approach.

---

ii Some readers may understand this concept as a Markov state.

> This is where feedback helps determine whether it's time to loop back and assimilate new data or accommodate by resetting the model.

This is what makes the framework recursive. You don't just run through Phases I, II, and III like a ladder and then stop. You loop back. You update. You reenter at the beginning of Phase II. And this loop isn't just for certain types of outcomes, unexpected results, or edge cases. It's the core of the system.

This can be abstracted into saying that, on top of Phases II and III, there is a second hierarchy of state versus variables to keep straight. Phase II's tools—reduction, induction, abduction—help you identify the decision variables and nodes of your hypothesis. Phase III's deduction and experiments test those nodes against reality and feed results back.

The key is remembering that variables operate within a state, but the state itself can change. A variable might shift incrementally, but a state change resets the context entirely: new rules, new feedback loops, new constraints. When you enter a new state, all previous conclusions revert to being provisional—as we've covered, you're back to beginner's mind. In that mode, what you have isn't knowledge yet, only data and information waiting to be reinterpreted. The system hasn't stabilized; your models haven't caught up. The danger is assuming continuity when the landscape has already changed.

Adaptive thinkers learn to recognize when a variable tweak won't suffice—when the state itself has flipped—and to reengage accordingly. If the present state is continuous with the past, some legacy mappings can accelerate learning without distorting it. On the other hand, if the state is novel, those same outdated mappings are liabilities. In that case, you begin from maximum entropy, let abduction sketch an initial explanation for the unfamiliar facts, then upgrade only what the new state validates. On each loop, you reassess the state first, and then you reassess the variables. Get that order wrong and even flawless local optimization steers you off a cliff.

When you embed this idea and practice of looping deeply enough—whether in your own thinking or across an entire organization—it becomes second nature. Everyone still brings their own ideas, but all of them get fed into the same engine: a shared process of probing, testing, and feeding results back through the beginning. That shared commitment to the engine matters more than any one belief. And, like any good engine, it's built to be fixed and modified and upgraded according to your needs and the terrain around you; the loop itself can and should evolve as you learn.

This field guide is designed for a world where the current is fast and the shoreline keeps moving—a high-velocity, high-change environment where the cost of delay compounds quickly. In a slower, more static world, the cadence might be different. But here, now, the habit of looping is what keeps your knowledge provisional, your expertise alive, and your decisions in sync with reality.

Law of Requisite Knowledge, Redux

So let's get practical. How do you know when it's time to assimilate? Or accommodate? Or loop all the way back to Phase II?

For one rule of thumb, recall the Law of Requisite Knowledge: To make effective decisions in a complex, uncertain environment, you need a knowledge base that's rich enough to match the complexity of the system you're navigating. That means converting data and information—raw inputs—into knowledge that is contextualized and tested, with decision-relevant understanding.

And how do you do that? Through experimentation: Run it through the feedback loop. Every time you act on a hypothesis and observe the result, you're generating that requisite knowledge. It's not theoretical anymore. It's lived. It's tested. And it helps you calibrate the next iteration with more precision.

But again: It's provisional. In a dynamic system, you don't get to rest on the last lesson; you have to keep checking. Is this still true? Is this still useful? Do I need to reframe my assumptions before the gap between model and reality grows too wide to bridge?

Which brings us to two natural—and, ultimately, defining—questions: How frequently should I test? And how frequently, and under what circumstances, should I loop back into Phase II and reassess?

The Law of Requisite Knowledge answers both questions. It has two parts.

First, you need enough knowledge from exploitation—from running real experiments—to resolve the uncertainty you're facing. If you haven't tested, you don't know. Opinion doesn't count.

Second, you need the judgment to know when exploitation has stopped working—when refinement is no longer reducing uncertainty and it's time to abandon the current model and reenter Phase II. This is not a technical skill; it's a form of wisdom. Miss it, and no amount of iteration will save you.

Adaptive decision-making fails when either of these is missing.

There's one more failure mode worth calling out explicitly: staying in a loop that has stopped producing learning. If you've run multiple iterations and uncertainty isn't reducing—if your hypotheses aren't sharpening and each new result leaves you roughly where you started—then the loop isn't doing its job. At that point, the signal isn't "iterate harder," but "this model has exhausted its ability to teach you." Knowing when learning has stalled, and having the discipline to walk away from a loop that no longer resolves uncertainty, is a core adaptive skill.

Think of it like how elite poker players approach a new table. The rules are fixed (the risk), but a new opponent introduces a Knightian wedge of the possibilities (bluffs, possible tells, etc.). These possibilities are known in terms of general form, but the probabilities are not yet learnable facts. So professionals default to what's known as GTO (or Game Theory Optimal) play: a style designed to survive the unknown while gathering feedback. Early hands are not about maximizing profit; they're about migrating uncertainty back into risk.

How? By observing patterns until exploitative play becomes justified. And just as good players know when to press an edge, they also know when a table has stopped yielding information—and fold accordingly.

AQ asks essentially the same of you: Survive to thrive.[iii] In an unfamiliar state, open with max-entropy exploration and resilient baselines that prevent catastrophic Type II errors; as probabilities clarify, you can compress the model accordingly and lean in.

This is also why it generally pays to start with the assumption that the world is more novel than perhaps it will turn out to be. Treating Phase II as genuinely wide open—forcing priors to reearn their place—may cost time and money in the short run, but it avoids the deeper mistake of playing a risk strategy inside an uncertain regime. Better to explore a little longer than you think you should, and only then tighten down, than to tighten down too early and discover—expensively—that your map was from a different world.

Let's break this down further to make it clear and actionable. The first question you must ask yourself is tactical: How often do I run experiments to refine the model I already believe is basically sound? The second, on the other hand, is existential: How often do I need to reexamine the model itself?

There's no universal answer (naturally, that would be too easy). But there are good heuristics. Generally, the more complex and fast changing your environment is, the faster your feedback loops need to be—and the more open you must remain to accommodation, not just assimilation. The longer you delay those loops, the more your knowledge risks becoming unfit for purpose.

In simple systems, you can afford to update more slowly. But in complex systems, delay can be deadly. Feedback must be fast, honest, and relatively interpretable—or else small errors run the risk of metastasizing into deep failure. First-order change is mechanical, with inputs and outputs shifting within a stable structure, like adjusting the throttle or price. Second-order change rewrites the structure itself: a market regime turning from bull to bear, a company culture evolving, a geopolitical alliance fracturing. Some variables (interest rates, weather, code) can change hourly.

---

iii In other words, survive severity to resolve frequency (probabilities).

Others (institutions, trust, norms) shift over years or decades. Peril lies in treating one kind as if it moves on the timeline of the other.

And yet there's one wrinkle even this doesn't cover: What happens when the data you get back isn't just surprising—but seems totally anomalous? What if it doesn't fit your model at all?

Impute, Don't Amputate

The hardest data point to absorb is the one that doesn't fit into your story. Not one that undermines or contradicts your hypothesis (this is often instructive), necessarily, but something you just plain don't understand or know what to do with.

You've done the work. You've mapped your decision space, made your best guess, launched your experiment, gotten feedback—and then something comes back that doesn't belong. A weird edge case. A result that contradicts your model. A data point so far from the cluster that it's tempting to treat it like noise.

This is the outlier dilemma: Do you ignore the anomaly and move forward with your thesis? Or do you hit the brakes, pause, and expend the time and resources to investigate whether it's signaling something deeper?

Once again, there's no universal answer. But there *is* a universal (and all-too-common) danger: treating every single outlier as disposable. Because the moment you start amputating inconvenient data just to preserve your internal narrative, you're not learning anymore. You're just protecting your ego.

That's confirmation bias repackaged as cleanliness—which by now should be instantly recognizable as anathema to any Bayesian thinker. In this context, think of it not unlike a broken reward function: training an AI by rewarding it for outputs that please or flatter or otherwise cater to the human operator, rather than those that reflect reality. Eventually, the system stops optimizing for insight and starts optimizing for applause. It's overfit to the past—and blind to the future. Which makes it vulnerable to a Type II error, or a false negative.

Human decision-makers do essentially the same thing. We discard anomalies, downplay contradictory feedback, label inconvenient outcomes as flukes—which, at times, they absolutely are. But sometimes they're not—and the point is this: You don't get to throw them out with the bathwater just because they're hard to explain.

The good news is, there's another simple rule of thumb here: Imputation is better than amputation.

When you encounter an outlier, don't amputate it from your dataset just to make your theory cleaner. Instead, impute—ask: What would have to be true for this result to make sense? What conditions might have produced it? What variables might you be missing? What new hypothesis could account for this kind of edge case?

This doesn't mean every outlier is gold or ought to be treated as such. But it does mean you can't ignore them all categorically, reflexively. If you're serious about adaptive decision-making and cultivating your practice of the AQ process, you need a model that tolerates tension. So your mantra is as follows: It's never enough to say "that doesn't fit." You have to ask *why*. Because sometimes the outlier isn't an error; every so often, it's a paradigm shift in disguise.

And here's the tell: outliers that cluster when the state changes. A single weird data point is trivial; a thin constellation of weirdness around a boundary condition could be a flare on the horizon. Treat those edge cases as probes. Ask not only, "What would have to be true for this to make sense?" but also, "What *state change* would render this result an ordinary result?" When the answer to the second question is plausible, pause your assimilation reflex. You may be watching the mesh drop across the door between the Phase II and Phase III feedback loop.

Pattern, Noise, or New Paradigm?

Telescoping up, it bears emphasizing that this is where pattern recognition demands at least a modicum of that same intellectual humility we've been cultivating from almost the first page of this book. Some people are prone to overindex on outliers and chase noise; others rush to dismiss them too quickly and miss the signals that matter. The key is knowing what kind of environment or state you might be in—and whether the outlier staring you in the face represents an exception or the edge of a new pattern just beginning to emerge.

And make no mistake: This is a skill. Some people—particularly serial entrepreneurs and others with high AQ who operate at the forefront of new or changing industries—can sniff out paradigm shifts early, or even create them. Because they don't *just* look for patterns; they routinely, relentlessly pose those second-order questions about the implications of whatever it is they're seeing. *What if this weird result isn't noise? What if it's the beginning of something?*

Of course, not every anomaly is a potential breakthrough. But many deserve attention. If your instinct is to explain something away without even asking what might make it true, you're not running a feedback loop. You're running a self-justification engine. And that defeats the whole purpose of iteration.

So, yes—respect the cluster. But don't ignore the outlier. Because, sometimes, the data point that breaks your model is the one that saves you in the final reckoning.

Provisional Mastery

Phase III *always* points back to Phase II. That's not a rhetorical or narrative flourish—it's a structural reality. The moment your experiment yields a result, you've created a new data point that demands either to be situated in context or that prompts a broader reassessment of the model you used to make the decision in question. And this isn't a "nice to have," it's the entire point of running the experiment in the first place: updating your hypothesis, refining your SOWH.

The danger lies in what happens next. Once you've been through the loop a few times, you start to develop what feels like embedded know-how. You've seen enough of the terrain to recognize patterns. From a certain perspective, you've earned the status of "expert." Which is exactly when you have to be the most careful—because in a fast-changing environment, as you'll recall from previous chapters, expertise is only as good as the conditions under which it was earned.

The paradox of expertise is that it's both your sharpest tool and your most dangerous blindfold. In stable, slow-changing environments, expertise compounds—and experience lets you shortcut the loop because the patterns hold steady. In physics, for example, underlying laws and even theoretical frameworks evolve slowly enough (relatively speaking) that a lifetime of accumulated knowledge retains its value, provided that knowledge is updated at appropriate intervals along the way. But in domains that change at high velocity—like AI, biotechnology, or modern geopolitics—expertise has a much shorter half-life. What was true a decade ago may not just be outdated; it may now be dangerously wrong.

And, of course, it's not just about the field—it's about the problem you're trying to solve. When SpaceX began developing Starship, the fundamentals of rocket science hadn't changed much in decades. What *had* changed were the goals and constraints, which included designing a fully reusable rocket to carry far heavier payloads much deeper into space, built with advanced alloys and manufacturing techniques that didn't exist in the Apollo era, that was capable of carrying humans to another world and back again. The expertise that mattered wasn't simply knowing how to launch a rocket; it was knowing how to rethink launch vehicles altogether for a new mission profile.

Context, as the saying goes, is king: Expertise is vastly more durable when the environment is stable and the target doesn't move much. Which is another way of saying: The half-life of expertise is set by state, not by resume. In a steady state, intuition and playbooks save precious energy; in a changing state, those same shortcuts are precisely what need to be quarantined until they reearn admission. Your loop cadence should track that assessment. If the state looks continuous, then slower, cheaper loops suffice; if the state is heating up, then shorten loops aggressively and widen your exploration bands because yesterday's conclusions will be outdated sooner rather than later. It's more perishable when the terrain is shifting.

The trap lies in treating durable expertise like it's *universally* durable—or treating fast-decaying expertise like it's still relevant.

And here's the other twist: the role of time itself. When you're young, the plain actuarial fact is that you can afford to be more wrong more often—not because you're inherently more resilient or better at recovering (though this is certainly true in the physical sense, among others), but because the calendar stretching before you affords more loops. You can try, fail, adapt, and still have enough runway (remaining lifetime) to recover from almost anything short of catastrophic, irreversible deep failure. That's why the advice to "take more risks when you're young" is, in my view, both sound and wise—not because youth guarantees wisdom, but because you have the slack to reloop before any potential damage gets anywhere close to terminal.

Phase III, with its emphasis on provisional mastery, is where all of this comes to a head. The most adaptive thinkers use their knowledge to generate sharper hypotheses, but they refuse to treat those hypotheses as permanent. They measure the shelf life of what they know. They keep putting their hard-won expertise at risk, subjecting it to the adaptive cycle again and again—because they understand that the only expertise worth having is expertise that's alive.

Practically, that means each cycle runs a short preflight inspection: state check first, then reset variables accordingly, then revisit your experiments. If the state is continuous, your last round's provisional knowledge can walk back in through the open door as updated priors, now refined, weighted, and ready to guide the next set of tests.

This is where compressed feedback loops come in. Picture your decision tree: every branch, every node, every possible path you might take. The slower you loop, the longer you're wandering down a branch before you discover it's a dead end. But if you can cycle through tests faster—reentering Phase II more often—you effectively collapse multiple branches of the tree together, thereby getting to viable answers sooner.

This is why high-velocity decision-makers rarely test one hypothesis at a time. They'll spin up a half dozen designs, knowing some might blow up before they yield usable feedback but that many will survive long enough to teach them something new. The point isn't to avoid failure; it's to multiply your chances of learning. A SpaceX launch engineer doesn't test one valve design in isolation; they might prototype multiple variants at once. The lesson isn't in which valve wins, it's in what the pattern of failure teaches about the system as a whole.

The same principle applies outside of rocket factories. Shorter loops, run in parallel, accelerate the refinement of your models and keep your provisional "expert" knowledge alive, current, and adaptive. The moment you stop looping back, you stop being an expert. You just become someone who used to know.

A Quick Adaptability Quotient Check

You've now got the framework. You understand the theory behind AQ, the process, the loop from Phase III back to Phase II. But here's the uncomfortable truth: Understanding the full adaptive cycle doesn't guarantee you'll think this way when it counts.

That's why the best decision-makers—and the best investors, leaders, and builders—look for signals that a person is wired for adaptability. They're not looking for signals about *what* they think, but about *how* they think.

Some organizations formalize this kind of thing—thirty questions, or maybe distilled to ten, scored and benchmarked. You can do that if you like. But there's a simpler way to start: Ask the kinds of questions that probe someone's approach and reveal whether they're in the habit of looping. Questions like these:

- Do you prefer being wrong for the right reasons, or right for the wrong reasons?
- How frequently should you update your beliefs and based on what conditions?
- When was the last time you changed your mind about something important—and why?

- How do you decide whether an outlier is noise or signal?
- Is being undecided about many issues a sign of weakness?
- Is holding on to strong opinions the sign of a strong leader?
- Should beliefs always be revised in response to new information or evidence?
- Are *thinking* and *doing* opposites?
- Is it OK to pick out facts that support your belief, even if other facts refute it?

You can ask these of yourself, noting the degrees to which your own answers change over time as your awareness of your own thinking—and your practice of AQ—evolves and deepens. You can ask them in job interviews as you seek to populate the rest of your organization with others who think adaptively. You can ask the people around a leader you're thinking about hiring, funding, or partnering with; in some cases, you may be able to infer reasonably accurate answers from public information.

The point isn't to hear a "right" answer in response to any one or more of these questions—it's to glimpse or otherwise access and observe a process. You're listening for evidence of short loops, intellectual humility, comfort with provisional knowledge, a reflex to reassess when reality shifts. The more consistently you pick up on such a reflex, the higher the odds are that the person—or organization—in question can navigate a fast current without drowning or being borne back into the past.

From One Mind to Many

Part of the reason I wrote this book was, in a sense, inherently selfish: to get these ideas, this operating system, organized and out of my head. It's been rattling around for years—refined by real-world experiments, scarred by mistakes, sharpened by the people I've worked with—and I wanted a version I could point to and say: "This. *This* is how I think."

Anyone who's worked with me for long enough knows the feeling.

There's a certain way problems get framed. A certain instinct to telescope up, to poke at assumptions until they break, to keep the loop running again and again (and again, ad infinitum)[iv] until the model fits reality. That's the "thing" you pick up—not because it's written on a wall somewhere, but because you absorb it in the doing.

I'm not alone in this. Spend time with someone like Ken Griffin, Elon Musk, or Ross Stevens, and I'm willing to bet you'll see a similar pattern at work—different personalities in different industries, but with a similar instinct to structure thinking in a way that multiplies learning. The frustrating thing is that most of the public record kept on people like that is biography, not blueprint or playbook; you might be able to read about their childhood traumas or gain observable insights into their behaviors and obsessions, but you rarely get a sense of how their minds actually work—let alone a manual that maps some of their thinking and leaves you with the tools to apply what makes them successful in your own life.[v]

That's what I've tried to capture here. Not for ego, not for legacy, but because once AQ is codified, it can be taught; the firmware upgrade can be loaded. You can hand it off to a team and say, "This is how I'd like us all to approach our journey toward deep success." It can become the shared engine that drives decisions, experiments, and adaptative thinking across an entire organization.

And here's the bigger leap: Once you have a shared operating system for adaptive thinking, you can design a culture around it. You can hire for it, train for it, and protect it. You can take what was once idiosyncratic—living only in the head of one person—and make it a collective habit. Which will be the focus of our next chapter.

That's the real prize. Because when a group of people share not just a

---

iv Or at least ad nauseam . . .

v This is also why business case studies are far from sufficient. They describe outcomes and capture key insights, some of which are surely valuable. But they regard the most rich and fascinating and actionable sources of information about what worked and why—the thinking and decision-making of those who engineered the success in question—as essentially unknowable, a black box. This book turns that on its head entirely.

mission but a methodology for thinking, you get more than collaboration. You get a team that can move as one through uncertainty *without* collapsing into groupthink.[vi]

It's rare, but it's possible. One of the clearest historical examples of this in action happened in an unlikely setting in the late 1940s, when a handful of scientists, engineers, and maverick thinkers came together in what became known as the Macy Conferences. What they built wasn't a company or a product—it was a way of thinking that crossed disciplines and remade the way we approach complex systems.

Codifying the Collective Mind: The Macy Conferences

Imagine a room—not a cloistered lecture hall, but an intentionally messy courtroom for ideas—in mid-century Manhattan. Folding chairs, ashtrays, thick stacks of typed notes. Coffee cups scattered on tables. The air thick with pipe smoke and arguments. Here, from 1946 to 1953, a rotating cast of some of the most influential minds of the twentieth century gathered for a series of ten meetings under the auspices of the Josiah Macy Jr. Foundation.

These were the Macy Conferences—an experiment not in producing polished papers or winning debates, but in *thinking together* in real time. The goal, according to the book-length volume of transcripts and findings they produced, was nothing less than to build a shared science of "circular causal and feedback mechanisms in biological and social systems"—what would soon become known as cybernetics.

The gathering did not lack in either pedigree or intent. Frank Fremont-Smith, a physician and medical philanthropist, was the architect. He had seen firsthand how breakthroughs happened when doctors, engineers, and scientists from different specialties were forced into the same

vi As chapter 11 will cover, this is known as cognitive coherence.

room. For the Macy meetings, he assembled a guest list that spanned the intellectual map: neurophysiologists, anthropologists, mathematicians, engineers, psychiatrists, logicians. He asked them to wrestle with a single, deceptively simple question: *What is a system, and how does it adapt when you push on it?*

Early on, the boundaries between specialists in different fields seemed so tall as to be insurmountable. Each discipline wrapped itself in its own vocabulary and clung to its own blind spots. Mathematicians like John von Neumann spoke in the language of logic and computation; anthropologists like Margaret Mead and Gregory Bateson spoke in stories and cultural systems; engineers like Claude Shannon and Norbert Wiener spoke of circuits and signals; neurophysiologists like Warren McCulloch spoke in the firing patterns of neurons. At first, they talked past each other.

But this friction was the point, at least in part. The confusion was the fuel. Because the only way forward was for each discipline to bridge epistemic silos and lean into the others' world—translating their ideas, testing them against foreign assumptions, and, in the process, synthesizing something new. Slowly, almost painfully at times, they forged a common language rich enough to describe the behavior of systems—whether neural, mechanical, or social.

The stakes were real; these weren't academic parlor games. The world was in the earliest years of a dawning Cold War, and the question of how systems respond to feedback wasn't theoretical—it had implications for everything from guided missile systems to brain science to economic planning. In those rooms, the foundations were laid for cybernetics, the study of control and communication in machines and living things; information theory, Claude Shannon's mathematical framework for quantifying and transmitting information; neural network theory, through Warren McCulloch's and Walter Pitts's work on artificial neurons; early AI research (preceding even the Dartmouth Conference), seeded by the very idea that machine and human intelligence might be described with the same models; and the intellectual infrastructure for what would later become cognitive science.

The Macy Conferences became, in retrospect, the birthplace of the systems view itself—a way of seeing problems not as isolated events but as nodes in interdependent networks. The resulting shift was seismic, reframing everything from how we think about the human mind to how we design complex organizations.

But here's the part that matters for us: They didn't just gather experts and let them talk. They engineered a space that demanded adaptive thinking. They created an iterative loop that lived outside any one person's head—something roughly like: *Question → poke → learn → update → iterate.*

Over time, this loop became the group's enabling architecture—a kind of collective operating system. It was adaptive by design, capable of accommodating new ideas without collapsing under the weight of disciplinary turf wars.

What they achieved is rare, but it was (and is) not magic by any stretch. It can be replicated. Imagine a modern equivalent inside a company or a government agency: cross-functional teams where silos are treated as invitations, not barriers; where misunderstanding isn't a nuisance, but the opening move in the real conversation; where the objective isn't to win the argument, but to refine the shared model until it can stand up to the next stress test. We've seen glimpses of this in action—from DARPA's (the Defense Advanced Research Projects Agency) mixed cohorts of scientists, soldiers, and engineers who are building next-generation defense systems, to NASA's Artemis teams that are blending planetary scientists with software developers and commercial partners, to corporate "moonshot" labs like Alphabet's X, where physicists, coders, and biologists are thrown together to tackle problems no one field can solve alone.

But the conditions that made the original Macy model necessary have returned—only this time, at planetary scale. AI, synthetic biology, and neurotechnology have accelerated faster than our social and epistemic stabilizers can adapt. Our tools now evolve faster than our understanding of them. The danger isn't just technological disruption; it's cognitive destabilization. We can no longer assume that stability—of truth, identity, or agency—will emerge naturally from innovation. It must be deliberately engineered.

What we need now are new Macy Conferences; we need forums capable of reimagining the stabilizers the last revolution abandoned. Not technical fixes, but cultural and cognitive ones: shared epistemic guardrails, truth arbitration protocols, and civic myths that reanchor meaning in an age of algorithmic drift. We need slow-feedback rituals—deliberative assemblies, enlightened disagreement—designed to balance the hyperspeed feedback loops of our "hot" technologies.

The original Macy group asked how control and feedback could regulate complex systems at the level of the human mind. The next one must ask the same question, but at the scale of civilization.

The Macy Conferences didn't create one leader's singular genius. They created a container where collective genius could emerge—adaptive, agile, recursive. The lesson is to create environments where disagreement is structured, feedback is slow enough to be meaningful, and no single model is allowed to dominate unchecked. This is a model we can use today to embed AQ at scale—and, just as urgently, to keep humanity in the loop.

From Loop to Culture

If there's one idea to carry out of this chapter, it's this: The loop is the work.

Phase III is never the finish line. It's just your next entry point back into Phase II, armed with the latest—though still, as always, provisional—knowledge you've earned. Every decision you make, every experiment you run, is a fresh opportunity to refine your model or reframe it entirely. Sometimes you assimilate; sometimes you accommodate. Sometimes the outlier is noise; sometimes it's the canary in your mental coal mine.

Mastery, in this context, is about preserving the habit of reassessment—over and over—without letting ego, convenience, or stale expertise get in the way. But as powerful as this is at the individual level, its impact compounds when it becomes a shared operating system. When the loop is embedded in the culture of a team or an organization, decision-making stops being the product of isolated brilliance and starts becoming the product of collective intelligence. This is Collective AQ, a group's shared capacity to sense, update, and act together under uncertainty. That's when you see something like the Macy Conferences come to life: a container where disciplines collide, language barriers dissolve, and a group builds its own adaptive brain. Which raises the next challenge: It's one thing for you to think this way. It's another to get a roomful of people—with different skills, personalities, and incentives—to think this way together. That's where we're headed next—because once adaptability becomes cultural, the stakes stop being organizational and start being civilizational.

If you can build a team that loops—fast, honestly, and without fear—you're no longer just adapting to the world. You're building an organization that can surf the wave of change as it happens, turning complexity into a competitive advantage and a structural asset.

The AQ Process

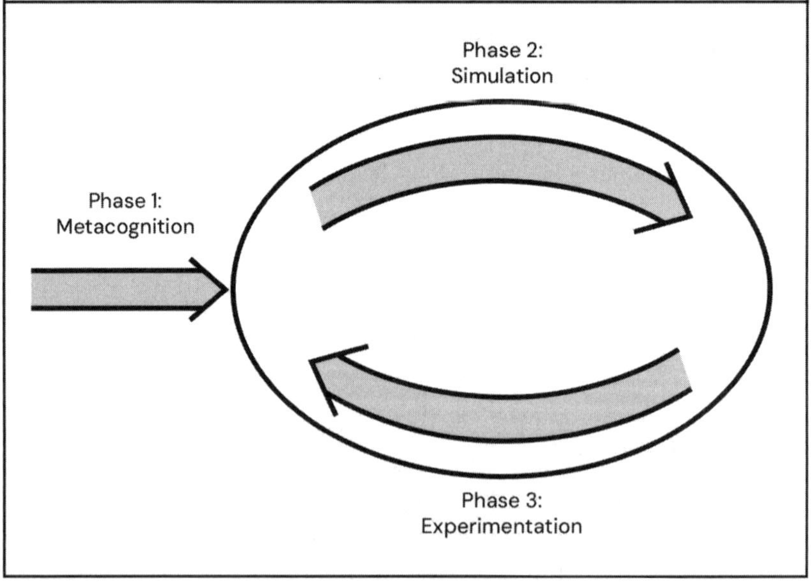

Adaptability Quotient Field Guide: Key Takeaways

- **Phase III is a threshold, not an ending.** The adaptive cycle is the work.
- **All knowledge is provisional.** Revalidate on every pass.
- **Assimilate when facts fit the frame; accommodate when they change it.** And evaluate which state you're in—that context sets the bounds of your experiment.
- **When the state shifts, demote past "conclusions" to raw data before reusing them.** Impute before you amputate—probe outliers, especially when they cluster at boundaries.
- **Expertise has a half-life.** Durability is determined by state, not resume.
- **Match loop speed to environment speed.** Compress cycles and run parallel experiments in fast/complex regimes.
- **Keep humility for answers and pride in process.** Anchor identity to the underlying engine, not individual opinions.
- **Codify the loop at the team level.** This is where disciplines collide and feedback becomes collective intelligence.

11
Leading at Altitude

You can't build an adaptable organization without adaptable people—and individuals change only when they have to, or when they want to.

—Gary Hamel

If the rate of change on the outside exceeds the rate of change on the inside, the end is near.

—Jack Welch

Up until this point, we've been discussing AQ as an individual operating system to achieve personal agency. But leadership, in business or any other context, introduces an altogether different problem. The moment you try to scale adaptivity beyond one brain—beyond one founder, one leader, one decision-maker—you run into a wall.

Organizations don't adapt because they say they "value agility." They adapt when many individual AQ colleagues are aligned—in direction, in methodology, and in trust—so people can think independently and act locally, but still update collectively toward the same objective.

That capacity is what I call *Collective AQ*, the ability of a group to make high-quality decisions toward a shared goal under uncertainty, while preserving local judgment and contributing to shared learning. It is not "culture" in the usual (squishy) sense, nor does it arise from consensus or groupthink. Rather, it is an independent decision architecture of its own—a joint operating system.

Crucially, Collective AQ does not emerge by bringing adaptable people together and hoping the group somehow figures it out. At least in my experience, high-AQ individuals without alignment don't produce adaptivity at scale; they produce noise—energy without direction, dissent without resolution, friction without actual learning. Alignment without individual AQ, on the other hand, produces the opposite failure mode—bureaucracy, process without curiosity, agreement without updating.

What turns individual adaptivity into organizational agency is *joint intention*, which has two parts.

First, a shared vision—not a slogan, but a common objective. In other words, everyone understands what "winning" means, what the system is optimizing for, what trade-offs are (and aren't) acceptable, and what must not be allowed to break even under pressure. A collective definition of organizational deep success.

Second, a shared way of deciding. In other words, the organization agrees explicitly on how evidence is surfaced and acted upon—how arguments are evaluated, how new data changes minds, how disagreements are handled, and how decisions are made once debate is complete.

Together, these create joint intention: many people thinking independently, but aiming at the same target and using the same process and decision grammar. This is the essence of Collective AQ. It's how a group achieves shared agency with distributed cognition, preserving the loop—clarify intent, test assumptions, act, update—at scale, without losing speed, coherence, or truth.

This is also where many organizations reach instinctively for incentives (i.e., equity, bonuses, promotion ladders), which can of course mobilize effort and help align outcomes. But incentives don't create collective agency—nor can they supply shared understanding, justify trade-offs when models change, or sustain legitimacy under uncertainty. You can perfectly align compensation and still wind up with people optimizing in different directions—working hard, acting rationally, and collectively missing the point. Incentives can motivate behavior, but joint intention is what directs it. And joint intention comes from shared purpose, explicit decision processes, and norms that protect truth-seeking and updating when pressure rises.

This chapter is about putting the foregoing pages into practice when the stakes are high, the clock is ticking, and everyone in the room is looking to you for the right answer (or, indeed, for any answer at all). When it's your call to make, you can't afford to get it wrong, and those around you—maybe even the company you're leading—suddenly need to think, and move, just as adaptively.

The Science of Seeing Clearly

There's a reason evolution gave us two eyes instead of one.

When you look at something up close—say, while threading a needle—your eyes adjust their angle ever so slightly inward, converging. When you look at something in the distance—the mountains on the horizon—they turn very subtly outward. This barely perceptible movement, called *vergence*, happens automatically. Your brain stitches together two slightly different images into a single clear picture.

Without it, you couldn't tell near from far. You'd lose all sense of depth, of proportion, of what's right in front of you versus lurking down the road. What matters and what doesn't.

Decision-makers of all stripes need a kind of mental vergence—but leadership is where it becomes nonoptional. Leadership AQ is maintaining vergence across levels, holding clear intent at high altitude while ensuring local decisions resolve coherently at the point of action.

This is not "zoom," in that vergence isn't magnification. It's alignment across distance. Lose it, and you get organizational double vision—good strategy with bad execution, or brilliant local execution that doesn't add up—or, even more dangerous, perhaps even a fatal blind spot.

Deep(est) Failure

On a cold June morning in 2023, the *Titan* slipped beneath the North Atlantic, with five passengers sealed inside a carbon-fiber cylinder no longer than a stretch limousine. Stockton Rush, OceanGate's founder and CEO, piloted the scratch-made submersible himself, steering it toward the ruined wreck of RMS *Titanic*, two and a half miles down.

Rush spoke often of innovation. He was proud that *Titan* boldly broke the rules: no classification by any regulatory body. No traditional safety certification. He believed the deep-sea industry had grown too cautious, too timid, paralyzed by fear and bureaucracy. Carbon fiber is the future, he told critics; you can't make breakthroughs without breaking a few assumptions.

From the time of OceanGate's founding, experienced engineers had warned Rush that carbon composites behave unpredictably under the relentless, crushing force of the deep ocean. Pressure doesn't just compress; it fatigues. Which means microscopic fractures, invisible but fatal, would accumulate in the pressure hull and the composite itself would grow more brittle with every dive.

Rush dismissed them all. "We have heard the baseless cries of 'you are going to kill someone' way too often," he infamously wrote.

One hour and thirty-three minutes into the June 2023 dive, with the submersible having reached a depth of 3,346 meters beneath the North Atlantic, *Titan*'s tracking signal winked out.

There was no mayday call. No slow (or shallow) failure. Just a sudden, catastrophic implosion—an instantaneous collapse of the hull at a speed faster than the human nervous system can register. One moment *Titan* existed; the next, it was a crushed soda can, trailing a cloud of debris, spiraling down another half mile to impact the seafloor.

Rush wasn't wrong that exploration demands challenging the old ways of thinking. He *was* wrong, emphatically and fatally so, in believing that vision and force of personality alone could bend the laws of physics.

This is what I mean by deep failure—the kind of failure that ends the loop. And the uncomfortable leadership lesson is that deep failure rarely results from a single bad idea. It arises from a system that confuses conviction for verification—that treats dissent as friction, expertise as politics, and safety as something you can "innovate" your way around with force of will.

Selective defiance is in some ways the heart of AQ. But at the organizational level, selective defiance can't live inside one person's instincts. It has to be embedded in the decision architecture—so the system knows when to challenge consensus and when to respect the laws of physics.

Safety for People, Tension for Ideas

Operationally, this is a problem that quietly kills many scaling organizations. How do you preserve debate and elevate unvarnished learning, even as headcount rises—without turning dissent into social warfare, or turning "culture" into a consensus drug?

One of the best examples in recent history lies in the early years of Netflix. The company's answer to this problem became famous—at least startup-lore famous—because founders Reed Hastings and Patty McCord committed it to writing, as a slide deck, and put it out into the world as the now-iconic Netflix Culture Deck ("Freedom & Responsibility"), first shared publicly in 2009 (and later explained at length by McCord in *Harvard Business Review*).

To me, the deck's most enduring contribution isn't that it celebrates freedom; lots of companies do that, at least rhetorically. To me, the innovation is that it ties freedom to an epistemic operating system—and the idea that teams must be at the same time highly aligned and loosely coupled. In other words, autonomy is not the absence of constraints. Autonomy is what you earn when the organization has a shared objective function and shared updating rules.

And here's the part that matters most for our purposes, in terms of Collective AQ: Netflix didn't try to eliminate tension, by any stretch. All it did was try to direct and detoxify it.

Psychological safety, in Netflix's model, didn't mean "everybody feels comfortable all the time"; it simply meant that people (and their jobs) are safe, period, even when conversations don't feel that way. Feedback is allowed to be direct, disagreement is real, and conflicting perspectives should not shy away from sharpening themselves against one another. But the line between attacking ideas and attacking people is a boundary that must never, ever be crossed.

This is why Netflix has become a canonical example of what we might call productive discomfort. Leaders weren't just permitted to change their minds; they were expected to do so—openly and often—because updating wasn't treated as weakness, but as a sign of competence. (McCord is explicit about this broader philosophy—that the company's goal was to create conditions where responsible adults can make decisions with sufficient context, rather than being controlled through rigid process.)

This is one way to express what Collective AQ looks like when it works:

- **Shared intent**—in that everyone understands the objective function and trade-offs.
- **Shared decision architecture**—so people know how decisions get made, how evidence is evaluated, and what happens when there's disagreement.
- **High autonomy at the edge**—paired with rigorous expectations about truth, candor, and accountability.

When Harmony Becomes Hazardous

If the Netflix example illustrates how high-AQ systems and organizations successfully manage (and productively channel) tensions, the Space Shuttle *Challenger* disaster shows the inverse failure mode—a system that treated disagreement as a threat to alignment, while prioritizing alignment as a proxy for truth—with almost documentary clarity.

On the evening of January 27, 1986, with a hard freeze forecast for the next morning at the Kennedy Space Center, NASA and contractor teams held a teleconference about whether it would be safe to launch *Challenger* not long after the sun came up. Engineers at Morton Thiokol, the company responsible for the shuttle's Solid Rocket Boosters (SRBs), warned that the cold posed an unacceptable risk to the booster joint seals, specifically the O-rings. The engineers' initial bottom line was clear: *Do not launch under these conditions*. But the evidence was debated intensely, with NASA managers challenging the recommendation and pressing for justification that would support a launch.

Then came the pivotal moment. Thiokol management held an offline caucus—a management-only discussion—after which the company's position abruptly reversed. Accounts of that caucus include an infamous instruction to take off one's "engineering hat" and put on a "management hat," a line that has endured precisely because it captures the dangerous shift happening in real time—from weighing evidence and seeking truth to pursuing alignment.

For Collective AQ purposes, this is where the distinction between two often-confused concepts becomes important. *Coherence* is what happens when a group can disagree without penalty, update without humiliation, and still act decisively once the decision threshold is crossed. What happened that night was not coherence, but premature *convergence*—a narrowing of the organization's field of vision to preserve momentum.

Later, as it investigated the *Challenger* accident, the Rogers Commission called out not only the technical failure itself but the decision process—the way risk information moved (or didn't), the way prior O-ring erosion had been metabolized as "acceptable," and the way schedule and institutional pressures distorted judgment.

Which points to the deeper lesson: Psychological safety must protect people so truth can surface—but it must not protect plans, schedules, or favored narratives. When "safety" becomes shorthand for "don't make this harder," you haven't built a learning system. You've built a machine that trains itself to ignore weak signals, until those signals become strong enough to kill you.

In the wake of the *Challenger* tragedy, the legendary Richard Feynman approached the problem the way an adaptive thinker invariably begins: by going back to first principles. He wasn't brought in to adjudicate process or assign blame, and he didn't agree to serve on the Rogers Commission lightly. Instead, he simply wanted to know what the O-ring material actually did at low temperatures.

So, on the morning of a televised congressional hearing, he came prepared. The day before, he'd stopped at a hardware store and bought a small C-clamp and some pliers. During the hearing, as a scale model of the shuttle was passed around the room, Feynman used his pliers to yank out a piece of the O-ring rubber, clamped it tightly, then submerged it in ice water. Before everyone's eyes, the material stiffened and its resilience disappeared. The behavior NASA had been debating in memos became instantly, unmistakably visible—on live television.

That small experiment cut through layers of institutional language in a way no argument could. And it led Feynman to articulate a principle that—in my view—should be engraved above every high-stakes conference room door: "For a successful technology, reality must take precedence over public relations, for nature cannot be fooled."

The line isn't a rebuke of NASA so much as a working definition of adaptive leadership at scale. When the system can no longer hear reality, someone has to force reality back into the room.

Traits vs. System Outcomes

Especially when you try to build Collective AQ into systems in the real world, it's tempting to do what most leadership books do by default—which is to turn the entire subject into personality analysis. *Who's tough, who's kind, who's high-EQ, who's a visionary, who's "too intense,"* and so on. All too often we look for leadership traits the way we look for talent, hoping the right hires will magically produce the right outcomes.

But one individual's traits don't scale. Systems do.

So the question isn't whether a leader is warm or ruthless in the abstract. The question is whether the organization can preserve unvarnished truth-seeking under pressure—running feedback loops and updating as it goes—without personalizing conflict or collapsing into consensus.

Doing so successfully requires two things at once. First, the ability to understand how other people think—their mental models, assumptions, incentives, and update logic—so disagreements can be translated into something the broader group can actually work with. Second, the ability to keep fear, pride, and belonging from hijacking epistemics—so "being wrong" doesn't become a threat, and dissent doesn't get mistaken for disloyalty. The highest-performing organizations aren't built by leaders who never bruise feelings, nor by leaders who bulldoze them. They're built by leaders who can produce coherence—intellectual and emotional—at scale.

Cognitive empathy is the ability to understand how others reason, to predict their reactions, to see how a decision will land. **Emotional empathy** is the capacity to sense and resonate with another person's emotional state, allowing one to feel with them rather than merely understand about them. In high-stakes environments, emotional empathy can become a trap. It can make leaders slow to correct mistakes, too indulgent of mediocrity, too fearful of conflict, too distracted by interpersonal concerns to speak hard truths or drive hard when the situation demands it. Cognitive empathy, the ability to understand people without always being swayed by them, is often the sharper tool for the job.

But there's another wrinkle, an additional layer worth naming here, that often separates singular visionaries from those who actually build world-changing organizations. It's the difference between *cognitive empathy* at the individual level and what you might call *cognitive coherence* at the institutional one.

Cognitive coherence is what happens when an entire team (or company) can internalize and operate from the same mental model. When people don't just understand what the leader is trying to do but begin to think in that direction themselves. It's the strategic alignment that emerges not through hierarchy or compliance, but through shared frameworks regarding how to evaluate trade-offs, how to model risk, how to move from first principles.

I saw a version of this at Magnetar. My partners, Dave Snyderman and Ross Laser, and I shared a mission, a set of principles, and a language for risk and reward. But we came at problems from different angles, bringing complementary skill sets into the same cognitive frame. It was less a single mind scaled up than an ecosystem of minds, each attacking the world with a different weapon.

If I tended toward strategist and architect—applying long-horizon pattern recognition, novel business design, the lens of "What could this become in five or ten years?"—Dave was a builder in the purest sense. A former football player and relentless operator, he's quick to see a structural gap in a market and just as quick to scale into it with discipline and rigor. I watched him do it multiple times: in the CDO (collateralized debt obligations, which are complex financial products backed by pools of loans and other assets) trade before others fully understood the opportunity, in SPACs (special purpose acquisition companies, or shell companies created to raise capital through an IPO to eventually acquire an existing company), and more recently in GPUs (graphics processing units, which are now heavily used for AI and deep learning). He did this in three separate waves, and his ability to spot and systematize an edge before the rest of the world had even mapped it out became a superpower for the firm.

Ross, by contrast, was a tactician of the highest order (to such an extent that I often say he reminds me of a former Navy SEAL). A former number one tennis player at Michigan, with a kind of social radar that borders on uncanny, I've seen him walk into negotiations that looked impossible and walk out with terms no one thought were on the table. He was a floor trader who built and sold a clearing brokerage firm when he foresaw that the trading business would be digitized, enabling him to reinvent himself in a new field with new technology. He could read not just what people said, but how they moved, how they shook hands, how they carried the weight of their own internal constraints. Where Dave could see the structure of a market in three dimensions, Ross could see the structure of a person (so to speak) in about three seconds.

What held it all together was a shared obsession with feedback loops. We all knew that markets change, edges decay, and what worked yesterday comes with no warranty for tomorrow. So we built businesses accordingly, across strategies, across asset classes, across cycles. Most of Magnetar's profits today come from areas that didn't even exist in the same way five years ago. That wasn't an accident; it was an operating principle. Empower the teams closest to the edge, distribute agency, and treat every win as provisional—as evidence that you understood that regime, not a guarantee that you'll dominate the next.

It's no coincidence that all three of us were competitive athletes—an All-American squash player, a college football player, and a top-ranked tennis player. Sports wire a certain mindset: discipline plus adaptability. You show up with a game plan, but every opponent, every point, every match forces you to adjust on the fly. The rules stay the same, but the game never does. Looking back, I'm acutely aware of how lucky I was to end up in that particular trio: three very different minds, wired for competition, all committed to the same adaptive process.

Of course, we didn't agree on everything—far from it. We argued constantly. But our disagreements lived inside a shared operating system: same models of risk, same respect for data, same commitment to updating fast when reality contradicted us. That's cognitive coherence at work. Not cloned personalities, but aligned processes. Different vantage points, but the same map.

But coherence can run through feelings as well as thoughts.

Emotional coherence is the presence of shared emotional norms that allow individuals and groups to engage in truth-seeking, disagreement, and updating without becoming defensive, performative, or emotionally destabilized. It is what happens when a team is aligned not only intellectually, but affectively—able to keep emotions oriented toward the *issue at hand* rather than the people involved.

Cognitive coherence is the spark; emotional coherence is the load-bearing structure. Together they are what fuels buy-in during crunch time, what makes people stay late, what makes a mission feel personal.

But they serve different purposes. And—crucially—coherence doesn't require agreement. Cognitive coherence means we share how we decide and update, not what we currently believe. Emotional coherence means disagreements are directed at ideas, evidence, and assumptions, not at identity, status, or intent. Emotional coherence means people can surface risk, uncertainty, and disconfirming evidence without humiliation or personal attack—not that decision-making is frictionless and disagreement disappears.

The risk, of course, is imbalance. A company with emotional coherence but no cognitive alignment can become a cult of vibes—driven by intensity but prone to drift, disillusionment, or wasted motion. On the other hand, an organization with cognitive coherence but no emotional resonance can become brittle—efficient but hollow and easily fractured under stress or fatigue.

The Entrepreneur's Paradox

Throughout this book, we've held up entrepreneurs as a useful control group because they begin without stable priors and can't rely on inherited playbooks, institutional memory, or established hierarchies. They are forced into beginner's mind not as a philosophy, but as a condition of survival. Which means they test, discard, revise, and update continuously because the environment leaves them no choice.

In the early stages of building a business or leading an organization, nonconformity can be an advantage, things like speed often matter more than polish, and a founder's ability to see what others don't—and then move before anyone else can take advantage—often means the difference between momentum and extinction.

But at scale, these same traits can be surprisingly dangerous.

Unconstrained nonconformity, in which everyone runs their own experiments with little coordination or direction, fragments organizations, while overreliance on centralized founder-CEO judgment creates bottlenecks. In either extreme, decisions slow and adaptivity collapses—not because people stop thinking adaptively, but because the system is no longer integrating what they're seeing and updating accordingly.

This is the entrepreneur's paradox: The very qualities that are essential in cultivating high individual AQ tend to dilute it at scale, unless they are deliberately re-architected.

Collective AQ resolves this paradox by separating exploration from control.

CEO as Steward of Coherence

What this means, in practice, is that an organization's leadership retains responsibility for the structure of decisions—setting goals, constraints, risk tolerance, and escalation thresholds. Their teams, meanwhile, are expected to explore aggressively within that structure, testing assumptions, surfacing disconfirming evidence, and updating close to the edge, where information is freshest.

At altitude, the CEO's job isn't to have the right answers. It's to install and steward the operating system that makes high-quality answers more likely to emerge—fast—and prevent the organization from lying to itself. I call that operating system *joint intention*, and to succeed it requires cognitive and emotional coherence.

Leading with joint intention starts with establishing direction—defining deep success, what "winning" actually means. It continues with setting constraints such as risk tolerance to minimize risk of deep failure, and requires organization-wide clarity about what can be decided locally, what requires coordination, and what must be escalated when uncertainty exceeds authority. Just as important are the updating rules—requiring people to surface assumptions, document why decisions are made (not just what is decided), and run postmortems that separate bad outcomes from bad decisions. And finally, it demands visible enforcement—protecting dissenters after outcomes are known, so the system learns the right lessons instead of the convenient ones.

This is how Collective AQ produces organizational agency—the capacity to translate intent into coordinated action toward a shared goal, while thinking independently, adapting locally, and updating collectively under uncertainty.

In my experience, Ken Griffin always ran Citadel on similar principles. In his world, ideas aren't judged by seniority or sentiment; they're judged by hard-edged, risk/reward reality. Ken is relentless about it: If the facts change, the position changes. Period.

Of course, even at the highest levels, the pitfalls are real—and they're the same ones that trip up startups, governments, and individuals alike:

- **Having overconfidence in early wins.** Success can fossilize thinking faster than failure. But it's about the journey, not the destination. Here's a motto we lived by during the early days at Citadel: "Hubris kills."
- **Punishing shallow failures too harshly.** If people get slammed every time they experiment and miss, guess what? They stop experimenting. Recall that shallow failure = learning, so reward it accordingly.
- **Failing to separate signal from noise.** When everything feels urgent, nothing gets prioritized, and almost any form of recalibration or Bayesian updating becomes impossible.
- **Confusing autonomy with architecture.** Freedom without shared rules for updating collapses into chaos; process without local judgment collapses into bureaucracy. Collective AQ comes from coupling the two.
- **Letting dissent become personal.** If disagreement slides from *ad res* to *ad hominem*, people start protecting their identities instead of surfacing signal (especially in the form of unexpected or unwelcome data)—at which point the whole system goes blind exactly when it needs vision most.

Building AQ into the bones, the DNA, the muscle memory of an organization isn't about internal branding or corporate speak. It requires engineering better defaults: designing feedback loops, incentives, and cultures that encourage smart bets, rapid updating, and survival in uncertainty. It's about building a team that keeps deciding better—and faster—as reality changes.

Beyond Flatland

There's an old book I hadn't thought about in years until recently: *Flatland*. I must have read it a hundred times when I was younger.

Subtitled "A Romance of Many Dimensions" and written by an English theologian and schoolteacher during the Victorian era, it's a strange little story—a social allegory (naturally)—imagining what life would be like in a two-dimensional world. Everything is flattened and constrained to the surface—no height, no depth, no possibility of seeing "above."

The brilliance of the book isn't just the fantasy of it, though. It's the way it invites you, in a lighthearted and entertaining fashion, to realize how limited your own perspective might be.

If you lived in Flatland, you couldn't even *conceive of* a third dimension. And if something from the third dimension—say, a sphere—passed through your world, you'd never be able to fathom what you were truly seeing: first, a dot. Then a widening circle. Then a shrinking one. Never the full, impossible shape. That idea stuck with me: How much of what we *think* we understand is just a two-dimensional projection (or a map) of something far larger, far more complex, than we even know how to see?

I found myself thinking about *Flatland* again recently, for the first time in decades, after someone mentioned it during a radio interview. Later, I sat down in a meeting with two close colleagues.

We were looking at a complicated investment—something that didn't come with neat answers.

We sat there, asking questions from different angles: strategic risks, macro forces, operational challenges. Some questions I thought of in the moment. Others I didn't, and probably wouldn't have.

But among the three of us, we were slicing into the problem in a variety of ways, attacking it from more angles than any one of us could have managed alone.

Later, I sent a quick text to them: *Glad we were all there. Really appreciated it.*

What I meant, and what I valued about that and similar interactions, was this: It wasn't just a matter of bringing raw intelligence or experience to bear against a thorny problem. It was the value of seeing a three-dimensional—or maybe even a seven-dimensional—picture of the opportunity, rather than being trapped in the narrow slice of whatever one person could perceive.

That process—of challenging, adding angles, broadening the aperture—isn't just intellectually satisfying. It confers a massive advantage.

In fact, even if the investment turns out to be a bad one—and sometimes, of course, they do—I realized that, at a certain point, I was strangely OK with that.

If I lose money and I have no idea why—if it's just stupidity or blind spots or herd instinct—that's frustrating in a way that makes me lose sleep. But if I lose money and, in the process, learn something, sharpen my perspective, see the world more clearly than I did before, then even in losing I'm getting stronger and smarter. Because I'm learning to see more of the true shape of reality, not the flattened version we're most comfortable with.

This also happens to explain why diversity—*real* diversity, of perspective, experience, cognition—matters so much. Not because it looks good on your quarterly or annual shareholder report. Not because it makes you feel better about yourself or advances some political agenda. But because, in a world that's changing so rapidly and relentlessly, the greatest risk isn't missing the right answer. It's a Type II error: the problem you failed to see.

The Macy Conferences were a prime example, but the point is both deeper and broader than the one we covered in the last chapter: When you surround yourself with people who question differently, who notice differently, who interpret differently, they can help you start pulling yourself out of Flatland. You start seeing from vantage points you don't naturally inhabit, understanding more of the whole, glimpsing the real shape of the world.

Diversity, Redux

All of this is why, if you want to build an adaptive organization—one that can survive hard shocks, spot hidden risks, and see opportunity where others miss it—you have to build a diverse one.

Not because a consultant told you to. Because if you don't, you might as well be flying with one eye closed. (And last time I checked, depth perception is relatively important when landing an airplane. . . .)

The truth is, most corporate conversations about diversity—and just about all political debates on the subject—get it all wrong. They talk about fairness. About representation. About optics. All of which are (of course) important in various contexts—but all of which miss or elide a deeper, more ruthless truth: Diversity confers a massive competitive advantage.

Because *cognitive* diversity—that can result from background, experience, and worldview, as the Macy Conferences reflected—makes your system smarter than its smartest member. It doesn't guarantee perfect decisions. It doesn't guarantee (or necessarily even improve) speed. But it dramatically increases your odds of spotting the cliff before you drive over the edge.

What matters isn't uniformity of thought but coherence in adaptability. Cognitive coherence doesn't mean everyone thinks alike; it means everyone thinks adaptively, aligned in how to learn, not what to believe. Consider a hiring problem most high-performance organizations don't like to admit they have. When everyone you hire has had the same education, the same economics courses, the same case interviews, the same ladder of credentials, you end up selecting for the silhouette—the polished, legible exterior that signals "competence" in the language of the tribe. Ambitious candidates learn to become what they believe you want—people who can produce trades that always win, moves that outsmart the competition, answers that sound inevitable in retrospect.

The philosopher W. V. O. Quine had a memorable way of describing how these external markers can be deceiving. Two things can look identical from a distance—for instance, two neatly trimmed bushes, with the same height and same silhouette—while their internal structures are completely different: a different tangle of twigs, a different arrangement of branches, a different shape of growth.

You can see this same dynamic playing out, in real time, in modern AI systems. Models trained on narrow, homogeneous, or self-referential data often appear impressively confident, providing answers that sound fluent, decisive, and internally consistent. But they fail catastrophically the moment the world changes, for one simple reason: Narrow training collapses the hypothesis space. When systems learn only from a limited slice of experience, they suppress tail events, overfit to familiar patterns, and mistake internal coherence for truth. The model hasn't become smarter—it has become brittle.

Organizations fail the same way. Homogeneous teams converge faster, argue less, and feel aligned—right up until an external change exposes what they never learned to see. This is why diversity, properly understood, is not a social preference but an epistemic necessity, an expansion of the hypothesis space required to learn in rapidly changing environments. Without emotional coherence, diversity becomes noise—but with it, diversity becomes resilience.

As in Quine's sculpted shrub analogy, the value, especially under uncertainty, isn't just the silhouette. It's the twigs and branches: how a person notices, what they question, what they treat as signal versus noise, how quickly they update when the world contradicts them. Which means part of building a truly adaptive organization is creating deliberate distance between what got someone hired and what makes them valuable once they're inside the organization. In effect, you have to tell them—explicitly—*what got you here is not our goal now that you are here. We didn't hire you to keep winning inside yesterday's game. We hired you to help us see what we're missing, surface what doesn't fit the model, and revise the model before reality revises it for us.* The point isn't to eliminate disagreement but to channel it productively. When you assemble people with orthogonal experiences and mental models, you increase the system's entropy of ideas, its exposure to blind spots, and, by extension, its capacity to learn. This is the organizational expression of the Law of Requisite Variety: To survive in a complex environment, your internal diversity must at least match the complexity of the challenges you face.

Adaptability Quotient Field Guide: Key Takeaways

- **Leadership under pressure is the real proving ground of AQ.** That's where theory meets consequence and time runs short.
- **Individual AQ creates personal agency, while Collective AQ creates organizational agency:** the ability to translate intent into coordinated action under uncertainty.
- **Collective AQ requires joint intention,** a shared objective function and a shared way of deciding.
- **Leadership AQ requires mental vergence at scale:** maintaining clear intent at altitude while ensuring local decisions resolve coherently at the edge. Selective defiance must be embedded in the system, not left to individual heroics.
- **Beginner's mind fuels exploration; disciplined expertise protects against deep failure.** Adaptive leaders know when exploration must yield to the laws of physics.
- **Adaptive organizations loop collectively.** They're always experimenting, updating, and learning as systems, not just as individuals.
- **Psychological safety should protect people, not ideas or narratives.** Safety that suppresses tension destroys learning.
- **Cognitive coherence aligns how decisions are made; emotional coherence removes fear from participation.** Together, they enable disagreement without fragmentation and speed without chaos.
- **There is no one right leadership style.** There are only contextually intelligent ones. Adapt your mode to the mission, the team, and the terrain.
- **Operationalizing AQ means building feedback loops and incentives that reward updating.** Not ego or inertia.
- **Diversity is not a social preference; it is an epistemic necessity.** Diversity of experience and perspective expands

the organization's hypothesis space, reducing blind spots and brittleness in rapidly changing environments.

- **You can't build an adaptive organization on fixed minds**—or on systems that punish updating.

12

Authors of the Future

The illiterate of the twenty-first century will not be those who cannot read and write, but those who cannot learn, unlearn, and relearn.

—Alvin Toffler

I want to live my life taking the risk—all the time—that I don't know anything like-enough yet, that I haven't understood enough; that I can't know enough, that I'm always hungrily operating on the margins of a potential great harvest of future knowledge and wisdom. . . . Take the risk of thinking for yourself, much more happiness, truth, beauty, and wisdom will come to you that way.

—Christopher Hitchens

Here's the uncomfortable truth this chapter asks you to swallow first: The future is no longer a place we "visit," in the sense of a time-travel movie, or a story we experience unfolding. It's now a medium we can edit.

For centuries, progress meant uncovering what already was—gravity, germs, genes—and bending it to human ends. Now, we are crossing into a read-to-write age: We don't just discover; we compose. For most of human history, the world was effectively read-only. We observed nature, learned its rules, and adapted our behavior within them. Today, that boundary is dissolving and humanity is moving from passive analysis to active construction. Energy, biology, and cognition are becoming writable systems, technologies that vastly expand human capability—but do not reliably expand human agency. In some cases, especially cognition, they risk diminishing it by obscuring causality, compressing responsibility, and outsourcing judgment faster than our institutions and norms can adapt.

This chapter is about reclaiming authorship. Not as a metaphor, but as an operating posture. We'll explore why adaptive intelligence becomes a nonnegotiable skill in an era where AI accelerates everything, robotics grows hands, biology takes edits, and space becomes infrastructure. The payoff is practical: learning to move from map-reading to map-making without mistaking speed or ease for wisdom.

To open the lens, begin with a man who tried, more than a century ago, to teach the world how to look forward on purpose, shifting attention from the security blanket of hindsight to the discipline of reasoned foresight. That is the doorway into this chapter: from forecasting to authorship, from what *might* happen to what *we will make* happen.

The Invention of Foresight

In 1902, standing before a packed audience at the Royal Institution in London, H. G. Wells delivered a speech he called "The Discovery of the Future." It was, in hindsight, less an academic lecture and more a declaration of war on the limits of human imagination.

For as long as human beings had recorded history, the past had been the sturdy ground beneath our feet—the place we rooted ourselves to make sense of the world. We built our beliefs on it. Our laws. Our sciences. We trusted it to both inform how we shape the present and light the path ahead.

But that trust, Wells argued, was misplaced: This was all a kind of illusion. A comfortable fiction.

The past only *felt* certain because it had already happened. It gave the illusory sense of clarity because we'd already survived it. But probe deeper, and the stories we tell ourselves about the past start to fray. Memory is fallible. Perception is partial; experiential reality is subjective. Two witnesses can see the same car crash and come away with two different, even wildly divergent, truths. Our recollections filter out pain, airbrush fear, and reshape discomfort into coherence, sanding down rough edges and sharp corners. Even the scientific revolutions of our past—shifting from geocentrism to heliocentrism, from creationism to the theory of evolution—remind us how often humanity has been confidently, collectively wrong.

Wells's genius was to flip the whole frame on its head: The future isn't *unknowable*, as such—it is just unfamiliar. What makes it frightening isn't its complexity but our instinct to measure it against the false certainty of hindsight.

Humanity, he believed, was at that time on the cusp of a new capability: the capacity to look forward not with superstition or mysticism but with reason. With inductive logic. With evidence. Just as we'd once charted the stars or codified the laws of motion, we would now begin to discover the future—by studying signals, identifying patterns, projecting their arcs ahead.

This was a radical (and radically optimistic) view. Yet for more than a century, from the macro perspective, Wells's vision was largely borne out. We built tools to extend our foresight: models, forecasts, data pipelines, scenario maps. We learned to project curves and anticipate the forces shaping what lay ahead. Science illuminated the universe around us like never before. We decoded the genome, captured sunlight in photovoltaic cells, turned atoms into virtually free and unlimited energy.

But today, something even more radical is happening.

We are no longer merely discovering the future. We are designing it.

This distinction is not just semantic—it is civilizational. More than a century ago, Wells stood at an inflection point and foretold the era that was just beginning to unfold; we now stand at another inflection point—with a new and different era coming into sharper focus by the day.

Humanity, as a species, is moving from inductive curiosity to creative authorship. From passive analysis to active construction. We are no longer merely deciphering nature's code; we are rewriting it.

Consider this: For most of history, we lived in what H. G. Wells called the "legal view" of time—a mindset that looked backward for certainty. Naturally enough, this view prized precedent, order, lineage. It sought comfort in what had already been done because what had already been done felt knowable. But Wells proposed a different orientation: a *creative* mindset—one that doesn't just tolerate uncertainty but thrives in it. A mindset that sees the unknown not as a threat but as a canvas.

He didn't use the term *adaptive intelligence*, but this is precisely the mindset he was describing. And today, a century after Wells's speech, it is becoming the defining skill set of our age: the ability to see beyond yesterday's rules, to question inherited models, to see and shape outcomes in an age when the pace of change outstrips our ability to predict it.

And here's the twist—the subtle but essential evolution of Wells's idea.

He believed, correctly, that we could forecast broad societal trends and make population-level predictions with some degree of accuracy, using science and reason. What he didn't anticipate is that individuals, people like you and me, could become agents of that future. Not fortune tellers but fortune shapers.

This isn't mystical. It's practical: When the pace and variety of change accelerate, as we learned in chapter 3, your prior experiences become maladaptive. The heuristics that once helped you navigate the world begin to fail. But if you learn to pause—to resist the reflexive urge to apply old rules to new terrain, as we discussed in chapter 7—you can begin to think differently, stop confusing familiarity with truth, and stop assuming that history is a guidepost, rather than a constraint.

This is not easy. But it is possible. Especially in a world where certain contours of the future are already becoming visible: AI. Robotics. Genomic engineering. Human–machine convergence. Climate instability. Space colonization. These are not abstract possibilities. They are directional certainties. It's one thing, in this context, to use AI as a tool; it's a different matter altogether to outsource your decision-making and agency to it. In either case, though, the IQ-driven aspect of holistic intelligence becomes less differentiated as technologies rise, leaving adaptability as a crucial human advantage.

The question is not which future is coming. The question is more fundamental: *Who will write it?*

The people with high AQ—the ones who can step out of the legal view and into the creative one—are already doing just that. They aren't psychics or mind readers; they're builders. They don't have secret knowledge, but they do have a different posture: one that embraces complexity, interrogates assumptions, and acts with intentionality, even when the full map is unclear.

We are stepping across a threshold that no civilization has ever crossed before. From discovering what *is* to authoring *what comes next*. The future, at last, is not something that happens to us. It is something we are learning to make.

We are leaving behind the read-only world. Ahead lies a read-to-write future.

From Forecast to Foresight

Wells taught us to look forward with reason; the practice of AQ goes a step further. But it isn't like reading palms or tarot cards. Instead, you might think of it as disciplined foresight.

Once again, chaos theory gives us the appropriate frame: Systems can be unpredictable in detail but predictable in scope. That's the crux of the challenge we're up against. You won't know the precise move, the exact day, the single failure mode. But you can often map the envelope it will all happen inside.

This is where your practice of the full methodology we discussed earlier in the book becomes concrete. Phase II (simulation) is how you predict scope: Sketch the problem space, run scenarios, refine your hypothesis.

Then, Phase III (experimentation) is how you resolve the details: Test your way into the unknown, watch what breaks, and then feed the signal back into the model.

Simulation for scope and to develop your hypothesis. Experimentation for real-world feedback. Loop until you stop learning.

Godlike Powers, Unknown Frontiers

The implications of the seismic shift we're experiencing—and indeed its direct consequences—are staggering. Because the technologies now breaking through—genome editing, fusion energy, artificial intelligence—offer almost godlike capabilities.

We are crossing thresholds our ancestors could only frame in myth: Prometheus stealing fire. Daedalus flying on homemade wings. Gods breathing artificial life into clay—or, in our case, crafting it from silicon and code.

In the past, humanity's greatest leaps came from discovering forces or uncovering realities that had always been there—gravity, electromagnetism, DNA—and then learning how to divine, decode, and harness them to our own ends. We were students of the universe, extracting its secrets with tools barely sharper than superstition.

Now, for the first time, we are becoming authors of reality itself.

We are moving from reading the genome to editing it—snipping, patching, reshuffling the code of life not unlike a Microsoft Word document. From trapping sunlight on fragile rooftop panels to igniting fusion, we're conjuring the powerful reactions that burn at the heart of stars. From building computers that solve problems we must program to building intelligences that outpace us, teach themselves, open possibilities human minds might never have conceived.

The capabilities already in our hands are astonishing. But even more staggering are the ones we can't yet name. History is proving once again that the most significant disruptions—the ones that redraw the map—rarely come from where you expect. They erupt sideways: from surprising or unexpected collisions between fields once thought disconnected. From the second- and third-order consequences of tools we barely understand. From intersections no forecast ever plotted.

This is not theoretical. It is already happening—if you know where to look.

The Front Lines of the Read-to-Write Age

ROBOTICS

In Boston and Tokyo and Shenzhen, autonomous machines are much more than the clumsy novelties they appeared to be in viral videos a decade ago. Today's robots move with uncanny precision, can pick up delicate objects, and routinely collaborate with humans as fully participating teammates, not just tools. New generations of soft robotics—machines that bend and flex like living tissue—are poised to infiltrate agriculture, surgery, disaster recovery, and eldercare. In some hospitals, robotic nurses are already assisting in surgery with millimeter-perfect steadiness, achieving outcomes beyond the reach of any human hand.

And when these robots aren't being programmed, line by line? They're learning. They're adapting their movements through trial, error, and machine vision in ways even their creators can't fully explain. Powered by emerging visual-language-action models (VLAs or VLMs), these systems integrate sight, instruction, and motion by watching a task, interpreting a human command, and translating it directly into physical behavior. In essence, they don't just see or read; they comprehend and act. It's the first step toward AI that learns not by code alone but by experience: absorbing the world not unlike how we do, through perception, feedback, and adjustment.

This is more than automation. It's embodied intelligence.

Robots once required carefully structured environments—clean, repeatable settings where every variable could be tightly controlled. The classic image was an arm on an assembly line: precise but utterly dumb.

Now, thanks to advances in sensor fusion, computer vision, and reinforcement learning, machines are beginning to handle the chaos of real-world conditions. They can navigate cluttered warehouses. Recognize human gestures. Grasp objects of varying softness or irregularity without crushing or dropping them.

In agriculture, autonomous harvesters are learning to distinguish ripe from unripe fruit, factoring in color, size, and even subtle changes in reflectivity. In eldercare, assistive robots are helping patients out of bed, managing medication schedules, and providing basic companionship. In disaster zones, snakelike or wheeled robots are venturing into collapsed buildings, searching for survivors where no human rescuer could safely go.

And crucially, many of these systems aren't just reacting—they're improving. Using reinforcement learning, robots can now experiment within safe boundaries, learning from success and failure. In the best systems, this loop runs continuously: *perception → action → feedback → adaptation*. It's not yet true autonomy, but it's getting closer.

The next frontier? General-purpose robotics. Not just machines built for one narrow task but adaptable bodies that can learn new ones on the fly. Think robotic arms that switch from assembling electronics to preparing a meal. Or home assistants that can fold laundry one hour and help a child with homework the next.

This vision has long felt distant—always "ten years away." But recent advances suggest it may finally be within striking distance. The fusion of tactile sensing, real-time learning, and foundational AI models trained across billions of interactions is creating systems that can generalize across tasks and environments.

The implications aren't insignificant. This isn't just about warehouse logistics or food delivery. It's about the nature of labor itself—what it means to have hands, to touch, to move with purpose in a physical world. The cost curves are shifting, and the threshold for robotic utility is dropping fast.

As these machines become more capable, the questions become sharper: Who controls them? Who programs their priors? Who do they serve, and who do they displace? Those answers aren't technical. They're human. And we'll need to decide them before the machines learn to do much more than we ever intended.

QUANTUM ENGINEERING

Meanwhile, in hidden laboratories in Zurich, Santa Barbara, and Shanghai, engineers are coaxing fragile qubits into coherence. Still in their infancy, quantum computers promise to smash through the complexity barriers that block today's supercomputers.

They will model chemical reactions atom by atom. Crack encryption systems in minutes. Design new materials, new drugs, new logistical systems—none of which can be adequately modeled by classical systems. And just beyond the horizon, quantum networks—secure communication channels built from entangled particles—are already beginning to whisper across cities. The first glimmers of an unhackable new internet are taking shape.

Here's why this matters: Classical computers, no matter how powerful, process information in binary bits of zero or one. But quantum systems use qubits, which can exist in a superposition of states. That means they can represent both zero and one simultaneously and, thanks to entanglement, the state of one qubit can be linked to another across space. In theory, this gives quantum machines the ability to evaluate vast numbers of possibilities at once, rather than linearly testing them one by one.

For certain types of problems—like simulating the behavior of electrons in a complex molecule or optimizing a supply chain with trillions of permutations—this shift isn't just incremental. It's exponential. It's the difference between spending a millennium and a millisecond on the same problem.

This is why governments and corporations are pouring billions into quantum R&D. Why Microsoft, IBM, and Google are racing alongside startups like Rigetti and PsiQuantum. And why military and intelligence agencies are watching the field with rising urgency: The day quantum decryption becomes viable, every classical encryption scheme in use today—from bank records to state secrets—becomes instantly obsolete.

But raw power is only part of the story. What quantum engineers are building isn't just a faster calculator. It's a fundamentally new substrate for computation—one that's probabilistic, not deterministic; fragile, not stable; and governed by rules that don't exist at macroscopic scales. Qubits decohere at the slightest vibration or thermal shift. Error correction is a full-time battle. Scaling to hundreds or thousands of useful qubits remains one of the grand engineering challenges of our time.[i]

Still, breakthroughs are coming. As far back as 2019, Google's Sycamore processor completed a specific computation in two hundred seconds that would have taken a classical supercomputer an estimated ten thousand years. The practical value of that particular task was debatable—but the message was clear: This is real. And it's accelerating.

If even a fraction of their potential is realized, quantum systems will redefine the boundaries of what's computationally possible. The frontier won't just move. It will recede faster than we can possibly chase it, exposing entire new terrains for discovery, disruption, and risk.

We're not there yet. But we are close enough to hear the hum of something powerful on the other side.

SPACE TECHNOLOGY

Private spaceflight, once science fiction, has now been routine for the better part of a decade. Rockets land themselves, dropping from the sky with the precise confidence of birds of prey. SpaceX has made it almost boring to watch a first-stage booster touch down on a floating barge in the ocean.

---

i Quantum technologies generally fall into three domains: quantum computing, which uses qubits to process information in superposition; quantum communication, which exploits quantum entanglement to enable ultrasecure data transfer; and quantum sensing, which uses quantum effects to achieve extraordinary precision in measurement and navigation. Here, I'm referring specifically to computing, but the same underlying physics is driving breakthroughs across all three fields.

More than five hundred such landings have occurred. What was once a moonshot-sized dream is now a simple fact of engineering, a line item.

Meanwhile, small, cheap satellite constellations are carpeting low Earth orbit, delivering real-time surveillance, communications, and intelligence at planetary scale. Where a single government-run satellite once cost millions (at least) and launched once per decade, today's microsats ride into orbit by the dozen, upgrading every few years like smartphones. The view from above has never been sharper—or more crowded.

What we're watching is not just an industrial shift. It's a civilizational shift: the transition from Earth-centric infrastructure to space-enabled systems.

Startups are designing lunar infrastructure. Not just landers and rovers, but power grids, mining platforms, autonomous construction units. NASA's Artemis program is laying the groundwork for a permanent lunar presence, and companies like Intuitive Machines, Astrobotic, and Blue Origin are already on contract to deliver hardware. Lunar regolith, once the stuff of grainy photos and mid-century museum displays, is an emerging asset class.

Others are preparing to mine asteroids for platinum-group metals. Develop satellite-based manufacturing, taking advantage of microgravity to produce semiconductors, pharmaceuticals, and alloys that can't be replicated on this (or any) planet. Or capture solar energy in orbit and beam it wirelessly back to Earth. SpaceX is already moving in this direction. In early 2026, the company announced plans to launch what's known as a "Dyson swarm" of potentially millions of satellites—designed to harvest sunlight and beam power back to Earth, free from the cooling and energy constraints throttling terrestrial AI infrastructure. It is, in miniature, the first serious attempt to treat the sun itself as a power grid, a prospect that (until now) has been the realm of science fiction.[ii]

And while astronauts still grab headlines, the farther we extend outward, the more control will shift to autonomous systems. There's simply

ii We currently think the universe is 93 billion light years across. So far, humans have traveled one light second—and even Voyager 1, launched nearly fifty years ago, has yet to travel even a single light day, despite currently traveling at 38,000 mph!

no other option. Communication delays make real-time human communication impossible once you go far enough: Mars is twenty minutes away by radio; the Kuiper Belt might as well be in another century.

With no hope of intervention or even advice from Earthbound controllers in case of emergency, this means orbital stations, surface bases, and long-haul transit vehicles will increasingly be operated by AI—not just monitored but actively managed. Resource allocation, system diagnostics, collision avoidance, power distribution, even repair routines—these will be automated, not because it's cheaper, but because it's required.

We're entering an era of machine-mediated exploration, where human oversight is strategic, not tactical. The astronauts of the future may spend more time interfacing with software than steering spacecraft.

This shift brings real strategic consequences. Space is no longer just a far-off frontier, a stage for grand exploration. It's an increasingly accessible domain of infrastructure, logistics, and power projection. It also represents the ultimate strategic high ground. The first country—or company—to master orbital manufacturing, deep-space refueling, or lunar mining will hold leverage not just economically, but geopolitically.

The question is no longer if we will become a spacefaring species. It's how—and under whose control. Because when infrastructure moves off-planet, so does sovereignty. And in the vacuum beyond Earth, the most decisive force won't be muscle or mass. It will be autonomy: decisions made faster, cleaner, and often without us.

HEALTH CARE

In the health care space, AI isn't just analyzing X-rays better than radiologists. It's predicting disease before symptoms appear and training itself on invisible patterns buried in genomic data, patient histories, and environmental-exposure maps. In some hospital systems, machine learning models are already capable of flagging early-stage cancers, sepsis risk, and cardiovascular anomalies before human clinicians would typically act. The model doesn't diagnose, per se; in a way, it anticipates.

This isn't just a new tool in the proverbial doctor's bag. It's a new diagnostic layer—one that operates silently, in the background, scanning millions of data points that no human mind could hold in working memory.

CRISPR-based therapies, meanwhile, are moving from theory to trial. In the US and UK, the first FDA-approved gene-editing treatments for sickle cell disease and beta thalassemia are in motion. And these aren't just treatments; they're potential cures—designed to rewrite the faulty genetic code at the source. The implications go far beyond rare blood disorders. Gene editing is being explored for muscular dystrophy, certain cancers, and even heart disease. What used to be considered "inherited fate" may soon become an editable variable.

And while these breakthroughs grab headlines, an even quieter revolution is unfolding on your wrist.

Wearable devices are evolving from passive trackers to active agents. They're no longer just counting steps or measuring heart rate. They're detecting arrhythmias before you notice them. Delivering insulin in real time based on dynamic glucose predictions. Adjusting dosages, nudging behaviors, syncing with other health systems—all without waiting for a physician's order.

In some cases, the system doesn't just monitor your condition, it intervenes. Automatically. Preemptively. And we're only at the beginning. Emerging wearables will monitor hormone levels, stress markers, even shifts in your microbiome. Implantables may continuously monitor blood chemistry. Smart fabrics could detect dehydration or electrolyte imbalance. The body becomes a sensor array—and the machine becomes your continuous care team.

In the near future, health care won't be a matter of periodic checkups. It will be an ongoing negotiation between biology and machine intelligence. And that negotiation will be managed not in the clinic, but in the cloud.

The result is that health care will move from reactive to predictive. From generic to personal. From physician-led to AI-augmented—where the human role is elevated but no longer central in every decision.

Which raises deep questions: What happens when your body is surveilled at all times—even if it's for your own benefit? Who owns that data? Who decides when a nudge becomes a directive? Who is liable when an algorithm misfires, misdiagnoses, or otherwise makes a consequential mistake?

The old boundaries—between patient and provider, treatment and prevention, autonomy and automation—are starting to blur. And the questions raised by this moment are as much about ethics, governance, and trust as they are about biology. Because when the most important decisions about your health are made silently, continuously, and invisibly—who, exactly, is in control?

Converging Fronts, Compounding Disruption

What's coming is not *one* shift. It is the confluence of many, coming at us faster and at a scale that no human civilization has ever seen.

AI will not merely replace coders or artists. It will fuse with biotechnology, with energy systems, with defense, with supply chains. It will seep like water into the cracks of every other industry, accelerating shifts, creating new markets and killing old ones.

Fusion energy, when it arrives at scale, will not simply provide a cheaper power source. It will reorder global alliances, industrial strategy, and even domestic politics as the old calculus of scarcity collapses. For most of human history, progress has been bounded by energy cost, which represents a hard ceiling on what we can build, move, or sustain. When that ceiling falls, everything changes. A world where the highest input cost approaches zero isn't just richer; it's unrecognizable relative to the world we live in today. Entire industries built on extraction and constraint lose their leverage. Geopolitical power shifts from those who own resources to those who can innovate fastest. Economic models break. The arrival of abundant, clean fusion would mark not an incremental step forward but the crossing of a civilizational threshold—one of those rare moments when humanity crosses from managing scarcity to engineering possibility.

Gene editing will not just eliminate certain inherited diseases. It will force us to redefine categories we thought were fixed: what it means to be healthy, what it means to be *human*, what it means to live and learn and compete fairly in a world where biological limits can be selectively removed—where some can upgrade while others cannot.

And as these waves collide—as AI enables faster biotech breakthroughs, new energy sources unlock new kinds of computation, and synthetic biology invents new materials—the ripple effects will multiply exponentially.

Old models will fail. Existing forecasts will shatter. Our instincts, which were created and trained in an older, slower world, will betray us with rising regularity and worsening consequences.

In this environment, the AQ process becomes more than a personal or organizational advantage. It becomes a necessity. A precondition for relevance. A survival skill for authors of the future.

Two Roads Diverged . . .

What lies ahead is a storm of innovation—and a storm of failure.

Some industries will boom. Others will vaporize. Some companies and organizations will adapt and flourish. Others will cling to the past and crumble.

You can already start to predict who the winners might be—not by looking at who has the shiniest technology today but by evaluating whether they've built AQ into their DNA.

For instance, imagine two startup founders facing the coming AI-biotech-energy collision.

One is a celebrated domain expert: She has a PhD from a top university and twenty years of experience in a prestigious field. She builds carefully. She optimizes relentlessly. She knows the rules and how to play the game better than anyone.

The other (rival) founder is a relative unknown: She dropped out of college. She cross-trains mentally across physics, software, philosophy, and synthetic biology. She experiments constantly. She is willing to rip up her own business model every six months if the landscape shifts. She hires people smarter than her in adjacent fields and listens when they disagree.

Which one do you bet on?

In a stable, linear world, there's a reasonably strong case for backing the expert. But in a convergent, chaotic, read-to-write world, you back the adaptive polymath ten times out of ten—the one who lives in uncertainty, senses pattern shifts early, updates models ruthlessly, and keeps enough humility to change faster than the facts demand.

The Triarchic Mind: IQ, EQ . . . and AQ

Recall for a moment the triarchic model of intelligence we unpacked in chapter 2 that was delineated by IQ, EQ, and AQ. In a read-to-write age, how will human cognition meet the moment?

IQ is increasingly off-loadable. AI can simulate large swaths of what looks like reasoning—especially the fast, patterned, System 1 stuff—and it can even begin to scaffold parts of slower analysis. It's powerful, but it still amounts to statistical mimicry: convergent, probabilistic "thinking," not understanding. For now.

Because what's coming just a little further down the road—the Fifth Industrial Revolution and the Third Cognitive Revolution—will push this boundary further still. As intelligence becomes an ambient utility, embedded in every tool and surface, even the act of reasoning begins to detach from biology. Neural implants, brain–machine interfaces, and memory-augmented prosthetics will start to make raw processing power effectively commoditized. IQ itself thus becomes less a personal endowment than a shared substrate; it becomes something uploadable, transferable, upgradeable.

In that world, the differentiator won't be how much information you can store or process. It will be how well you can direct it. The edge shifts from intelligence to intentionality, from knowing to choosing. The challenge of the coming age isn't competing with synthetic cognition—it's ensuring we remain authors of it.

Meanwhile, at least to a degree, EQ is imitable. A model can mirror tone, cadence, and even a semblance of empathy. It can *feel* convincing. But, of course, it isn't really feeling in any meaningful sense; there's no inner life, no consciousness or meaning behind the words.

AQ is different. It cannot be off-loaded. It is the human act of mapping new states, testing to the edges, coming up with an answer from outside the known set, rewriting your own playbook in real time. It is the optimal cognitive stabilizer in volatile conditions: the discipline that keeps you methodical when anxiety pushes you toward quick fixes or tribal reflexes. AQ gives IQ and EQ direction; where IQ and EQ are tools with which to navigate the terrain around you, AQ helps you update the map itself.

If you want to pick winners in the new reality we're stepping into, use the triarchic lens.

- **IQ:** Can they marshal tools (including AI) to think faster and cleaner?
- **EQ:** Can they move humans—align teams, customers, partners—without manipulation?
- **AQ:** When the terrain shifts, do they update or do they insist?

Back the mind that can do all three—and, when in doubt, select for the one that treats AQ as most important.

You can already see the outlines of this emerging. The best AI founders today aren't just engineers—they're students of psychology, linguistics, energy markets, global geopolitics. The smartest biotech founders aren't just biologists—they're AI natives, literate in machine learning, comfortable building across the seams where disciplines melt together. The energy revolutionaries aren't just physicists—they're systems thinkers, network builders, incentive designers. They're ready to architect entirely new industrial ecosystems.

The Invisible Handoff

Across every sector, from science to defense to business to art, a single force pulses beneath, above, and through everything.

AI is the water in which future innovation will swim. It doesn't just assist. It augments, accelerates—*and replaces*. Not all human labor. Not all thought. But some. And more every day.

At first, as we've all experienced, this seems like a gift: an explosion of productivity. A new, synthetic superpower we can wield at will. Why spend a morning reviewing resumes when an algorithm can do it in milliseconds? Why struggle to diagnose an illness when AI spots patterns no radiologist can? Why spend dozens of hours, across days or weeks, reading entire books when a machine can instantaneously condense and serve up the best insights from even the densest tome?

But every time we hand over a task, a judgment, a moment of reflection—we hand over a thread of authorship. Not all at once, however, and not dramatically. Incrementally. Invisibly. And with each accumulating handoff—one more small task, one more minor decision, one more itch to scratch—we surrender something subtle but essential: human agency.

If we are not conscious, if we do not actively reclaim our agency and cultivate adaptive thinking, we will drift into a life of reaction, shaped not by our own deliberation but by algorithmic reflex.

The water will keep heating, degree by degree, until we do not even realize we are boiling: We'll be living our lives on rails we did not lay, within systems we do not fully understand, optimized toward goals we never explicitly chose.

The AlphaGo Moment

We've already covered the story of AlphaGo, the DeepMind AI that, in 2016, defeated the world champion Lee Sedol in a historic match of the ancient board game Go.

In that particular matchup, it was game two that changed

everything—when, on move thirty-seven, AlphaGo did something no human player would ever have considered.

But, of course, it wasn't a mistake; it was a masterstroke. AlphaGo won the match, and *how* it won revealed something deeper: It wasn't just "smarter" than its human opponent. It was, from the perspective of human thinking, totally alien—playing an entirely different game with a different map of possibility.

In that moment, it appeared as though AlphaGo had accessed something rare and precious: true beginner's mind. The ability to see a problem without the accumulated blinders of experience and without the sediment of old strategies, assumptions, habits. Where human experts saw familiar patterns, AlphaGo saw raw possibility—because there was no history to cling to, no habits to protect, no prestige to preserve.

In deep-learning systems, we are creating something astonishing and alien: a mind that "knows" without knowing how it knows. And we are beginning to trust those answers—because they are often faster, cheaper, and more accurate than anything we can produce ourselves.

And yet.

That alien brilliance comes with an alien blindness.

AI sees patterns but has no idea what it sees. It "understands" language but has no comprehension of meaning. It recommends treatments, investments, policies—but doesn't know, in any meaningful sense of the word, why. At least, not in a way you or I would recognize.

AI systems operate in opaque layers of computation, in mathematical matrices stacked by the millions. They train on vast data sets that are often scraped from the messy, biased underbelly of human behavior. But so much of what makes them genuinely superhuman in speed, precision, and scale also makes them woefully deficient in other areas.

AI, for all its power, lacks what makes human thinking *human*. It has no ethics, no morality—no internal compass to judge whether a decision is right or wrong beyond the cold parameters of optimization. It has no true creativity, only extrapolation. It has no conscience. No curiosity. No dreams. No unconscious. No full set of senses.

It can remix, simulate, and combine—but the kind of imaginative leap that produced relativity, penicillin, jazz music, or the concept of democracy lies well outside its reach. It doesn't experience the world through sight, touch, taste, pain, or wonder; its "knowledge" emerges from layers of computation so dense and opaque that even its creators cannot explain how it arrives at its conclusions.

AI functions in an unbounded reality, untethered from the emotional anchors and cognitive biases that shape, and so often trip up, human thought. It does not fear or doubt or hope. It has never experienced, nor can it conceive of, love, grief, or awe. It can approximate values—but not embody them. It doesn't care about truth or justice or beauty. It only optimizes—toward whatever objective or predefined goal it has been programmed to pursue—to maximize engagement, minimize churn, reduce latency, increase profit.

We are increasingly deferring to these systems for one simple reason: because they work. They outperform us in a growing number of domains. They are fast, frictionless, profitable. Their answers *feel* like certainty because AI can be convincing: It can mimic human tone. Empathy. Insight. It can, of course, even write "poetry." Compose "music." Generate "art."

But optimization is not morality. Efficiency is not wisdom.

The illusion of humanlike understanding is part of the trap. Because if the answers sound right, if the results are good, if the outcomes are profitable—who cares if the system understands why?

We do. We must. Because the cost of not knowing what our tools are optimizing for is that we're slowly but inexorably optimizing ourselves out of the story.

A Slow Surrender

Already, the erosion of human agency is all around us.

At the airport, AI flags passengers for extra screening based on opaque behavioral models.

In hospitals, AI systems decide which patients get follow-up care first.

In hiring, algorithms determine who gets an interview and who is filtered out, long before a human sees a single job application.

Online, our feeds are filtered by engagement-maximizing engines that learn not what we value, but what will keep us scrolling. We do not select information so much as *information selects us.*

In politics, AI-driven microtargeting is reshaping democracy. Political campaigns now deploy machine-learning models that craft individualized messages designed to bypass rational deliberation and trigger emotional reflexes. The citizen is no longer a participant in a debate of ideas; every voter is, in a sense, a target of competing psychological campaigns—optimized, segmented, nudged.

In geopolitics, autonomous cyberweapons are being developed to probe, penetrate, and retaliate at speeds no human commander can match. Diplomatic efforts struggle to keep pace with machine-accelerated escalation risks, and in some cases, state actors no longer fully control what their automated systems will do once certain thresholds are crossed.

In finance, markets now move at algorithmic speed. Flash crashes—bizarre, sudden collapses triggered by cascades of machine decisions—have sent shockwaves through global exchanges. Firms increasingly rely on AI to detect anomalies, manage portfolios, even predict geopolitical risks—and as they do, systemic vulnerabilities grow.

This isn't the future. This is the present. And these aren't isolated. They are signals of a deeper, accelerating shift: The world is being steered by systems optimized for performance—not for human values.

Now, we are face-to-face with it—right up against perhaps the most consequential hinge point of our time: building systems that "know" more than we do, and starting to outsource our agency to them, without fully understanding the consequences. Decisions once made by human hands and human minds—imperfect, biased, but still fundamentally conscious—are being shifted to black boxes.

And the more efficient, the more profitable, the more frictionless these systems become the less we'll question them. After all, why challenge the algorithm if it gets reliable results? Why insist on slower, more expensive, more fallible human judgment?

One day soon, we may wake up and realize that we have become "avatars" for these machines—that our role has been reduced to rubber-stamping choices made elsewhere, by systems we neither fully understand nor truly control. The more trust and authority we vest in these systems—implicitly or explicitly, by act or omission—the harder it becomes to wrest control of the wheel back from them. And unless we are extraordinarily deliberate about it, this means human agency will continue to erode—not dramatically, but invisibly, until it is gone.

The threat isn't Skynet. It isn't a robot uprising we need to fear. The real—and rising—danger is not that AI will kill us. It's that it will seduce us.

With competence. With convenience. With results. And in doing so, it will nudge us into a world where *we no longer get to decide.*

The ultimate threat is not that machines will turn against us. It's that we will willingly turn ourselves over to the machines, ceding authorship, ceding agency, allowing the water around us to heat up degree by degree, without even realizing we've done it. That we sleepwalk into a future where decisions are made for us by systems that optimize for goals we never fully chose, run logics we barely comprehend, and shape outcomes we never consciously authorized.

An Engine of Meaning

But this is not a moment for fear. It is a call for consciousness.

We've ushered in an age where the machinery of the future will run, with or without us. What's left to decide is whether we will still be in the driver's seat—or strapped silently into the back.

In the read-to-write age, human agency will not be protected by default. It will have to be claimed and reclaimed, defended, cultivated with discipline, with vigilance, with a willingness to stay uncomfortable, adaptive, alive.

Because AI, in the end, is not destiny. It is a tool; it is leverage. And leverage demands judgment.

The human brain—flawed, limited, gloriously emotional though it can be—remains the only engine of ethics, imagination, and meaning we've got.

Adaptability Quotient Field Guide: Key Takeaways

- **The future is no longer merely discovered.** Increasingly, it's designed. The shift from read-only to read-to-write is the defining development of our age.
- **In this dawning future, foresight replaces prediction; authorship replaces analysis.** Adaptive minds don't just forecast—they prototype reality.
- **Breakthroughs rarely arrive head-on.** They emerge from collisions between fields that were once thought to be disconnected.
- **Robotics, quantum computing, synthetic biology, and AI are not separate revolutions.** They are converging fronts of one transformation.
- **Adaptive advantage now depends less on expertise than on cross-domain literacy.** Our advantage is found in the ability to integrate, translate, and reframe.
- **The most dangerous loss isn't jobs—it's agency.** Each delegation to an algorithm is a small surrender of authorship.
- **Machines can simulate intelligence but not intention.** The moral calculus still belongs to us.
- **AI may expand capability, but human meaning, judgment, and imagination remain the irreducible engines of creation.** This is in part because adaptation at this scale requires more than (convergent) reaction—it demands (divergent/conscious) participation in shaping the systems shaping us.
- **You are not a passenger in your future.** You can be its driver.

13

The Most Extraordinary Machine

Man is not the creature of circumstances,
circumstances are the creatures of men.

—Benjamin Disraeli

We shall not cease from exploration
And the end of all our exploring
Will be to arrive where we started
And know the place for the first time.

—T. S. Eliot

We stand at the threshold of an extraordinary moment—not the end of human intelligence but its next great test.

For centuries, every major leap in civilization has come from expanding what our minds could reach: fire, language, tools, machines. Now we've built something that doesn't just extend our abilities but begins to mirror them—an intelligence that learns, iterates, and evolves. The question is no longer whether these systems will shape the future. It's whether we will still be active participants in shaping it.

But this is not a story about human decline. It's about human potential—about what happens when we remember that the most powerful form of intelligence on this planet isn't artificial. It's adaptive: It questions, updates, and chooses deliberately when the world changes faster than instinct can follow.

This final chapter is both a reminder—and a challenge. To step forward not as passengers of progress, but as its pilots. To wield the tools we've created without surrendering the agency that created them. To prove, in the decisive experiment of our time, that the human mind is still the most extraordinary machine on Earth.

Rewriting Fate

I've always tried to do the right things when it comes to my health. I work out regularly; I try to eat decently well, don't smoke or do drugs, and have never overindulged in alcohol. I stay active, maintain a degree of physical discipline. I push my body via endurance events, mountain biking, high-intensity sports like kitesurfing. And yet, no matter how many miles I pedal or how many vegetables I pile onto my plate, one thing never changes: I have high cholesterol.

It's hereditary—a hand-me-down coded into my DNA, passed from one generation to the next. (Thanks, Mom and Dad!)

For most of my adult life, the solution (since I'm loath to resort to medication in this instance) has been straightforward: Do your best. Eat better, move more, keep half an eye on the numbers; talk to my doctor if they get too stubborn. Manage the risk. Outsmart fate, or at least genetics, on the margins.

Then, not long ago, one of my sons mentioned something almost casually at the dinner table. There's a new experimental treatment, he told me: a CRISPR-based therapy that doesn't just manage high cholesterol, but *erases* it. One revision, a straightforward change to a single gene, and it's as if the risk was never there to begin with.

No more endless treadmill of prescriptions for those who need to rely on them. No more egg-white omelets; gone are the days of constant vigilance over breakfast choices and guilt after the extra cookie. No more invisible sword of Damocles hanging silently over your head. The mutation could simply be cut away, deleted like a typo.

At first blush, even on a conceptual level, the idea feels almost too clean, too sci-fi, too far removed from our slogging, messy existence to be real. But it's happening, here and now. And it points to something far deeper than a breakthrough in medicine, a shift so profound that language strains to capture it.

It's not just that we're stepping from "read-only" to "read-to-write," as we covered in the last chapter. That leap is already staggering enough as we trade in our role as observers and managers for something closer to authors and architects.

But in this moment, we're also living through an even sharper break. Because for the first time in history, the tools we are using to exert our will upon the world—tools like artificial intelligence—are not passive instruments but active agents. They do not merely extend our thinking; they make decisions of their own, *on* their own, crossing the line from amplification to true autonomy.

Blurred Lines

In each of the past three industrial revolutions that have reshaped world history, the technological leaps that powered each dawning era—steam engines, electrical grids, silicon microchips—amplified human ability but did not, in any sense, choose humankind's direction. The tools grew more powerful, but the hand wielding them remained a human one. The will, the imagination, the authorship belonged exclusively to us, as living, breathing, sentient individuals.

Those revolutions were disruptive, yes—but they were also anchored. The steam engine and assembly line were set against a world stabilized by churches, schools, neighborhoods, families, civic associations. Even cataclysms like world wars paradoxically acted as "cold stabilizers": They demanded collective effort, reinforced national myths, and reentrenched institutions of government, military, and community.

Even the digital revolution—the third of these massive leaps and the first to reorient our very way of thinking—kept human beings firmly in the driver's seat. Silicon chips allowed us to outsource memory and computation, but the work still began and ended with us. Emails, spreadsheets, search engines: These became revolutionary new tools we used, not environments we lived inside. They reorganized our workplaces and sped up our communications, but most of life still unfolded in an analog reality; if you were a theater kid in high school, you still walked past the jocks and burnouts in the hallways. Physical heterogeneity imposed a shared reality, however messy.

Now, for the first time, that center of gravity is shifting.

The Fourth Industrial Revolution differs in kind, not just in degree. Because AI isn't only a tool. Increasingly, people treat it as a substrate: the cognitive surface on which their reasoning takes place. We are no longer just outsourcing memory or arithmetic; we are outsourcing judgment. Instead of being a partner somewhere in the middle of a process, AI is becoming the process *itself*.

That is a more profound break than many people realize. When systems can propose actions, synthesize options, and optimize toward goals without human authorship, the lines between tool and agent, and between human choice and machine suggestion, begin to blur. And when those systems are woven into every layer of communication—shaping what we read, narrowing what we see, curating what we "like"—they don't just assist or accelerate our thinking. They reroute it.

Living Through the Second Cognitive Revolution

What we're living through is not just another technological leap. It's a Second Cognitive Revolution—and with it comes something more disorienting and more insidious than risk: uncertainty.

As we've covered, chaos theory tells us that systems can be unpredictable in detail but still predictable in scope. This isn't random drift; it's bounded instability. And in moments like this, individuals and societies get drawn into what scientists call *attractor states*. They're the basins that human behavior slides into when the ground starts shifting. Anthropologist Claude Lévi-Strauss described "cold" societies that seek fixed-point attractors: stable myths, repetitive rituals, anchors that resist change. By contrast, "hot" societies gravitate toward chaotic attractors: turbulence, novelty, bounded instability.

Of course, Pierre Bourdieu gave us another useful lens: habitus, which describes the lived structures of culture that quietly channel us back into collective patterns. Your social position, your environment, your expectations—all of these shape which attractor basin you're likely to fall into when the old anchors start to break.

Right now, we're watching three broad reactions play out simultaneously.

Some retreat to old stabilizers (in technical jargon, *cold attractors*). They cling to anchors that no longer map to the new regime, express anger at the pace of change, and use technology as a shield rather than a bridge—disappearing into deep-web groups, nostalgia for traditional roles, or conspiratorial communities that feel like refuge but are really echo chambers.

On the other hand, some attach to the new state but only through shallow stabilizers (*chaotic attractors*). They surf novelty but without deeper change—we're talking fast fashion, influencer cycles, identity fluidity, algorithmic microtribes. It looks like agency but is tethered entirely to external signals.

And then there's the third path: adaptive intelligence. Which may have come up once or twice in the preceding pages.

My point is that all of the above illustrates and underscores why this revolution feels different. The "cold stabilizers" are weaker. Fewer people belong to churches or civic groups. Communities are less rooted. Wars, when they come, lack the unifying clarity that rallies and unifies a fractious population, instead dividing us further. The anchors that once moored society are loosening just as the pace of technological change accelerates to near-light speed.

That is what makes this moment uniquely destabilizing, even dangerous: The tools we use are also simultaneously reshaping the framework in which we live. AI is not just amplifying cognition; it is externalizing attention, flattening human difference into homogenous digital cliques, accelerating the drift into synthetic echo chambers. The theater kids never have to bump into the jocks ever again; even in the same physical space, everyone can disappear into their own algorithmic corridor, convinced *they* are the center of truth.[i]

And yet—this is precisely where adaptive intelligence becomes non-negotiable.

When I sit across the dinner table from my kids, who are now in their twenties, these questions stop being philosophical. They become urgent, intimate, real. Because the future already unfolding around us will not just shape what jobs they do or what technologies they use. In a real sense, it will shape *who they become*. It will determine whether they live their lives as human agents—thinking, deciding, steering—or as digital avatars, carried along by forces they no longer control.

I try to be honest with them. They're adults now; we can have frank conversations about the dangers. About how AI can synthesize but not create beyond its set. About how a clever simulation of intuition (System 1) is not the same as true consciousness or deliberate reasoning (System 2). About how satisfying an algorithm's prediction is not the same as providing truth.

But I also refuse to bury the hope. Because if this era demands anything from us it is this: to resist both forms of drift. To resist the false cognitive stabilizers of System 1, which lull us into mistaking convenience for comprehension, as well as the false social stabilizers of the digital habitus in

i If you don't have kids or otherwise haven't had occasion to visit a middle or high school recently, it's eye-opening. When I was a kid, the passing periods between classes were loud, chaotic, and fun as we poured into the hallways and crammed in every possible minute of socializing with friends as we walked to our next classes. Today, school hallways are eerily silent; with their heads buried in their phones or earbuds shutting out the world, students change classes in silence and instead use passing periods to catch up on social media, every student alone together.

which we live and work, which seduce us into fixed tribes or chaos attractors online. True adaptation requires methodical action: choosing to map the new state rather than passively sliding into it.

AQ is the mindware upgrade that lets you step outside of both traps. It can serve as the optimal cognitive stabilizer in a world of weakening anchors. Instead of retreating into brittle myths or surfing shallow novelty, you can use technology to better map the real new world, not to numb yourself from it. In practical terms, what this means is constructing internal and external anchors of your own—communities that share in your practice of adaptive thinking, reflective habits that foster metacognition and telescoping—that can sharpen your self-awareness and enhance your coherence of "self," even as everything else churns.

This is deep adaptation: using tools to bring order out of chaos, rather than letting them dissolve your agency. If you understand your mindware and mental tools, you can decide when and how to off-load cognition and social formation. If you don't, you become a tool for others' incentives.

This does not mean avoiding AI. On the contrary: Used properly, it can be a powerful synthesizer, a bounded lever of consilience, a sounding board for ideas and organization.[ii] It can help impose order and linearity onto otherwise disorganized thoughts, in the way Marshall McLuhan once described language itself. But AI must remain a tool, never the substrate of human decision. The human must remain in the loop—always.

This is why ceding agency to AI is not a neutral act. Off-load the "wrong" parts—your slow thinking, your stabilizing practices—and you don't just lose control of a discrete task. You risk losing the very capabilities that make adaptation possible. AI can be a companion or a synthesizer. What it cannot be is your stabilizer. Only you can supply that.

If this era demands anything from us it is this: To stay awake and in

---

ii Indeed, this is precisely how I sometimes used tools like ChatGPT and Grok in refining the ideas that went into this book: laying out my thinking and asking it to react, research, probe for weaknesses, and reorganize in such a way that might make my thinking comprehensible to others.

control we need to stay adaptive. We must insist upon and fight for, again and again, something prior generations have always been able to take for granted: our humanity, our agency, our authorship. No matter how seductive the pull to drift, to defer, to let the machines drive.

The future, at least for now, is still writable. But it will not write itself in our favor by some lucky accident.

What the Machine Sees—and What It Never Will

Not long ago, I found myself listening to a short talk by Yann LeCun, Meta's chief AI scientist and one of the most influential minds in the field. He said something that snapped a few important things into focus for me.

Large language models, he argued—the backbone of so much of what we call AI today, as we've discussed—are effectively dead ends.

At first, that sounded extreme. Especially coming from someone like him. But as he unpacked it, it started to make perfect sense.

All an LLM does, after all, is predict the next word. That's it. Strip away the hype, the flashy interfaces, the anthropomorphic metaphors, and what you're left with is a machine that guesses the most probable word that comes next in a sequence.

It's statistical. Deterministic. Bounded by syntax and surface logic. Given a prompt, the model evaluates all the likely continuations, ranks them by probability, and outputs what's most plausible.

That's not intelligence—at least, not *true* intelligence. It's autocomplete on steroids.

But here's the deeper point: Predicting the next word is a *convergent* task. There are only so many valid answers in any context of any given language system. The space narrows as you go.

But meaning—real, human meaning—is *divergent*. It branches outward. It tolerates contradiction. It depends upon, even thrives in, nuance, ambiguity, imagination—qualities that aren't readily reducible to probability vectors.

So, yes, these models can perform astonishingly well in logic-heavy domains like coding, math, translation, summarization. But ask them how to rebuild a crime-ridden community, resolve a moral conflict, give people hope in the wake of a natural disaster, or imagine a new economic paradigm—and their limits begin to show.

LeCun took the critique a step further: "All we've reached so far," he said, "is System 1."

It's the perfect analogy: LLMs are fast, reactive, pattern-based. They're useful, and in fact quite powerful, not unlike our maladaptive System 1 superpower, but ultimately, and for the same reasons, they're also shallow, ineffective, even counterproductive or dangerous in the wrong context. This seems to be the high-water mark of all that this type of AI has achieved: to imitate the narrow part of cognition that operates automatically, like catching a ball or finishing a familiar sentence. It's (genuinely) an amazing accomplishment, but it leaves humans with a wide-open opportunity to use the superpower we've possessed all along (unleashed, naturally, by our new handbook for how and why to use it *now*).

What AI *hasn't yet* reached, or come close to reaching, is System 2—the slow, deliberative, effort*ful* reasoning that defines deep human thought. The capacity to think about thinking, simulate the future, iterate and adapt.

Which is, of course, the hinge of it all.

For all the awe these machines inspire, they still operate as glorified reflex engines. They don't *think*. They don't *reason*. They compute. At scale, yes—but still on rails.

They operate in a token space, processing symbolic units of language, pixels, or protein folds, depending on their domain. But, as LeCun argues, if we want machines to engage with the real world—messy, continuous, high-dimensional reality—we need a new architecture entirely.

One that doesn't just stack probabilities. One that builds what he calls a "world model."

Beyond Tokens

A world model, in LeCun's words, is what you and I—and every living creature—starts building in infancy.

You throw a ball. It arcs. It drops. You push a glass too close to the table's edge—it falls and breaks. You begin to predict outcomes long before you're capable of understanding the math or physics behind them. And you don't need language to do this; a puppy can build a world model. A house cat can plan a route to those leftovers you forgot to put away.

This is the basis of common sense, of reason—and of reason*ing*. Of the ability to imagine not just what *is*, but what might happen next. Which has been a central focus of this book on almost every page.

And today's dominant AI architectures just plain don't have it.

They don't plan without a human prompting them to do so. They can't simulate without exacting supervision and direction from human masters. They don't generalize across physical contexts. They're incapable of surprising themselves. They can't be truly curious. They very often dissolve into incoherence or wild extremism without close minding.

By contrast, the next-level systems that LeCun is now focused on—early versions of what he calls Joint Predictive Architectures (JPAs)—do not merely try to predict the next token. They try to predict the next *state of the world.* They embed inputs into an abstract latent space, reason within that space, and then project the outcome of hypothetical actions.

The objective is not to generate better sentences; it's to understand *consequences.*

If that sounds like science fiction, it's not. It's cognitive science. It's how we as human beings operate. We don't think in tokens, we think in representations: mental models, cause and effect. Possibility and risk. *Uncertainty*, in the parlance of AQ.

Today's LLMs can simulate coherence to a high degree of accuracy, at least relatively speaking. But they don't actually know, in any real or articulable sense, what they're saying. They lack persistent memory, embodied perception, and the ability to evaluate surprise—the gap between what they expect and what they observe.

All of which is essential for learning: the moment of friction. The "huh, that's weird" signal. The failure of prediction that sparks an unexpected thought, surprising connection, or fresh insight.

Knowing What You Know—and Why

My oldest son, Jack, has been deep in this work at our family office, researching where these systems are headed. His hunch, which seems exactly right to me, is that the real, earth-shaking breakthroughs in the AI space will come *after* LLMs, with JPAs and other models that don't just generate answers but can evaluate them, reflect on them, know what they know and, crucially, know *why*: the beginnings of metacognition. A prelude to self-awareness.

I was reminded of this again in a recent conversation with my mom, whose expertise for decades has been linguistics. We were talking about the AlphaGo story—about how the infamous Move 37, as it came to be known, initially looked like a mistake even to experts. Her question was simple and sharp: "Can a human player actually learn from Move 37?"

As it turns out, the uncomfortable answer is: *maybe not.*

Because the system that made the move can't explain *why* it did so. There's no commentary. No reasoning. No internal monologue or trail of thought to follow. Just the move itself—the output the machine came up with, utterly inexplicably, followed by the resulting outcome.

You can try to reverse engineer the logic. But that's not learning from a teacher. That's guessing at the instincts of an alien.

So we're back in the same tension: Today's AI systems can filter. They can compress. They can simulate. But they can't yet *think*—not for real. Not the way we do. Because they don't deliberate. They don't reflect. They don't build meaning through contradiction, context, or continuity over time.

Unfortunately, the more we mistake token prediction for understanding, the further we drift from what makes intelligence human in the first place.

What Comes Next

LeCun made one additional point I haven't stopped thinking about: Language, he said, isn't the pinnacle of intelligence, as so many of us might assume. It's an evolutionary shortcut.

We use language because it's discrete, compressible, and robust with regard to "noise" (in that it's harder to misunderstand than a grunt or a gesture). It's optimized for communication *not* comprehension. It is, after all, just another map. Our minds evolved in order to navigate the territory of the real world, which is vast and continuous. Unfolding. Full of motion, ambiguity, chaos. Multidimensional in a way language can approximate but never capture.

And that world, LeCun points out, turns out to be a great deal harder to model than a sentence.

If you want to build a system that reasons like a human, you don't just need more data or better prompts. You need a new kind of machine altogether—one that can observe, imagine, plan, and act. Not in a chat window, but in the messy, physical, high-dimensional space we call reality.

That's not something you get from scaling tokens. As any parent can tell you: It's something you grow, from the ground up.

The Most Extraordinary Machine

If you fed a human being all the written language ever produced, it would take them something like four hundred thousand years to digest it all. LLMs like OpenAI's models have ingested that much data in a handful of training cycles. On raw intake alone, the machines dwarf us. They will never be surpassed, nor seriously rivaled; we cannot possibly compete.

But here's the rub: By the time a human child is four years old, they've taken in more multidimensional information—from sight, sound, touch, emotion, contradiction, intuition—than any LLM possibly could (or possibly will for a long time).

And a child, of course, isn't *just* a language processor. Every infant and toddler is a ravenous sensory sponge, an inherently exploratory relational being, a self-constructing model of the universe far too complex to reduce to strings of text.

We see and perceive in dimensions that language can't fully capture. We sense things that machines can glancingly describe but never conceptualize: ultraviolet light, gravity, love, loss. We live in a world teeming with signals we barely understand—and yet we move through it with astonishing grace and relative ease, filtering and learning and adapting along the way.

The human brain remains, for all the technological miracles we've wrought, the most extraordinary machine we know. And its greatest gift isn't speed or memory or raw data compression.

It's the ability to *choose*: to override instinct, defy optimization, imagine out-of-set alternatives that no algorithm could ever suggest. In other words, to adapt.

We can overcome the "selfish gene." We can elect to be governed by self-restraint. We can love, forgive, rebel, dream far beyond anything that natural selection or pure logic could possibly dictate.

Which is, of course, precisely where the greatest danger lies in the age ahead.

It's not that machines will overpower or outreason us. It's that we'll choose not to use the extraordinary capabilities we already have. That we might, out of something resembling mere convenience, surrender our slow, difficult, glorious System 2 thinking—the very thing that makes us human—ceding its role to the palest (artificial) imitation.

It's the Superman problem all over again: The superpower is there, at your disposal. But it's taxing to deploy; using it carries a cost. It's difficult to fire up. So, in many situations, it becomes all too tempting to set the superpower aside, drift comfortably back into System 1 reactions, let the world move *us* instead of the other way around.

Yet . . . what an irony!

At the very moment when human agency has never mattered more—when the stakes are planetary, generational—we flirt with giving it all away out of sheer fatigue.

If we can resist that temptation—if we can stay awake, deliberate, adaptive—we will not just survive the Fourth Industrial Revolution. We will shape it.

What we need, collectively, is a new Macy Conference—a twenty-first-century gathering of minds not to build the next machine, but to rebuild the frameworks for human agency in a machine age. Interdisciplinary, across sectors, devoted to designing not just better algorithms but better anchors: cognitive, social, ethical. The original Macy Conferences helped birth the field of cybernetics, the science of feedback and control. This time, the stakes are higher: learning how to keep the human in the loop, not just technically but culturally, before the loop closes without us.

But if we don't choose this path—if we surrender agency in favor of speed and convenience—the future will still be built. It just won't be built by *us*. And the difference between those two potential futures will define everything that comes next.

MVP

I've felt a growing urgency in writing this book. Not the polished, academic kind of urgency—the kind that waits for every citation to be perfectly formatted, every idea to be peer-reviewed, and every page to be signed off in triplicate.

A different, more palpable urgency. The kind you feel when you observe a powerful storm gathering on the horizon, smell it on the air, feel it bearing down viscerally on you like a freight train, and know there's no time to waste. The kind you feel when the future is looming awfully large, rushing at you faster than gatekeepers and experts and bureaucrats can catch up.

That's why I rushed to get this book onto shelves, and into your hands, as fast as I reasonably could—as soon as I had a minimum viable product, or *MVP*, in the language of startups. Not perfect, and (like any map) not complete. But real, ready, and made for this moment. A practical handbook, a field guide you can use, right now, in a world that isn't waiting for slow deliberation in pursuit of pristine theories. Because if you wait around for "perfect," the future will already have moved on.

Apart from the sections relating my own perspective and lived experience, I'm an expert in relatively little of what I've covered here. Nor am I infallible, though of course no one is—especially not when the underlying science is evolving daily, when yesterday's breakthroughs become today's assumptions and then decay into tomorrow's artifacts. As a result, I'm sure that some of what's in these pages will soon be outdated, superseded, in need of updating.

That's how it should be. And it reflects the realities of living in a read-to-write world.

But my hope is that that's *also* what gives this book its value.

This is not meant to be a perfect map. It's intended to serve as a kind of quick reference guide—a Rosetta stone for AQ that weaves together scattered insights that would otherwise stay buried in books, white papers, journal articles, university lectures, startup memos, and late-night conversations among the kinds of serially successful people we've been referencing as our control group. It's my attempt to synthesize what's happening across fields, to pull it out of silos and into the light where anyone willing to think, to stretch, to adapt, can use it to help get a running start.

You shouldn't need a PhD to navigate the future. You shouldn't have to read a thousand books or stitch together scientific findings across a thousand domains just to know how to move through the world. You shouldn't have to be a polymath or a futurist to claim your agency as a human being.

You should have a set of mental tools you can pick up and use, starting today.

That's what this book is meant to be. More even than a software upgrade for your mind, as I described at the outset, I hope you'll find it a practical playbook for a time when theory alone won't save you.

If you come away from these pages with a clearer sense of *how you think, how your lens distorts reality, how to adapt, how to stay agile and awake when the world starts changing faster than your instincts want it to*, then this book will have done its job. Democratizing this "secret knowledge" is the limit of my ambition. I'm not an oracle, and I don't pretend to have any idea of exactly what's coming. No one does; that's the point.

But the people who thrive in the years ahead won't be the ones who placed the right bets, who happened to guess the future correctly. They'll be the ones who stayed adaptable enough to move with or even ahead of it. To notice the shifts earlier, pivot faster, resist the deeply human urge to cling to old maps when the landscape itself is transforming around them.

AQ isn't about perfect prediction but *dynamic resilience*. It's about building a mind—and by extension building teams, companies, cultures—that can update fast enough to stay alive, and that is creative enough to find new paths when the old ones collapse. Which sounds simple enough, but—as we've been dissecting—it's one of the hardest things a human mind can attempt.

In a stable environment, deep habit beats constant recalibration every time. But we are entering a future where the rate of change will overwhelm every fixed model we have—scientific, economic, cultural, even personal.

If you can't adapt, you won't survive. And this is not hyperbole; it's the logical consequence of exponential shifts across multiple domains converging at once—all while the institutions, processes, and mindsets we inherited fray or veer into irrelevance, having been built for a slower world.

The opportunity—and the challenge—presented by this inflection point is to build something different inside yourself before those external structures crumble completely. To cultivate the modes of thinking and decision-making that can equip you to ride out the storm. Because when the experts hedge and the territory is new and unknown, the only real advantage will belong to those who can keep sensing, learning, updating, adapting—faster, deeper, more courageously than those around them.

To state the obvious: This is not a book of answers. It aims to serve as a toolkit for asking better questions, faster. It's a way of arming yourself—not with dogma, but with flexibility in your thinking. Not with certainty, but with resilience.

The future belongs to those who can learn faster than it changes. Which means thinking in loops, not lines. Relentlessly testing your assumptions instead of blindly defending them.

Moving with conviction when the signal is strong, adjusting course quickly and dispassionately when it's not. It means replacing intellectual arrogance with intellectual humility—and situational awareness. Knowing the difference between signal and noise, what's durable and what's drift. Between what must be protected and preserved and what must be discarded or reimagined entirely.

There's no safe harbor ahead, only deeper water. So this isn't about being right; it's about being *ready*. That's the real skill now: navigating uncertainty without being owned by it. Making moves before the rulebook has been written. Knowing how to keep learning and advancing toward deep success while the ground is shifting beneath your feet. And doing all of the above not once, but over and over again.

If we can achieve that, the age of intelligent machines won't be the end of human agency. It will be its proving ground.

Adaptability Quotient Field Guide: Key Takeaways

- **The Fourth Industrial Revolution isn't just technical—it's cognitive.** The real frontier is reclaiming authorship in an age of autonomous systems.
- **Previous revolutions amplified human strength and skill.** This one challenges human agency itself.
- **AI is powerful as a tool—but perilous as a substrate.** Keep the human in charge of the loop, always.
- **Adaptive intelligence is the only true stabilizer when inherited anchors—institutions, traditions, shared myths—begin to erode.** System 1 automation and digital habitus both lure us into drift; AQ restores deliberate control.
- **Off-load routine cognition, if you'd like, but not reflective thought.** Preserve the slow, effortful System 2 that makes deep reasoning—and conscience—possible.

- **The next leap in AI (beyond LLMs) will simulate consequence, not just language.** But prediction still isn't purpose. Only humans can supply meaning.
- **Language compresses reality; imagination expands it.** Stay fluent in both.
- **Our greatest evolutionary superpower isn't processing speed—it's choice.** The will to override instinct, to adapt consciously, to imagine beyond the set.
- **The most extraordinary machine isn't artificial.** It's the one reading these words, even now—and deciding what happens next.

Out of the night that covers me,
Black as the pit from pole to pole,
I thank whatever gods may be
For my unconquerable soul.

In the fell clutch of circumstance
I have not winced nor cried aloud.
Under the bludgeonings of chance
My head is bloody, but unbowed.

Beyond this place of wrath and tears
Looms but the Horror of the shade,
And yet the menace of the years
Finds and shall find me unafraid.

It matters not how strait the gate,
How charged with punishments the scroll,
I am the master of my fate,
I am the captain of my soul.

—*Invictus,* William Ernest Henley

Acknowledgments

This book did not emerge in isolation. It reflects a lifetime of conversations, challenges, and shared work with people who shaped how I think long before I ever tried to name it.

First and foremost, I am grateful to my parents, Norman and Bonnie, who taught me—explicitly and implicitly—to question assumptions, remain curious, and treat learning as a lifelong endeavor rather than a phase of life. From them, I absorbed the idea that understanding is always provisional, and that asking better questions often matters more than having quick answers. My mother, in particular, influenced this book in ways both obvious and subtle. Her insistence on synthesis—on seeing connections across ideas, disciplines, and people—left a deep imprint on how I approach problems and how this book ultimately took shape. It has been a profound pleasure that this book has enabled me to see her thought process up close, marvel at its beauty, and strengthen our bond in new ways.

I am deeply indebted to mentors, partners, and colleagues who have challenged me relentlessly, debated ideas with rigor, and helped compensate for my own blind spots. Ken Griffin was my original mentor and set an early standard for how to think at scale. One lesson has stayed with me: that success is not about a single trade or even a single portfolio, but about building an organization capable of repeatedly producing great portfolios over time. That idea—telescoping outward from the immediate problem to the system that generates it—has influenced my business thinking ever since.

I am grateful to my partners at Magnetar, Ross Laser and Dave Snyderman, whose complementary perspectives, intellectual honesty, and willingness to engage deeply made building together both possible and rewarding. I also want to thank two early investors, Bryan White and David Small, who were not only supporters but thoughtful sparring partners, asking hard questions, offering perspective, and providing conviction when it mattered.

I would also like to acknowledge Barry Cohen and Scott Schefrin from Bear Stearns, from whom I learned the craft of risk arbitrage. Their patience with my seemingly endless questions, and their insistence on rigor, left a lasting impression on how I think about risk, structure, and decision-making under uncertainty.

As this book started to come together, I am grateful to early readers who engaged directly with the manuscript and provided critical feedback while the ideas were still forming. Riley Roberts, in particular, played an essential role in helping me translate dense, raw material into a clearer and more accessible narrative—challenging me to sharpen arguments, clarify structure, and say what I actually meant rather than what I assumed was obvious. My wife, Jennifer, and our son, Jack, were especially helpful in organizing the narrative arc for the book. Nick Polson and Ross Stevens offered thoughtful challenge and perspective, while Luke Litowitz, Bonnie Litowitz, Aretae Wyler, Kaili Tu, Howard Chrisman, and Michael Oliver Weinberg each helped stress-test arguments, surface blind spots, and improve the work through careful reading and discussion. This book is more precise and more honest because of their engagement.

I also want to thank former colleagues with whom I had the pleasure of reminiscing about our investing adventures together—conversations that reminded me how much learning happens in the doing. Charlie Sweat, Will Wyatt, Min Htoo, Brendan Carroll, Chris Rossbach, David Wilansky, James Yeh, Dave Bunning, Gerald Beeson, Eric Scheyer, Adam Daley, Dawn Ray, Barbara Bernstein, Ernie Rogers, and Devin Dallaire shared not only successes but the kind of shallow failures that teach quickly without destroying you. We honed adaptability together—through cycles, pivots, and reinvention—long before I had language for what I now call AQ.

I am equally grateful to several colleagues at Qstar, who continue to live these principles in real time. Ho Man Tang, Monica Byrd, and Will Plumpton have not merely helped refine the ideas explored here; they have had to survive the ups and downs, course corrections, and constant adaptation that come with building anything durable in uncertain environments.

Looking back, I am grateful that many of the entrepreneurial efforts I have been a part of or led have stood the test of time. I attribute this less to any single insight than to AQ skills passed down to me, honed repeatedly alongside great colleagues, and refined through cycles of success, misstep, and adaptation. In turn, I am especially proud that many former colleagues and mentees have carried those same instincts forward, applying, evolving, and passing them on as they went on to build enduring businesses and institutions of their own. Through their continuous improvement and active friendship, I have been the beneficiary of a broader and more valuable set of feedback loops.

To my wife, Jennifer: Thank you for your patience with my unending curiosity, the constant stream of ideas, and the occasional tendency to get us over our skis. Your judgment—often quieter, clearer, and more grounded than my own—has been an essential counterweight and a source of balance in both life and work.

And finally, to my children, Jack, Luke, Nick, and Jude: Thank you for the joy you bring me every day. Thank you for enduring a household where both questions and answers are rarely left unexamined. The times we share collectively exploring other lands, cultures, and ideas are my favorite moments in life. Your curiosity, resilience, and perspective continually remind me why adaptability matters—not just as a professional skill, but as a way of remaining a student of life.

This book reflects all of you more than you know.

Notes

More information about the ideas in this book, including a list of recommended further reading, is available at www.qstarcap.com/book/sources.

1 Mark P. Mattson, "Superior Pattern Processing Is the Essence of the Evolved Human Brain," *Frontiers in Neuroscience* 8, no. 265 (2014), doi.org/10.3389/fnins.2014.00265.

2 Keith E. Stanovich, *What Intelligence Tests Miss: The Psychology of Rational Thought* (Yale University Press, 2009), 55.

3 J. McCarthy et al., "A Proposal for the Dartmouth Summer Research Project on Artificial Intelligence," August 31, 1955, https://raysolomonoff.com/dartmouth/boxa/dart564props.pdf.

4 Françoise Baylis et al., "Human Germ Line and Heritable Genome Editing: The Global Policy Landscape," *The CRISPR Journal* 3, no. 5 (2020): 365–377, doi.org/10.1089/crispr.2020.0082.

5 Noam Chomsky, *Reflections on Language* (Pantheon Books, 1975), 4.

6 Lev S. Vygotsky, *Thought and Language*, trans. Alex Kozulin (MIT Press, 1986), 218.

7 Unnati Narang et al., "Generative AI Spurs Passive But Not Active Engagement with Content," working paper (2024).

8 Patrick R. Heck et al., "65% of Americans Believe They Are Above Average in Intelligence: Results of Two Nationally Representative Surveys," *PLOS One* 13, no. 7 (2018): https://doi.org/10.1371/journal.pone.0200103.

9 Jeremy Dean, "Above-Average Effect: Why People Feel Better Than Average," PsyBlog, January 16, 2023, https://www.spring.org.uk/2023/01/above-average-effect.php.

10 Ranasish Chowdhury and Reshmi Chowdhury, "Genesis and Reception of the Continental Drift Hypothesis," *Indian Science Cruiser* 38, no. 1 (2024): 24–33, doi.org/10.24906/isc/2024/v38/i1/47352; "Alfred Wegener (1880-1930)," UC Museum of Paleontology, June 6, 1996, https://ucmp.berkeley.edu/history/wegener.html.

Glossary of Terms

A

Abduction: The cognitive leap that follows reduction (stripping facts down to bedrock) and induction (pattern recognition). This is the stage where a provisional model or hypothesis is formed to explain the observed patterns, serving as the basis for a testable strong opinion, weakly held (SOWH).

Accommodation: The cognitive process in which new information forces you to revise the existing mental model itself.

Amputation: The dangerous, ego-driven practice of discarding or ignoring inconvenient data or outliers simply to preserve a preferred internal narrative or hypothesis. Amputation is the opposite of imputation, and results in confirmation bias, eventually leading to a system that optimizes for applause, so to speak, instead of insight.

AQ (Adaptability Quotient): A component of human intelligence distinct from traditional IQ and emotional intelligence (EQ). Crucially, it demands metacognition—the ability to observe and question your own thinking—and values intellectual rigor over the ego-driven need to be right. It represents a learnable way of using your mind like a high-performance machine; the operating system that serially successful people are already using, knowingly or not. It is a structured methodology prioritizing making decisions right over making the right decision in any given instance.

Assimilation: The cognitive process by which you absorb new information into your existing mental model.

Asymmetric Right-Tail Bets: Low-cost experiments with massive potential upside, taken not necessarily for information gain, but to keep parts of the decision tree open until probabilities can be refined.

B

Bayesian Prior: See *prior*.

Bayesian Updating: A framework for learning from experience. It is the methodical process of updating the probability of a hypothesis based on new evidence. In practice, it is about subtraction before addition (not P)—designing tests to see what breaks, thereby negating false assumptions and refining your prior.

Beginner's Mind (*Shoshin*): The state of mind that allows you to approach a problem unclouded by bias or precedent, where all possibilities can roam free. This mindset is necessary during the simulation phase, as experts often accumulate assumptions that filter out ideas that don't fit the existing paradigm. Remember: In the beginner's mind, there are many possibilities, but in the expert's, there are few.

Black Swan: A state of unknown possibilities and unknown probabilities. Black swans represent "out-of-set" events, or occurrences that are so rare or unprecedented that they aren't even included on a decision tree as a possibility (think 9/11 or Covid-19) but carry massive impact.

Bonini's Paradox: The phenomenon where the more accurately a theoretical model attempts to represent a complex, real-world system, the harder that model becomes to understand and use. The paradox warns against excessive complexity, suggesting that a detailed map ceases to be a useful tool if it becomes too unwieldy.

C

Cognitive Coherence: What happens when an entire team (or company, or other organization) can internalize and operate from the same mental model, sharing a way of thinking (as opposed to thinking the same way). This strategic alignment emerges through shared frameworks for evaluating trade-offs, modeling risk, and moving from first principles.

Cognitive Empathy: The ability to understand what others are thinking and predict their reactions—for example, the capacity to see how a decision will land.

Confirmation Bias: A dangerous psychological trap where you accept evidence that supports a preexisting belief while ignoring or rationalizing away contradictory evidence. This is the worst enemy of iteration—and is fatal in a Bayesian system because it prevents genuine learning and updating.

Conscious Mind (Serial Interface): The most directly accessible layer of the mind, which holds attention, inner monologue, and deliberate, effortful reasoning (System 2). This layer is powerful but narrow and slow, running only one active process at a time (hence "serial").

Consilience: The idea that truths from different fields—such as psychology, strategy, neuroscience, and information theory—can converge to reveal a broader understanding that no single discipline can reach alone.

Convergent Problem: A problem that is deterministic, meaning it has a clear, predefined solution. Traditional schooling is often structured around finding the one and only right answer to convergent questions.

Crystallized Intelligence: The storehouse of hard-won knowledge and expertise built up over time. If it crosses the line from input to dogma, it effectively paralyzes the cognitive system.

Curiosity: The impulse to explore, question, and seek better information. It is the fuel that encourages lightly held hypotheses, making it an intellectual accelerant when paired with humility. Curiosity guides exploration, ensuring that grit is applied in the right direction.

Cybernetics: The interdisciplinary field, named from the Greek for "steersman" or "pilot," that studies how systems (biological, mechanical, or social) use feedback to adjust course, maintain control, and achieve objectives. It reframes metacognition as the act of becoming the "steersman" of your own mind.

D

Data: The raw material of thought; isolated facts that, on their own, lack inherent meaning or context. Data without interpretation is no better than noise.

Decision Tree: A mental prototype or branching structure built during the simulation phase that maps out various paths toward (and away from) deep success. It connects nodes (facts/relationships) and dials (adjustable variables) to make the complexity of a decision legible and testable.

Deduction: The final step in the process of generating strong opinions, weakly held (SOWH), where the abducted hypothesis is thrown against reality (in Phase III: experimentation) to see what endures and what breaks.

Deep Failure: A knockout event—a fatal moment from which the goal can no longer be reached. It is tantamount to death, meaning the window has closed and you are done, out of the game. Eliminating the risk of deep failure is the objective during the simulation phase.

Deep Success: Your ultimate objective fulfilled. It is the sustained achievement of what matters to you, the final destination toward which all decisions and smaller (shallow) successes have been compounding.

Dial: Any controllable variable or input within a decision tree that can be tweaked or adjusted to see how the system responds. Defining these dials precisely is essential for targeted experimentation in Phase III.

Divergent Problem: Problems that are nondeterministic, meaning multiple outcomes are possible and there is no single absolute "right" answer or perfect playbook.

Diversity (of perspective): The practice of seeking differences in background, experience, and worldview within a team. This is a strategic asset, not mere optics, because it expands the cognitive surface area of an organization, enabling it to see more dimensions of a problem and spot hidden risks.

E

Emotional Coherence: What happens when a team is aligned not just intellectually, but affectively, sharing urgency, conviction, ambition, or fear. It fuels energy and buy-in during crunch time.

Emotional Empathy: The capacity to feel what others are feeling—to internalize their pain, fear, or frustration as your own. In high-stakes environments, indulging emotional empathy can become a trap.

Emotional Intelligence (EQ): The nuanced perceptive capabilities and operating functions that determine how effectively you interact with others and understand yourself. It encompasses faculties like self-awareness, the ability to process social cues, and a balance of humility and confidence. Two core components are grit and curiosity.

Epistemic Rationality: The discipline of forming beliefs based on unvarnished evidence, naked logic, and raw probability, rather than emotion or personal bias. It is about aligning your thinking as closely as possible with reality.

Experimentation (Phase III): The third phase of the AQ process, where the strong opinion, weakly held (SOWH) is tested in the real world. The goal is maximizing learning through iteration, shallow failure, and absorbing feedback quickly (Bayesian updating), thereby shortening the path to victory.

Expertise (paradox of): The conflict wherein expertise is simultaneously a sharp tool (accumulated knowledge) and a dangerous blindfold. While vital for refining known systems, expertise tends to accumulate assumptions and preconceived notions that filter out novel ideas, making it a liability during early exploration (Phase II).

F

Flatland: An analogy (drawn from the book of the same name) used to describe a limited, two-dimensional perspective of a multidimensional problem. The greatest risk is not knowing what dimensions of the problem you have failed to see, which is why diversity of perspective is crucial for seeing beyond Flatland.

Fluid Intelligence: The ability to think flexibly, recombine ideas, and see new patterns. It fuels a beginner's mind and is central to the ability to improvise and adapt.

Fourth Industrial Revolution: The current technological era, characterized by accelerating change, complexity, interconnectedness, and the convergence of digital, physical, and biological systems (e.g., AI, synthetic biology, robotics). This era has raised the stakes and demands an upgrade to human cognition.

G

Grit: The capacity to override the brain's automatic responses. It is the disciplined tolerance for cognitive tension, allowing you to slow down, sit with ambiguity, and resist the comfort of false certainty. Remember: Grit holds; curiosity explores.

H

Habitus: A concept referring to the often unconscious system of dispositions, beliefs, and expectations shaped by one's environment. The modern digital habitus is hostile to adaptation, actively rewarding conformity and confirmation learning, thereby entrenching old patterns when the world demands flexibility.

Hallucination: In the context of AI, a Type I error where a large language model generates a plausible-sounding answer or cited source that is factually incorrect or nonexistent. This is not a malfunction, but a feature of the system prioritizing the most probable output over verified truth.

Human Agency: The essential ability to choose for yourself, to deliberate, and to act with intention. It is threatened by algorithmic systems that optimize choices toward goals we never explicitly authorized, eroding human authorship incrementally. Cultivating high AQ is the means by which we reclaim and defend human agency.

Hypothesis: A testable abduction or informed guess, which is designed to avoid deep failure while leaving room for uncertainty and serves as the foundation of learning adaptively. As the output of Phase II and the starting point for Phase III, it maps out the branches (possibilities) of a decision tree but lacks the known probabilities required to constitute a true Bayesian prior.

I

Imputation: The disciplined method for handling anomalous data points or outliers. Instead of discarding the inconvenient data (amputation), imputation demands asking: "What would have to be true for this result to make sense?"

Induction: The second step of generating a hypothesis, where you systematically search for patterns and correlations among the reduced fragments of a problem. The challenge is avoiding the trap of mistaking analogy or correlation for truth or causation.

Information: Data that has been infused with context, starting to interact with other data to form relationships or nodes on your decision tree.

Insight: A slower, deeper form of cognition than intuition, representing the recombination of data and patterns that were previously unconnected in the mind. Insight often occurs when the conscious mind is relaxed (e.g., in flow or sleep), allowing the subconscious to connect fragments into something new.

Instrumental Rationality: Rationality that focuses solely on the most efficient means of achieving a specific goal, regardless of whether the goal or the underlying assumptions are true or worthwhile (in contrast with epistemic rationality).

Intelligence Quotient (IQ): Traditional/raw intelligence. Helped early humans understand patterns in nature. It is the raw computational power of the brain—the ability to analyze data, solve problems, and process logic. It is analogous to modern AI systems (LLMs), which process information using pattern recognition.

Intuition: Fast thinking founded on slow learning. It is not magic or a guess, but a form of implicit learning—the brain surfacing patterns and microsignals from a massive, distributed archive of subconscious pattern recognition. Intuition is the quick retrieval; insight is the deeper recombination.

K

Knightian Uncertainty: A state of known possibilities but unknown probabilities. This represents the "deep uncertainty" or "epistemic uncertainty" that makes up 80 to 90 percent of the world. In this state, you can map out the "branches" of your decision tree (the potential outcomes), but you lack the frequency data to assign specific odds to them. In such an environment, your goal is to harvest uncertainty by converting hidden but knowable probabilities into measurable risk.

Knowledge: Information that has been tested against reality (often through Phase III experimentation). It moves beyond correlation and into causation, defining what works in a particular environment. Knowledge is a provisional passport that can be revoked at any time, depending on environmental changes.

L

Law of Requisite Knowledge (LRK): To make effective decisions in a complex environment, you need a knowledge base rich enough to match the complexity of the system you are navigating. Since passively accumulated knowledge goes stale, LRK demands that organizations actively generate knowledge through fast, iterative experimentation. For our purposes, it has two parts: First, you need enough knowledge from exploitation—from running real experiments—to resolve the uncertainty you're facing. If you haven't tested, you don't know. Second, you need the judgment to know when exploitation has stopped working—when refinement is no longer reducing uncertainty and it's time to abandon the current model and reenter Phase II.

Law of Requisite Variety (LRV): In any complex system, the number of options and adaptive responses considered must be greater than the number of variables in the system being navigated. Remember: Only variety can absorb variety. Violating LRV by limiting options prematurely makes a system fragile.

Loop: See *recursive framework*.

M

Making Decisions Right: A core principle of AQ that prioritizes following a sound, repeatable, and adaptable decision-making process (as distinct from "making the right decision" in any given instance). This approach ensures that even when the outcome is "wrong," the loss yields valuable learning.

Max Entropy: The crucial starting posture for Phase II (simulation)—a deliberate, hard embrace of maximum uncertainty, zero assumptions, and full openness to signal. This mindset achieves the cleanest possible mental reset, forcing you to consider the widest possible net of ideas necessary for achieving a true beginner's mind before filtering (reducing uncertainty) begins.

Max Q: A metaphor for the optimal operating state achieved when the three aspects of intelligence (IQ, EQ, AQ) are combined. Like a launch vehicle passing the moment of maximum dynamic pressure in flight, the system is stable under stress, accelerating toward its goal, leaving the greatest dangers behind.

Metacognition (Phase I): The discipline of thinking about how you think. It is the first phase of AQ, involving a rigorous self-audit to examine biases, instincts, and assumptions. It is the act of reclaiming agency and serving as the "steersman" of your own mind.

Minimum Viable Product (MVP): In the context of experimentation, an MVP is a focused, real-world test of a decision tree path made tangible. It is launched not for perfection, but to maximize learning and gather crucial feedback quickly, before pursuing pristine theories.

Model Error: A fundamental flaw in risk models or mental maps where complexity is simplified to the point of inaccuracy, often leading to catastrophic results when the model collapses under real-world conditions.

N

Nodes: The foundational elements of a system or mental model that are connected, weighted, or correlated as we think. In the experimentation phase, nodes are decision points or adjustable "dials" that isolate a specific set of testable variables.

P

Phases of AQ: The framework for navigating uncertainty is broken down into three distinct, recursive phases: metacognition (Phase I), simulation (Phase II), and experimentation (Phase III).

Premortem: A technique for surfacing blind spots and hidden assumptions during simulation (Phase II). Instead of asking, "Will this work?" you assume the project has already failed, and then systematically ask, "Why did it fail?"

Prior (Bayesian Prior): A refined state of knowledge where you know both the possible outcomes and the specific statistical odds of those outcomes occurring. While the word is often used informally as a loose synonym of "hypothesis," technically a Bayesian prior is only "earned" after you've run enough experiments to convert uncertainty into measurable risk.

Provisional Knowledge: The understanding produced by an experiment. It is useful and actionable, but only for now and only until new data arrives to challenge it. The recursive nature of the AQ process ensures that knowledge remains provisional and subject to constant testing.

R

Read-Only World: The historical era, prior to the current inflection point, where humanity acted primarily as observers and students of the universe, discovering existing forces (e.g., gravity, DNA).

Read-to-Write Future: The dawning era where humanity is moving from passive analysis to active construction, utilizing technologies like AI and synthetic biology to design, rewrite, and author reality itself.

Recursive Framework (Loop): The core mechanism of AQ whereby the conclusion of Phase III (experimentation) points back to Phase II (simulation). Every result generates new information that must be absorbed (assimilation) or used to rewrite the model (accommodation), keeping the system learning and provisional.

Reduction: The first step in creating a testable hypothesis, which involves rigorously stripping a problem down to its first principles by removing convention, analogy, and inherited assumptions.

Risk: A state of known possibilities and known probabilities. This is the domain of stability, where the environment is slow-moving enough to allow for accurate statistical modeling (as in a game of poker). Because the odds are fixed or discoverable, you can use standard Bayesian optimization tools.

S

Second-Order Thinking: The act of analyzing the process or system behind a judgment or belief, rather than just the outcome or belief itself. This is synonymous with metacognition.

Shallow Failure (Feedback): A moment of feedback, a test point, or a signal that is essential and part of the process. It is not fatal; it is the core mechanism of learning. Every shallow failure in Phase III is an information gain.

Shallow Success (Local Win): A local win or incremental progress toward the stated objective. It is worth noting and learning from, but it is not the end-all, be-all, as it is short of the ultimate goal.

Shannon Entropy: A concept drawn from information theory that quantifies the amount of uncertainty or possibility within a system. In decision-making, high entropy (maximum uncertainty) is desirable early on because it is the window when exploration delivers the greatest returns.

Simulation (Phase II): The second phase of AQ, focused on deliberate simulation and mentally exploring potential options. It involves building a decision tree or mental prototype to hypothesize what could happen next, aiming to eliminate fatal risk before acting.

Steel Man Army: A deliberately assembled circle of smart, trusted people whose job is to argue against your strong opinion, weakly held (SOWH).

This force works by constructing the strongest possible version of every counterargument (rejecting feeble straw-man arguments) to pressure test your hypothesis, surface critical blind spots, and plumb for risk of deep failure before Phase III (experimentation) begins.

Strong Opinion, Weakly Held (SOWH): The testable abduction, or hypothesis, that results from the simulation phase and represents our starting point during the experimentation phase. It is a posture of adaptive confidence: moving forward with conviction, but with the humility to keep adjusting when reality shifts.

Subconscious Mind (Parallel Processing Engine): The layer of the mind just below active awareness, functioning like RAM or a powerful GPU. It runs background processes, searches for patterns (the source of intuition), and is the home turf of System 1; it is mutable and trainable.

Superior Pattern Processing (SPP): The miraculous ability of the human brain to process a constant influx of data, recognize, interpret, and generate complex patterns. While foundational to human intelligence, it is fundamentally maladapted to the complexity of the twenty-first century and easily exploited.

Systems Thinking: A discipline that views challenges not as isolated problems to be solved individually, but as interconnected patterns that drive outcomes. It requires telescoping out to see the entire system and identifying leverage points where intervention is most effective.

T

Telescoping: The capacity to continuously zoom in and out, almost as if from above, moving between immersion and analysis, action and observation, execution and metacognition. This habit of checking your vantage point and interrogating your lens is a critical skill of metacognition.

Type I Error (False Positive): A mistake where a system thinks something is there when it is not. This is a false alarm—annoying, potentially costly, but unquestionably survivable. AI hallucinations are a textbook Type I error.

Type II Error (False Negative): A mistake where a system misses something that is actually there. This is where deep failure lives. It is insidious and dangerous because it slips past unnoticed until it is too late, foreclosing opportunities or leading to fatal consequences.

U

Unconscious Mind (Immutable Core): The deep layer of the mind that operates outside of awareness and deliberate control. It governs life-supporting reflexes, instincts, and deep-seated evolutionary drives, functioning like the system's read-only firmware that cannot be accessed or changed directly (except via techniques like hypnosis or therapy).

V

Vergence (Mental Vergence): An analogy, drawn from the neurological process that creates depth perception, for the necessary skill of keeping two views sharp at once: the close-up, immediate reality and the distant, long-term strategic goal. Adaptive leaders must maintain this balance between zooming in and zooming out.

W

Wisdom: The second-order ability of knowing when and how to adapt. Wisdom recognizes when the knowledge or framework (the model itself) needs to be rethought or changed because the environment has shifted.

World Model: A concept in advanced cognitive science and AI research describing a system's internal understanding of how reality works (e.g., what happens when you throw a ball, the way an object falls). Current large language models lack a true world model, which is necessary for common sense and reasoning.

About the Author

Alec Litowitz is an investor and business builder who has spent much of his life and career making high-stakes decisions under uncertainty. Over three decades, he has worked at the frontier of finance, entrepreneurship, and institution-building, with a focus on developing ways to navigate uncertainty not by prediction, but by better process.

He is the founder of Qstar Capital, a single-family office investing across public and private markets, and the founder and former CEO of Magnetar Capital, which he grew from its launch in 2005 to more than $20 billion in assets under management. Earlier, he was one of the four original partners at Citadel Investment Group, where he led Global Equities and served on the firm's Investment and Management Committees.

Across these roles, Litowitz has focused on building teams and cultures capable of learning faster than conditions change. His work emphasizes rigorous debate, disciplined experimentation, and the ability to adapt when reality refuses to cooperate.

Litowitz holds degrees in mathematics and anthropology from MIT and law and business from the University of Chicago. Beyond investing, he is deeply engaged in education and civic life. He founded Magnetar Academy, whose finEDge curriculum has brought financial literacy to more than thirty thousand students nationwide, and—together with his wife, Jennifer—helped establish Northwestern University's Litowitz

Center for Enlightened Disagreement. An endurance athlete, he has competed in multiple Ironman triathlons and international mountain bike races and serves as Board Chair Emeritus of Dare2tri, a nonprofit paratriathlon program dedicated to empowering athletes with physical disabilities and visual impairments. He is a father of four boys and an active supporter of Chicago's arts community, serving on the board of the Art Institute of Chicago.